The Future of Our Democracies

Also by Michael Bruter

CITIZENS OF EUROPE?

ENCYCLOPAEDIA OF EUROPEAN ELECTIONS (*co-editor with Yves Déloye*)

The Future of Our Democracies

Young Party Members in Europe

Michael Bruter

Senior Lecturer in European Political Science
London School of Economics and Political Science, UK

and

Sarah Harrison

Research Officer in Political Science
London School of Economics and Political Science, UK

First published 2009 by
PALGRAVE MACMILLAN

Palgrave Macmillan in the UK is an imprint of Macmillan Publishers Limited, registered in England, company number 785998, of Houndmills, Basingstoke, Hampshire RG21 6XS.

Palgrave Macmillan in the US is a division of St Martin's Press LLC, 175 Fifth Avenue, New York, NY 10010.

Palgrave Macmillan is the global academic imprint of the above companies and has companies and representatives throughout the world.

Palgrave® and Macmillan® are registered trademarks in the United States, the United Kingdom, Europe and other countries.

ISBN: 978–0–230–21973–1 hardback

This book is printed on paper suitable for recycling and made from fully managed and sustained forest sources. Logging, pulping and manufacturing processes are expected to conform to the environmental regulations of the country of origin.

A catalogue record for this book is available from the British Library.

A catalog record for this book is available from the Library of Congress.

10 9 8 7 6 5 4 3 2 1
18 17 16 15 14 13 12 11 10 09

Printed and bound in Great Britain by
CPI Antony Rowe, Chippenham and Eastbourne

Contents

List of Tables and Figures

Tables

Figure

Acknowledgement

The authors would like to thank the many people who, through their comments, help, and confidence, have made this project and this book possible.

Initial thanks are due to the Leverhulme Trust and the London School of Economics Seed Research Fund, which have financed this project, as well as the Economic and Social Research Council which has sponsored Sarah Harrison's doctoral degree.

We would also like to thank the colleagues who have helped us through their comments and suggestions, including the members of the Department of Government at the LSE (particularly Martin Lodge), those of the National Europe Centre at the Australian National University (in particular, Simon Bronitt, Dora Horvath, and Adam Berryman), and Prof. Susan Scarrow from the University of Houston.

We also owe an immense thank you to Guadalupe Machinandiarena, who, rather than a research assistant on this project, has really been an exceptional deputy researcher, a great helper and organiser, and has shown more dedication and support than anything we could possibly expect.

All our gratitude is also due to all our research assistants who have helped to translate our questionnaires and complete our interviews. They include, in particular, Szilvia Csanyi, Markus Wagner, Nikolas Astrup, Anne-Julie Clary, and so on.

Finally, we would like to thank all the parties and young party organisations and their branches, which have accepted to let us conduct our study without any reserve. These have included central party organisations and/or branches of the German SPD and Jusos, CDU and JU, FDP and Julis, the Spanish PSOE and JSE, PP and NNGG, the Norwegian Høyre and UH, the Hungarian MSzP, Fidesz, and Fidelitas, the British Labour Party, Labour Students, and Young Labour, Liberal-Democrats and Liberal Youth, UK Independence Party and British National Party, and the French Parti Socialiste and MJS, Les Verts and Souris Vertes, Parti Communiste Français and Jeunesses Communistes, Front National and FNJ.

We would finally like to thank Amy Lankester-Owen and Alison Howson from Palgrave Macmillan, as well as our anonymous referees for their suggestions on our book.

1
Introduction and Background

Introduction and object

Is this the end of democracy as we know it? Over the past three decades – and despite a small turn of fortune in recent French, Polish, and Irish elections – turnout has declined by an average 15 points across European democracies (IDEA, 2004).[1] In addition, the proportion of citizens enrolled in political parties has been halved between the early 1980s and the late 1990s (Mair and van Biezen, 2001).[2] A large number of studies conclude that membership in Western political parties is generally in decline (Mair and van Biezen, 2001; Pedersen et al., 2004; Scarrow, 2000; Seyd and Whiteley, 2004; Webb et al., 2002).

Hooghe et al. (2004) confirm that during the last 20 years, party membership has been declining in most liberal democracies (Dalton and Wattenberg, 2000; Mair, 1997; Mair and van Biezen, 2001). In the 1960s, roughly 13 per cent of the electorate were reported to be members of political parties, in the 1980s this proportion had shrunk to below nine per cent. In the 1990s, only six per cent of the electorate were registered as party members (Putnam, 2002: 406). A recent study of parties in all advanced industrial democracies reveals that, with the one exception of Spain, the trend in membership numbers is downwards (Webb et al., 2002). In the case of Britain, Seyd and Whiteley (2004) found that party membership and activism is declining among the three major parties; the Conservatives, Labour, and the Liberal Democrats.

Both the supply of political enthusiasts eager to join parties and the demand of parties for such enthusiasts seem to be waning (Seyd and Whiteley, 2004: 355). This widespread decline in traditional modes of participation may have been less worrying if it did not touch younger generations even more than their elder. In most European democracies, young citizens are first-in-line to express disenchantment with their politicians and their institutions. On average, in Europe, merely half of them still bother to vote.[3]

Of course, knowing that on average, young citizens are less active than before could hide a great variety of more subtle realities. Forty or fifty years ago, there was already a gap between the most eager young citizens, who decided to join political parties and get actively involved in membership organisations on the one hand, and those who preferred to take a back seat in their countries' democratic vehicles. Fifty years later, the disengagement of young citizens could correspond to a number of very different scenarios. Hypothetically, it could mean that both active and inactive citizens have assumed more distance from their countries' political lives without the distance between the two groups changing in any way. Alternatively, the proportion of 'back seat passengers' to 'drivers' may have increased, with the latter becoming an endangered species. Thirdly, the 'back seat passengers' may have remained the same while the 'drivers' may have become less mobilised. In a polar opposite way, however, this new reality could entail that an increasing gap has emerged between consistently motivated 'drivers' and 'back seat passengers' who have, in the meantime, altogether fallen out of the car.

While a lot has been written on the demobilisation and increased cynicism of the average European youth, little is known about those young citizens who still get involved in membership organisations and particularly in political parties. On the whole, we know that young people are not refreshing the ranks of political parties. Party membership has, over recent years, become decisively aged. Scarrow and Gezgor (2006) show that people over the age of 60 represent 61 per cent of party members, and only 24 per cent of the population in Britain.[4] Over the last decade, many citizens, and in particular, young people, have increasingly turned their backs on political parties but have instead preferred to join other groups or organisations in order to channel their participation (Whiteley, 2007). Young people are the future of old-style politics, and without their participation, some fear that our current model of governance might reach a point of no return.

Against this bleak picture – and apparently against the tide – a substantial proportion of young citizens perpetuate a classic tradition of political involvement by joining political parties. Parties welcome this precious new blood with great enthusiasm and hope that it will restore their fragile legitimacy. Yet, they also often suspect young party members of having very different preferences and priorities from older generations of activists. Out of choice or out of need, parties have often created specific institutional structures to incorporate them, have taken steps to protect their voices within the parties' structures, and have tended to fast track the promotion of some of them to prominent party positions in order to rejuvenate their image in the eyes of an increasingly sceptical public (Dalton and Weldon, 2005). This also means that if it is *not* the end of democracy as we know it, then, among these young party members, we will actually find those who will lead tomorrow's European nations. Would it not be important to understand what is in their hearts and minds before they make it to the front benches of national political scenes? Is it not essential to understand how they distinguish themselves from their parties' masses at this early stage?

This world of young party members is precisely the unknown and secretive universe that this book aims to explore. Over a period of three years, we have surveyed and spoken to these young party members. We chose a selection of six European party systems, and within them, 15 major parties, which cover the entire European ideological spectrum and all significant party families from the extreme left to the extreme right. In order to gain a valid insight into the hearts and minds of their members, we developed a mass survey, which was answered by nearly 3000 young party members, and then went back to over 500 of them in order to carry out in-depth interviews. The result is possibly the largest amount of data ever collected on young party members, a multi-methods, comparative spotlight cast over a whole category of young people who might come to play a major role in the political future of all of our democracies. In any case, they certainly hope to represent their future.

Ultimately, this book aims at understanding *who* exactly are young party members, *what* they seek, *how* they have come to join a political party, *what* being a party member means in their everyday life, and *how* they perceive politics, their party, their democracy, and their own political future.

Progressing from the existing literature

Our book sits at the crossroads between a number of important developments in the political science literature to which it contributes. These developments include the party politics literature, the political socialisation literature, the political participation literature, and general aspects of the comparative politics literature on political change.

For over a century, political parties have been considered a key link of representative democracy. As such, not only parties themselves but also their members have attracted considerable attention in the political science literature. Indeed, of the various forms of political activism, party membership is one of the most time and cost intensive. Party membership has suffered particularly severely as a result of a widespread public dissatisfaction with politics, ultimately resulting in a steady but consistent decline in levels of membership throughout Europe (Mair and van Biezen, 2001; Scarrow, 1996; Seyd and Whiteley, 2004). Despite – or perhaps because of – that sharp membership decline, fully understanding what drives some citizens in joining a party remains an interesting and important puzzle, and we believe that understanding how this works for young party members adds an important piece to our existing knowledge.

An extensive literature has been devoted to the question of membership incentives, identifying several competing models, first differentiating between material, purposive, and solidary incentives (Clark and Wilson, 1961) and then between selective and collective incentives (Seyd and Whiteley, 1992). In the first typology, by and large, material benefits correspond to specific spoils or advantages in money or in the nature the given party redistributes to its members. By contrast, purposive incentives correspond to the feeling of helping to pursue the goals of the organisation (such as the ideas of the party manifesto) via one's membership, and solidary incentives the benefits of social interaction with like-minded people. The second distinction separates those benefits of membership which can be enjoyed individually by the party member, and those which can only be enjoyed by a larger group, be it a specific group or the country as a whole.

The literature has shown that if party membership can be synonymous with material benefits (this was of course particularly the case in spoils-based systems such as the former Communist countries or the first Republic in Italy), solidary and purposive benefits tend to be predominant for a majority of party members. These benefits, referred to as collective by Seyd and Whiteley (1992) thus often relate to ideological and policy influence. The potential policy influence of party members is also now well documented. Panebianco (1988) argues that while the relationship between leaders and members is unequal, grass root party members can control organisational resources, which gives them some influence over local policy outcomes. Members are often regarded as the 'middle-level elite', with some (limited) agenda-setting powers, and serve as key intermediaries between the mass voters on the one hand, and the political elites on the other. In this sense, party members retain an 'ambassadorial role' within the community (Martin and Cowley, 1999; Seyd and Whiteley, 2004). Moreover, members can influence local policy outcomes by lobbying local elected representatives or run for office and become elected themselves albeit in junior positions. Thus, an individual may be motivated by a desire to see their preferred policy proposals and outputs enacted if they feel very strongly about certain policy proposals. May (1973) emphasises this ideological focus of party activists, and derives that party members tend to hold more extreme ideological views than voters and leaders alike. This often results in a 'pulling effect' of the party's policy proposals in the direction of the preferred policy position of the members.

What this party member's desire to influence public policy specifically amounts to in real terms is still subject to some controversy. Mueller (1989) suggests that citizens do not only consider their personal gain from party membership but also take into account the utility of other citizens. Along the same lines, Margolis (1982) develops a 'fair shares' principle that operates within the calculus of participation, largely echoing the distinction between selective and collective incentives. However, most of the existing research shows that collective incentives tend to take precedence over selective incentives for most members, to the point that the literature has coined the concept of 'altruistic incentives', which are listed to be the prime motivation of party members, be they of right-wing (such as the British Conservatives: Whiteley et al., 1994), or left-wing parties (Seyd and Whiteley, 1992 for the British Labour Party).

Overall, there is therefore a robust body of literature to help us understand why some people go beyond the paradox of collective action and decide to devote the time, resources, and energy that are required by party membership. Beyond that, however, it is important to question whether these findings fully capture the specific situation of *young* party members. Indeed, young party members are first and foremost 'young people', and as such, as explored by a vast body of psychological literature, they largely differ from their elder in a number of ways. Between 18 and 25, they are usually at the time of their life when they will define their long-term moral, social, and professional orientations. With regard to moral postures, Sigel (1989) notes that 'much of the foundation for political life – affect, cognition, and participation – is in place as the young person reaches adulthood.'

Research suggests that participatory habits tend to be picked up quite early during the life cycle (Fendrich and Turner, 1989; Galston, 2001; Hooghe and Stolle, 2003; Jennings, 1987; Jennings and Stoker, 2002; Youniss and Yates, 1997). There is a substantial body of literature suggesting that youth socialisation in the home and school has an effect on political attitudes and behaviour (Braungart and Braungart, 1990; Galston, 2001; Hooghe et al., 2004). Political socialisation experience is stronger at a younger age (Hooghe et al., 2004: 196).

Similarly, Cross and Young (2008) find that parents may play a key role in a young person's decision to join a political party. Youth members are twice as likely as engaged non-members to have a parent who belongs to a political party (2008: 353). This data suggests that partisan political activism is handed down from generation to generation. Young and Cross (2008) also find that one in five of the older party members who were asked to join a party were recruited by a family member. For party members 25 years and younger, half of those who were asked to join were recruited by a family member (2008: 354).

Socially, psychologists such as Salzinger et al. (1988), and Schaffer (1971) insist on the fact that no other age is more synonymous with the need to find one's own place with regard to others by building social networks, and defining one's human surroundings. Finally, the years between the age of 18–25 are when most young people will decide on and establish the path of their professional future, finalising academic and professional choices with profound long-term implications (Cannon, 1995; Gokalp, 1981).

This book argues that these fundamental concerns, prominent in the minds of young adults, are bound to have an impact on the way they conceive the prospect of their party membership. Thus, we suggest that to a certain extent, the incentive model that will apply to young people will be different from the general party membership incentive structure. To reflect what psychologists tell us are the main concerns of young adults, we therefore propose a model specifically tailored to young party members, which emphasises these three fundamental dimensions of moral, social, and professional concerns. Moreover, considering these three priorities are so widely described as 'prime' concerns of young adulthood in the literature, we suggest that not only do they give rise to specific incentives, which are slightly different from the material, purposive, and solidary incentives proposed by the general party membership literature, but that each of these possible moral, social, and professional incentive, when dominant, will create a specific 'type' of member. Each type of membership will lead to different approaches to membership and define a whole range of beliefs, motivations, perceptions, and attitudes. In other words, depending on which of these three dimensions is at the forefront of the party membership perspectives of a given young individual, we suggest that three different types of young party members exist, each with their own set of characteristics.

Over the next few paragraphs we discuss the context of party membership with regard to the existing literature and highlight some of the main paradoxes and puzzles that are relevant to scholars of political participation.

Young people in politics – mobilisation, participation, and socialisation – evolution and problems

As we have seen political parties face a difficult task in recruiting young party members to their rank-and-file. As a result, many parties face a widening generation gap within their organisation with most members being middle-aged to elderly. Pedersen et al. conclude in their study of Danish parties 'the young are strongly underrepresented and the old strongly overrepresented among party members' (2004: 372). Writing on the Irish case, Gallagher and Marsh (2004: 412) find that 'the members are middle aged, if not elderly, with an estimated average age of 52.' Cross and Young (2008) report the average age of a Canadian party member is 59. In addition, Seyd and Whiteley (1992) and Whiteley et al. (1994), also find similar patterns in their case study on the British Conservative Party. They state that the average age of a party member is 62. In a more recent study of party activism across 22 European countries, Whiteley (2007) finds that a lack of generational replacement explains the decline in party membership as existing party activists are not being replaced by younger cohorts of volunteers.

In particular, young people are the hardest to attract to join parties as they tend to be the most affected by disillusionment and apathy towards party politics. Traditional and mainstream parties are often seen as unrepresentative of the population at large with politicians viewed as 'out of touch' with the majority of the electorate but in particular with the youth. With regard to the decline of party identification, Dalton and Wattenberg (2000: 31) concludes: 'the decrease of partisanship in advanced industrial democracies has been disproportionately concentrated among the young.'

However, in contrast to this bleak picture of youth apathy and disillusionment, O'Neill (2001) and Gidengil et al. (2001) report more optimistic findings. They point to the fact that young Canadian citizens are not particularly disillusioned with politics in general and, in fact, in comparison with older age cohorts often indicate greater satisfaction with democracy and political institutions. In line with Inglehart (1990) and Nevitte (1996), there seems to be a value shift among younger cohorts of voters. Their argument essentially is that younger, post-materialist voters reject hierarchical forms of political participation but do not reject, or lack interest in, politics per se. As O'Neill (2001: 8) argues: 'Younger generations are more likely to engage in "new politics,".... and to be involved with non-traditional institutions and processes such as grass roots social movements and protest behaviour.'

Cross and Young (2008) have found that young people tend to prefer to express their cynicism of the agency of political institutions and distrust of party representatives via interest groups. These 'advocacy groups' are types of social movements that emphasise direct action and as a result bypass traditional structure of parties. Political parties have also had to compete with the more 'attractive' forms of engagement, for example, with the increase in the number of young people involved in more direct forms of participation such as protests, demonstrations, and so on. Whiteley (2007) suggests that 'Young cohorts of political activists prefer to get involved in single interest pressure groups and in other types of voluntary organisations, rather than in parties' (2007: 2).

Hooghe et al. (2004) find that young citizens are more likely to refrain from political activity, and in some cases the drop in civic engagement among the younger age cohorts has been responsible for the general decline in participation and turnout rates (Hooghe and Stolle, 2003; Gauthier and Pacom, 2001; Putnam, 2000; Rahn and Transue, 1998). While the age group 18–39 represented 37 per cent of the voters in 1998, it comprises only 17 per cent of all party members. People above the age of 60 made up to 26 per cent of the electorate as compared to 40 per cent of the members (2004: 372).

In Germany, where the Social Democratic Party once had a powerful youth section, the decline in youth party membership has been considerable (Offe and Fuchs, 2002: 216). Similarly, in Sweden, youth organisations lost more than 60 per cent of their members from 220,000 in 1972 to less than 50,000 in 1993 (Rothstein and Stolle, 2002: 294). Youth organisations are important in the recruitment of young citizens. They function as socialising agents for partisanship and aid the process of organisational learning. They also introduce young members to the ideology, ethos, and structure of the party. In addition, they function as a kind of learning school, where the members gradually grow acquainted with political and party life (Hooghe et al., 2004:

196). Despite the traditional role played by youth organisations of political parties in the recruitment of party members, these organisations have never been studied systematically.

Whilst parties are finding it harder to recruit members, the political marketplace is simultaneously becoming more competitive. There is simply a wider range of parties, social movements, interest or advocacy groups that vie for the participation and effort that citizens can offer and provide. Skocpol (2002: 131) suggests that in the US 'the professionally led advocacy group has emerged as a new and prominent feature of civic life.' (also cited by Seyd and Whiteley, 2004).

There is also an increased pressure on people's time, money, and effort. In addition, socio-economic and demographic changes have seen a decline of traditional working-class communities, the expansion of the suburbs, the decline of trade union membership and the growth of female employment. Politics has become more individualised. People are less willing to participate in collective forms of political activity (Pattie et al., 2004).

Scholars of party politics argue that this trend in declining levels of membership and the increase in levels of alternative group participation raises serious questions about the continued effectiveness of parties as bridges between civil society and government. This leads us to question the role of parties in democratic life. The prospect is that a corpus of professional leaders residing over a bare skeleton of a party shell. Professionalisation of politics, new technologies and political marketing are increasingly shrinking the linkage between civil society on the one hand, and the government and parties on the other. The literature on the decline of parties (see, for example, Dalton and Wattenberg, 2000; Meisel, 1991) and the literature on the professionalisation of parties reflect this risk of parties of becoming nothing more than member-less shells. Hooghe et al. (2004) state that the current decline in membership levels indicates the demise of mass-based parties in contemporary democracies. As a result of this development, parties have reacted to lower numbers of members by placing faith in new technologies over volunteer person-power (Butler and Ranney, 1992; Panebianco, 1988; Whitaker, 2001). Mass communications and marketing has enabled parties to reach voters directly, particularly at crucial times in the campaign calendar and of course in the event of elections. Seyd and Whiteley (2004) have found that parties have become less reliant on small subscriptions and now tend to increasingly depend upon donations from supporters and interested individuals Yet, whilst parties have other sources of finance and alternative communication channels, Scarrow (2000) observed that even in political parties that have become professionally dominated electoral machines, party members are still considered to be valuable as a resource in intra-party battles.

However, it must be remembered that members help provide parties with political legitimacy. They are an important testament to the fact that a party has support in the community and is rooted in the concerns and values of real people. In this sense, party members are often in contact with other citizens and as such may act as 'ambassadors to the community' (Scarrow, 1996: 43) or as 'representative figureheads in their local communities' (Whiteley et al., 1994: 4). Members that are visible in the local community convey 'the impression that a party is more than just an enterprise of the political elite' (Scarrow, 2000: 84). Members contribute voluntary manpower resources which can be crucial in times of elections and campaigns but their subscriptions also provide a non-negligible source of financial contributions. In addition, members and in particular young party members provide a pool of personnel from whom parties may recruit candidates for public offices at an array of different levels of responsibilities.

With their membership numbers dwindling, parties risk becoming increasingly detached from the voters they are meant to represent. Research on party members demonstrates that political party membership is generally unrepresentative of the electorate in terms of age, socio-economic status, education, and gender (Cross and Young, 2004; Gallagher and Marsh, 2002; Pedersen et al., 2004; Seyd and Whiteley, 2004). The 'professionalisation' of politics has led some to question the role of parties as the main linkage between civil society and government. Seyd and Whiteley (2004) suggest that the roles members have traditionally played as 'ambassadors' of the party in their community and their function as political communicators between civil society and the political party leadership are jeopardised by declining numbers of enrolees.

Whilst Mair and van Biezen (2001: 14) suggest that the general decline in party membership is paradoxical, as citizens 'appear to be as supportive of the idea of democracy as ever they were, they do not appear, however, to be quite so willing to involve themselves in actively maintaining the very institutions which democracy requires if it is to thrive'. This loss in interest and faith in political parties might signal that mass parties are losing ground in liberal democracies, only to be replaced by new types of political parties (Dalton and Wattenberg, 2000; Scarrow, 1996, 2000). Moreover, participatory politics is beset by another problem, that is, that the cost of participation generally outweighs the benefit received from the involvement. Therefore, parties find it hard to convince citizens to commit time, effort, and money to join their ranks and become party members.

Parties and young party organisations in Europe: The landscape

As explained at the beginning of this chapter, global levels of party membership have sharply declined in Europe since the 1970s. For instance, in the United Kingdom, the membership of the Labour party dropped from 666,000 in 1979 to 360,000 in 2001, that of the Conservatives from

1.35 million to 325,000 during the same period, while the Liberal Democrats were reduced from 145,000 to 80,000 at the same time. All three parties further declined between 2001 and now (see below for the latest figures). Table 1.1 gives a full account of this evolution between 1987 and 2000 using the work of Scarrow and Gezgor (2006). It gives the full extent of the collapsing attractiveness of European political parties on their national populations.

For instance, Table 1.1 shows us that in Norway, the part of the population enrolled in a political party declined from 13 per cent to 7 per cent between 1987 and 2000. In the same period, the national proportion of party members declined from 3 per cent to 2 per cent in the UK, from 4 per cent to 3 per cent in Germany, and from 10 per cent to 4 per cent in Italy. In short, almost all major European political parties have admitted a decline in their membership during this period.

At the same time, we also saw that the remaining party membership is also ageing. Table 1.2 looks at the over-representation of citizens aged over 60 in political party memberships as compared to the general national population.

Here again, the results are rather striking and in most European countries, citizens aged 60 and over are highly over-represented amongst party activists. This is, in fact, particularly acute in some of the six countries that we include in the study. In the United Kingdom, while people aged 60 and over only represent 24 per cent of the national population, they make up for 61 per cent of the country's party activists! Similarly, in Germany, they represent 58 per cent of party members across the country but only 33 per cent of the population. In France, these figures are 35 per cent and 23 per cent respectively, in Norway 33 per cent and 20 per cent, and, finally, in Hungary, 32 per cent and 25 per cent. Only Spain is an exception here, with a lower proportion of people aged 60 and over (16 per cent) in political parties than in the general population (24 per cent). Across Europe, Table 1.2 shows that Spain only shares this exceptional trend with Poland and Greece.

How big are political parties and young party organisations, then? Debates on the 'real' size of political parties has always been extremely controversial, with academics regularly taking the figures provided by political parties themselves with a (possibly generous!) pinch of salt. As it stands, typical membership figures in Europe vary very significantly. For instance, in Britain current estimates are of 208,000 for the British labour party, 290,000 for the Conservatives, about 70,000 for the Liberal Democrats, 16,000 for UKIP, and around 6,300 for the BNP. In Germany, by contrast, where the first prototypes of mass parties were to be found, there are still an estimated 530,000 members for the CDU (as well as 167,000 members of the CSU in Bavaria alone!), and comparable numbers of members for the SPD (approximately 540,000). Other German parties remain smaller with estimated memberships of 72,000 for the far left Linke, 64,000 for the FDP, and 44,000 for the Greens. However, membership figures are much lower

Table 1.1 Enrollment in political parties as per cent (%) of electorate (from Scarrow and Gezgor, 2006)

Country	Survey data		Party data			Evolution	
	Widfeldt 1989	ESS Combined 2002–2004	Katz and Mair 1987–1990	Scarrow 1994–1997	Mair and van Biezen 1997–2000	Survey 1989–2004	Party 1987–2000
Austria	–	13	21	17	18	–	–3
Belgium	9	7	9	8	7	–2	–2
Denmark	8	6	7	3	5	–2	–2
Finland	14*	7	13	11	10	–7	–3
France	**4**	**2**	–	**2**	**2**	**–2**	**0*****
Germany	**6**	**3**	**4**	**3**	**3**	**–3**	**–1**
Great Britain	**5**	**3**	**3**	**2**	**2**	**–2**	**–1**
Greece	12	6	–	–	7	–6	–
Ireland	4	5	5	3	3	+1	–2
Italy	7	4	10	3	4	–3	–6
Luxembourg	9	8	–	–	–	–1	–
Netherlands	7	5	3	–	3	–2	0
Norway	**12**	**9**	**13**	**8**	**7**	**–3**	**–6**
Portugal	3	4	–	–	4	+1	–
Spain	**3**	**4**	–	–	**3**	**+1**	–
Sweden	12**	8	8	7	6	–4	–2
Switzerland	–	8	–	9	6	–	–3***
CzechRepublic	–	4	–	–	4	–	–
Hungary	–	**1**	–	–	**2**	–	–
Poland	–	1	–	–	1	–	–
Slovenia	–	4	–	–	–	–	–

* 1987

** 1988

*** 1994–2000

Note: Evolution figures are not included in the Scarrow and Gezgor paper but have been calculated for the purposes of this book. Countries in bold are the six countries included in the analysis for this book.

Source: Scarrow and Gezgor (2006).

Table 1.2 The over-representation of the elderly in the population of party members

Country	Members % > 60	Population % > 60	Difference	Difference in 1990 (Widfeldt)
Austria	21	16	5*	–
Belgium	33	21	12*	−1
Denmark	40	23	17*	9
Finland	47	25	22*	3
France	35	23	12*	3
Germany	58	33	25*	0
Great Britain	61	24	37*	5
Greece	28	29	−1*	−7
Ireland	38	21	17*	−3
Italy	29	23	6*	−1
Luxembourg	31	15	16*	1
Netherlands	33	21	12*	14
Norway	33	20	13*	10
Portugal	26	27	−1	−4
Spain	16	24	−8	−5
Sweden	41	24	17*	9
Switzerland	37	21	16*	–
Czech Republic	40	23	17*	–
Hungary	32	25	7*	–
Poland	13	19	−6*	–
Slovenia	31	23	8*	–

*: $p < 0.05$.
Note: Countries in bold are the six countries included in the analysis for this book.
Source: Scarrow and Gezgor (2006), incluing reference to Widfeldt (1995).

for French, Hungarian, Norwegian, and Spanish political parties in absolute numbers.

Young party organisations are usually rather smaller affairs but vary significantly across countries. For instance, the membership of the UH, the young party organisation associated with the Norwegian Høyre claims 2,200 members aged between 14 and 30, including 63 per cent men and 37 per cent female. In Germany, where we have seen that political parties are quite large, the JU (young CDU) claim 130,000 members aged 18–35, JUSOS (young SPD) 70,000, and JULIS (the young Liberal Democrats) approximately 10,000. By contrast, the French 'Souris Vertes' (young Greens) only claim up to 2,000 members nationwide and the FNJ barely a little bit more.

It is worth noting that the relationship between young party organisations and the political parties they correspond to vary significantly across countries and parties. For instance, the Spanish NNGG and the French Jeunesses Communistes and right-wing Jeunes Populaires are very strongly related to their mother parties. This link is similar for the Hungarian FIDELITAS (young party organisation of the right-wing FIDESZ), and the Norwegian

UH, and even more pronounced for the young party organisation of the Hungarian MSzP, which has almost no organisational autonomy. By contrast, the German JUSOS has a tradition of great independence from the SPD and, in fact, of occasionally severe ideological disagreements with it. Finally, in some other cases, such as those of the French MJS, Spanish JSE, and most British parties, the level of autonomy or dependency between the young party organisation and the political party itself varies quite a lot according to the personality of the leaders of both organisations as well as their ideological majorities. Thus, while, for a certain time, the French FNJ seemed to follow quite a different 'route' from the FN, it was reined in quite severely in the 2000s. The French Parti Socialiste tried to do the same thing with the MJS in the mid-2000s but its attempts to regain control of the young party organisation were met with rebellion and fell through.

How do we do it?

In order to explore the world of young party members and make sense, not only of their whole, but also of their various sub-groups, the book will define an analytical model and typology of young party members. We will thus differentiate between three categories of young members, some of whom intend to become tomorrow's leaders, some who see themselves as grass root members, and some who see themselves as part of a social group. As explained, the original data collected from the six-country comparative survey of the young members of 15 parties, and the comparative in-depth interviews allow us to provide some important answers to the various questions we have identified above. After we define our trichotomous model of young activists characterised as moral, social, and professional-minded, we explore the significantly divergent trajectories, preferences, perceptions, involvement, and future prospects of the three types of members, unravelling what they believe, think, and hope for. We draw upon the wealth of quantitative and qualitative evidence we have gathered from the survey and the in-depth interviews throughout the book.

Altogether, this book will 'tell the story' of young party members' involvement, from the origins of their enrolment in a political party to their future dreams via a detailed account of the impact of their membership on their daily life, as well as an emphasis on their partisan, political, and democratic beliefs, preferences, and perceptions.

Approach and structure of the book

As we have detailed above, the scope and object of the book are vast and rather ambitious. Throughout the course of this 'journey' into the world of young party members, we want to give the reader an insight into the hearts and minds of young people that few of us really know anything about and understand. The images and preconceptions any of us might hold about young party members are undoubtedly as numerous as they are approximative. Some of us imagine dedicated ideologues, others ambitious and competitive careerists, when it is not brainwashed fanatics, skilled propagandists, glorified selfless idealists, or gifted communicators. In order to go beyond these conflicting stereotypes and to acknowledge the diversity and specificity of a group, which comprises of hundreds of thousands of young Europeans, our approach consists of mixing the big story with individual accounts. Our mass survey of young party members allows us to capture trends, types, and general tendencies. The hundreds of in-depth interviews that we carried out offer us the polychromatic world of ever changing individual stories, each corresponding to a unique life, and a unique way of living one's membership.

In a way, the book follows the trajectory of a young party member's life, starting from the origins of their decision to join, continuing onto a glimpse into their daily life as young activists, exploring their perceptions and beliefs, and finishing with their perceptions of their own future. Figure 1.1 sketches the journey through which our book will transport the reader, and depicts the trail that we will follow.

The result is the following structure.

Chapters 1 and 2 set the scene for our study. In the rest of Chapter 1, we place our research in its wider context. How does our book fit within the existing literature, what is the state of young party membership today, what sort of numbers are we talking about, how do parties integrate their young members, how are young party organisations structured, and so on.

Chapter 2 defines the trichotomous model of types of young party members and details how we intend to test the derived hypotheses. We discuss the logic of the trichotomous model and how it relates to and follows on from the incentives literature and the existing models of partisan involvement. This chapter also provides further details about the methodology that is used throughout the book. Finally, we test our trichotomous model using factor analysis and our mass survey results.

The next six chapters focus on different thematic dimensions of partisan involvement. To start with, Chapter 3 deals with the origins of this involvement. Where do young party members come from? What makes them join a party? Do they follow specific influences, and do we know anything about the critical moment when their decision to join a political party becomes effective. Chapter 4 details the daily life of a young party member. What are their activities and how do they vary?. Chapter 5 then looks at the impact of the commitment of young party members on their life. What sort of commitment represents the membership of a young activist? What is the impact of party membership on their relationship with their family and friends? In Chapter 6, we start exploring the beliefs and perceptions of young party members. How do relate to their party as a political

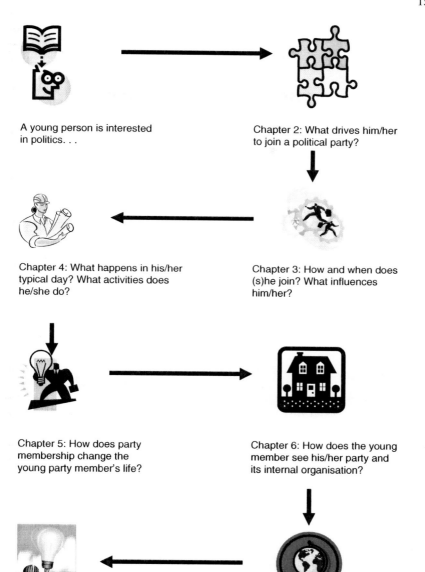

A young person is interested in politics. . .

Chapter 2: What drives him/her to join a political party?

Chapter 4: What happens in his/her typical day? What activities does he/she do?

Chapter 3: How and when does (s)he join? What influences him/her?

Chapter 5: How does party membership change the young party member's life?

Chapter 6: How does the young member see his/her party and its internal organisation?

Chapter 8: How does the young party member see – and dream of – his/her future?

Chapter 7: How does the young party member perceive democracy and want to change politics?

Figure 1.1 The journey

organisation? What are their priorities for their political party? How do they perceive its internal organisation? Do they feel efficacious, that is, do they have the impression that they matter within their parties? How do they see the relationship between young and less young party members, between members and leaders, and so on.

Chapter 7 evaluates young party members' attitudes towards their democracy. What are their policy priorities, what do they want to change in the life of others and how do they believe that they can manage. What do they believe is the place of political parties in democracies, do they think of politics as a profession, and what do they think of the apparent erosion of the attractiveness of political parties vis-à-vis non-partisan organisations such as pressure groups, citizens' groups, and so on? Then, in Chapter 8, young party members are asked to talk about their personal future. How do they see themselves in ten years from now? Do they expect their partisan involvement to continue, to change, to progress? Do they expect to run for election or take increasing positions of responsibility within their party? Do they expect their political involvement to be solely channelled by their partisan activism, or do they rather think that they will also choose to join another organisation, such as a pressure group or a union in order to support their political views?

Finally, Chapter 9 concludes the study and evaluates the impact of what we have learnt about young party members on what we can expect for our democracies themselves. Does the current generation of new young party members stand for anything different from their predecessors? Do they claim to have a different vision of the ills of our current political systems than what they perceive to be the vision of politicians in their 40s and 50s? Do they want to change anything? Can we already differentiate, at this young age, between those who will continue to represent the grass roots of European political parties, and a smaller nucleus of emerging leaders, and if yes what possible consequences will they have for the future of our democracies?

2
Model and Methods

We have seen from the previous chapter that young party membership as a phenomenon has largely been overlooked in a comparative manner and we have gained a better sense of the current challenges faced by political scientists who specialise in party politics in order to focus our attention on the complex nature and world of young party activists. In this chapter, we detail the ambition and scope of this book. We plan to analyse the underexposed world of young party membership in Europe in a way that will enable the reader to take a journey through the lives of young party members and offer them a glimpse into the hearts and minds of young party activists.

As explained in Chapter 1, our book is concerned with explaining: 'who exactly young party members are, what they seek, how they have come to join a political party, what being a party member means in their everyday life, and how they perceive politics, their party, their democracy, and their own political future.' Through this perspective, this chapter is the 'Ikea toolbox' of our book. This is where we explain what gap we try to fill in our disciplinary edifice of knowledge, the 'model' of what we believe goes through the hearts and minds of young party members and how we propose to test this model and characterise young party members' motivations, activities, perceptions, and preferences using a mixture of quantitative and qualitative methods. These tasks are taken on successively in this chapter.

We first outline the state of the literature on what we know about youth participation and why people decide to join a political party. We then expose our trichotomous model. In the third part of the chapter, we detail our methodology and the comparative spectrum of the project. We then finally test the proposed trichotomy used throughout the book by running a factor analysis of the incentives referred to by young party members in our survey.

Why people join parties

Party membership, one of the most time and cost intensive forms of activism, has suffered severely from widespread public dissatisfaction with politics. This has led to a steady decline in levels of membership across most of Europe (Katz et al., 1992; Mair and van Biezen, 2001; Seyd and Whiteley, 2004; Scarrow, 1996; also endnote 3) and its consistent ageing (Scarrow and Gezgor, 2006). Yet, in the golden age of mass parties, millions of Europeans from diverse backgrounds readily paid their dues to join their preferred party. Consequently, understanding what drives some citizens to join a party remains an important puzzle. In this section, we review some of the main models drawn from the literature to characterise membership incentives and explain one of the main contributions of our book – to move beyond satisfactory incentives models to categories of young party members per se.

Political science has long been interested in the specific characteristics of party members. In the particular case of youth participation, Cross and Young (2008) show that young activists tend to be more interested in politics, more likely to have an activist parent, and more trusting of parties' efficacy than members of advocacy groups.

There is also an extensive literature devoted to identifying competing models of incentives. It differentiates between material, purposive, and solidary incentives (Clark and Wilson, 1961) and between selective and collective incentives (Seyd and Whiteley, 1992). In the first model, material benefits correspond to specific spoils or advantages that the party redistributes to members. By contrast, purposive incentives correspond to the pursuit of the goals of the organisation (as per the party manifesto) via one's membership, and solidary incentives the benefits of social interaction with like-minded people. The second distinction separates those benefits of membership which can be enjoyed individually by the party member, and those which can only be enjoyed by a larger group, be it a specific group or the country as a whole. Overall, these typologies have proved their efficiency and correspond to intuitively convincing incentive categories. For instance, party membership can clearly bring material benefits. This was particularly true in spoils-based systems such as the first Republic in Italy or the former Communist countries.

Solidary and purposive benefits tend to be the predominant incentives for a majority of party activists. These benefits, referred to as collective by Seyd and Whiteley (1992) often relate to a well-documented ideological and policy influence of party members. Panebianco (1988) argues that while the relationship between leaders and members is unequal, grass root activists control some organisational resources, and gain influence over local policy outcomes with their (limited) agenda-setting powers. They serve as key intermediaries between voters and the political elites. In this sense, party members retain an 'ambassadorial role' within the community (Martin and Cowley, 1999; Scarrow, 1996; Seyd and Whiteley, 2004).

Party members are also sometimes the first to be consulted by politicians who want to test the likely effect of their proposals on the population before using focus group or other 'scientific' evaluations. In this sense, members can also lobby local elected representatives or run for office and become elected themselves albeit in junior positions. Thus, an individual may be motivated by a desire to see his preferred policy proposals and outputs enacted if he feels very strongly about certain policy priorities. May (1973) emphasises this ideological focus of party activists, and derives that party members tend to hold more extreme ideological views than voters and leaders alike and will try to 'pull' the party's policy proposals towards these more radical preferences. This theory, known as the May's Law of curvilinear disparity, implies that by definition, party members hold policy and ideological preferences that cannot be reconciled with those of the population in general. As an important consequence, not only are party members disconnected from voters' preferences, but internal party democracy, which is usually perceived as a 'good thing' in that it gives members an important say in the party's ideological programme, is paradoxically bound to result in a deterioration of the representativeness of political parties in a given democracy.

Margolis (1982) and Mueller (1989) show that these preferred policy positions are not just self-interested but correspond to members' genuine evaluations of what they believe to be the interest of society as a whole, and overall, the literature is unanimous to suggest that collective incentives take precedence over selective incentives for most members. This has led to the concept of 'altruistic incentives', which are sometimes considered to be the prime motivation of party members, be they of right-wing (Whiteley et al., 1994), or left-wing parties (Seyd and Whiteley, 1992).

A number of models propose variations on the types of incentives highlighted above and look at more specific reasons why people join parties. The first main motivation is a desire to pursue ideological preferences. This means that the young party member would want to express an interest in their particular preferences and try to help the party attain office and implement their preferred policies. Clark and Wilson (1961) formalise this particular incentive as purposive. Pedersen et al. (2004) confirm the importance of ideology and the support of policies as a key motivation of joining a party. In this sense, party membership is a means by which voters can communicate interests and viewpoints to party representatives in national, local and regional governments. Young and Cross (2008) also find that many youth members joined a political party specifically to participate in either a local candidate selection or a party leadership vote. In all, close to two-thirds of the youth members suggest that they were motivated to join their party because of one of these personnel recruitment contests (2008: 354). In terms of policy-seeking preferences, one in three youth members report joining a political party specifically to influence a public policy issue (2008: 354).

The second main inspiration to join a party is to follow a specific career path by attaining positions of responsibility within the party's structure and running for elections in an aim to secure office. This particular sense of following personal desires of professional development is commonly known as selective or material incentives (Clark and Wilson, 1961). It is not surprising to find that few party members mention the desire to have a political career as a key reason for joining a political party. This is tied to a dominant social norm about not promoting oneself. However, Hooghe et al. (2004) found that 41 per cent of the councillors they studied had started their career in a youth organisation. Networks tend to be important for any kind of political recruitment, and those who are strongly integrated into the party fabric will have a better chance of acquiring leading political positions (Diani and McAdam, 2003; Stouthuysen, 1991).

The final motivation that often underpins the decision to join a political party concerns the set of collective or solidary incentives (Clark and Wilson, 1961). This particular explanation of political participation emphasises the role of altruistic goals and the importance of group participation in order to make the world a better place or to help people who are less fortunate. This incentive often overlaps with the numerous aspects of social interaction, for example, some young people often decide to join a political party to meet new friends, engage in interesting debates and interact with like-minded people on a regular basis. This 'fun-factor' of taking part in a social organisation, such as a political party, is often regarded as an important aspect of party membership.

Pedersen et al. (2004) outline four main reasons that underpin the decision to join a political party. Firstly, members joined a party to promote specific ideological preferences. This factor accounted for 54 per cent of the respondents. Secondly, members who wanted to express their support for their preferred party accounted for 46 per cent of the respondents. Thirdly, a significant proportion of respondents wanted to express support for party policies, a reason for 31 per cent of the respondents. Finally, 40 per cent of the respondents wanted to oppose other parties such as the extreme right and the extreme left.

From incentives to members types: A trichotomous model of young party members

Overall, there is therefore a robust body of literature explaining why some people decide to devote time, resources, and energy to party membership. Beyond that, however, it is important to question whether these findings fully capture the specific situation of *young* party members. In the particular case of youth participation in Canada, Cross and Young (2008) show that young activists tend to be more interested in politics, more likely to have an activist parent, and more trusting of parties' efficacy than members of advocacy groups.

Alongside the specificity of the characteristics attributed to young party members, we want to investigate whether categories of incentives are equally shared by all members, or if, instead, individual members are driven by specific sets of incentives, which ascribe them to a membership 'type', with characteristic preferences, attitudes, and behaviours.

Without undermining the value of the types of incentives defined by the literature, we expect young party members to differ from their elder in terms of their perception of membership incentives because of what psychology suggests to be more 'dramatic' stakes associated with moral, social, and professional self-construction in young adulthood. Young party members are first and foremost 'young people', who are at the time of one's life when one defines his long-term moral, social, and professional orientations. With regard to moral postures, Sigel (1989) notes that 'much of the foundation for political life – affect, cognition, and participation – is in place as the young person reaches adulthood.' Thus, the ideological mindset of a young adult is likely to be experienced far more vividly than later, and the stakes associated with his moral positioning entail serious consequences in terms of self-identity definition.

Similarly, in social terms, Salzinger et al. (1988), and Schaffer (1971) stress that no other age is associated with a greater need to find one's place vis-à-vis others by building social and human networks. Finally, it is between the ages of 18–25 that most young people decide their desired path for their professional future, finalising academic and professional choices with profound long-term implications (Cannon, 1995; Gokalp, 1981).

In this sense, each type of classically defined membership incentive could take a more dramatic and original sense in the context of young party members. What for others would be a 'regular' collective incentive could be transformed into a crucial element of moral identification for a young adult defining his belief system. This would explain why the limited literature focusing on young party organisations in Europe – particularly in Germany and the UK (Bilstein, Hohlbein et al., 1971; Ellis, 2005; Merkl, 1977), systematically argues that young party organisations (and thus, by extension, their members) are more radical than their mother parties.

The selective incentives that lead party members, in general, to enjoy mingling with like-minded individuals are likely, in the case of young members, to be highlighted by their emerging social self-definition and need for belonging. Finally, while many established activists will think of material incentives as a few free concert tickets or a party's mobile phone, many young people may rightly or wrongly hope the 'prize' of their membership to be a whole professional future. Beyond these specificities, however, an essential claim of our model is that based on such dramatic potential implications, we should not simply think of membership incentives as randomly cumulating to explain the choice to join a party. Instead, we hypothesise that each member is characterised by the structural predominance of a category of incentives, resulting in three distinct types of young party members – moral-, social-, and professional-minded, who will differ in a number of attitudinal and behavioural patterns. Let us now consider these member types.

The moral-minded members

As we have seen, purposive incentives, including altruistic incentives and those centred upon ideology, tend to be prominent in the motivations of most activists in general. At the same time, social psychology suggests that young people tend to be more 'idealistic' than their elder (McCarthy, 2000; Samms, 1995), and that the importance they attach to their developing values may be reinforced by rebellious reactions to the perceived attitudes of family members, teachers, or young people in general. In general terms, the moral incentives of a young party member correspond to this idealistic value of membership and a specific desire to give more meaning and direction to one's life. In this sense, we expect the greatest share of young party members to be *moral-minded*, that is, to have predominantly chosen to join a party to express and assert their newly crystallised moral beliefs. In the context of their developing intellectual identity, party membership will be perceived as giving more meaning to their life and reinforcing a sense of helping others.

Considering the source of their motivation, we expect moral-minded members to embrace the logic of the May Law by seeing themselves as more radical (or at least more 'ideological') than their leaders. We expect them to wish to engage in other forms of organised participation – such as union or pressure group membership – that would also be a confirmation of their moral choices. These members will also be most likely to embrace radical modes of participation, such as demonstrations or the fight against other parties. We finally expect them to put the most emphasis on policy-seeking priorities and to be the least likely to consider politics as a profession.

The social-minded members

As explained earlier in this chapter, solidary incentives are likely to take a particularly critical meaning in the context of a young person's wish to feel integrated in a social group, and cultivate the 'entertainment' value of his party membership. As a form of social engagement, party membership provides young members with a chance to meet like-minded people, make new friends or simply exchange political opinions. As young adults are the most likely to feel socially inept or alienated, solidary incentives can predominantly explain the desire of many to join a party. We refer to them as *social-minded members*. For a social-minded member, attending local meetings where he or she can interact with like-minded people on a regular basis will be typically a core benefit of membership. Tullock (1971) theorised this 'fun' factor of organisational participation. We expect social-minded members to be the least involved of all young activists, and the least certain about their future political involvement. We also expect them to be the least efficacious of young members in that their allegiance will be pledged to their friends, rather than to the organisation or party ideology. Finally, we hypothesise that for the same reason, they will be the least active type of young members preferring to socialise on an occasional basis rather than on a daily routine.

The professional-minded members

Finally, it is with regard to material incentives that we expect to see the greatest difference between young party members and party members in general. Indeed, as young people are at an age to decide on their professional future, the potential material implications of a membership that could transform into a career path exceed any material reward that could be coveted by members already installed in a solid career path. The existing literature shows that regular members are only marginally interested in material incentives, which usually take the form of fringe material benefits gained directly or indirectly via unions (Clark and Wilson, 1961; Clarke et al., 2000; Young and Cross, 2002). These rewards will usually weigh little in the perceptions of young party members.

However, by nature, party membership can offer a number of professional and quasi-professional opportunities, which can be highly alluring to young people. The prospect of 'becoming a politician' (especially perceived as a 'profession') or simply deriving a job from one's political involvement, be it an internship, an administrative job in the party organisation or related groups (German foundations, British unions, French mutuelle-based insurance companies, etc) can be a very serious source of motivation for a young person. With an increasingly competitive job market, the decision to join a political party may thus be largely caught up in the desire to secure a career in politics. Regarding partisanship as a professional path will alter a series of perceptions and attitudes of the young party member, thus defined as a *professional-minded member*.

Becoming a young party member is *the* obvious path for young people who want to become politicians. A survey conducted by Hooghe, Stolle and Stouthuysen (2004) among city councillors in Belgium (Flanders) showed that 41 per cent of all councillors started their political career in a youth organisation. As such, this particular profile deserves special attention. Because there are ultimately a limited number of elected functions that a party can provide, we expect professional-minded young party members to be the smallest of all three categories. We suggest that they will have very different characteristics from their peers. As potential leaders, we expect them to be more moderate in terms of their ideological preferences than their counterparts (see reference to May's Law of curvilinear disparity earlier). They will be the least bothered about putting specific policies proposals on the agenda (policy-seeking) and will be ultimately, driven by a desire to seek an elected office. As a result, they will be the most likely to seek positions of responsibility in the future. Because the party represents their chosen career path, we also expect professional-minded young activists to be reluctant to 'distract' themselves with involvement in other organisations. They will be the most active (in order to prove their worth to the party) in terms of vote-seeking oriented participation (handing out flyers, trying to convince voters, sticking posters, etc), and the most convinced that politics is a profession. Finally, we expect professional-minded young party members to be the most efficacious of all.

Beyond these patterns, we hypothesise some differences across types of political systems. As seen earlier, in partitocratic systems, parties have traditionally enjoyed a great influence on citizens' daily life (Deschouwer and De Winter, 1998), which leads us to expect that professional-minded members should be more numerous in these systems. By contrast, fully or partly pillarised societies such as the Netherlands, Belgium, or Germany have a tradition of party-based social activities including young people's groups, and so on (Bax, 1990; Lijphart, 1968; Verkade, 1965). In such cases, we would expect social-minded members to be more prominent than elsewhere. Finally, the electoral literature has shown that cleavages and ideological commitments are more powerful in heavily polarised systems (Franklin et al., 1992; Hirczy, 1995), from which we derive that the more polarised the system, the higher the proportion of moral-minded members.

A model of young party members' preferences, behaviour, and attitudes: The hypotheses tested in the book

Our model suggests that there are three types of young party members, based on their dominant structuring incentives, and that they are characterised by different sets of preferences, attitudes, beliefs, behaviour, and perceptions of their party and their own political role. We also believe that there are three main competing paths to membership, which lead young people to join a party, as well as a number of 'catalytic' events that prompt their final decision to do so.

Our model includes (1) exploratory hypotheses on the characteristics of young party members in general, as well as cross-country and cross-party family comparisons, and (2) hypotheses on the impact of types of young member on a series of preferences, attitudes, and behaviour. Consistently with what we explained in Chapter 1, we organise the book's hypotheses in six different sections: hypotheses on (1) the trichotomous model of membership, (2) young party members' activities, (3) their path to membership, (4) their attitudes towards their party, (5) their attitudes towards democracy and their representative responsibility, and (6) their future. Altogether, we test the following hypotheses:

(1) HYPOTHESES ON THE TRICHOTOMOUS MODEL OF YOUNG PARTY MEMBERS:

H1: Three types of young party members: Young party members join political parties on the basis of one of three main dimensions of incentives: moral, social, and professional. Each respondent has a predominant structuring 'membership drive', which characterises him/her as a moral-minded, a social-minded, or a professional-minded young party member.

H1a: Imbalance: A dominant proportion of party members are moral-minded, a significant proportion are social-minded, and a smaller section are professional-minded.

H1b: Political system and members types: Types of political system influence the distribution of members across the three types. There are more professional-minded members in systems where parties can influence the distribution of public sector jobs (e.g. Hungary), social-minded members are over-represented in countries with a pillarised tradition of party-based societies, and so on. (e.g. Germany), and moral-minded members are more numerous in more polarised party systems.

(2) ON HOW SOME YOUNG PEOPLE BECOME PARTY MEMBERS

H2: Membership influence: Young people will join following the influence of their family, their friends, or based on their experience in other organisations. Family will be the dominant influence.

H2a: Process of influence: Influence can work either positively (imitation), or negatively (opposition).

H2b: The catalyst of joining: A young party member will often be able to identify a specific event as the catalyst of his or her enrolment in a political party.

(3) ON THE ACTIVITIES OF YOUNG PARTY MEMBERS

H3: Activism: Professional-minded members are most active in terms of 'electoral' activities (convincing others, handing out flyers, sticking posters), moral-minded ones are most active in terms of radical activities (demonstrations, fighting other parties), and social-minded ones are least active overall.

(4) ON ATTITUDES TOWARDS THE MEMBER'S PARTY

H4: Party objectives: When young party members are asked to prioritise between policy, vote, and office-seeking objectives, moral-minded members are most likely to emphasise policy-seeking objectives, and professional-minded members will highlight office-seeking objectives.

> *H5: Efficacy and satisfaction with party politics*: Professional-minded members are the most efficacious, the most positive about the party's organisation, and the most likely to think of politics as a profession. Social members are the most critical and least efficacious; moral members are least likely to think of politics as a profession.

(5)   ON ATTITUDES TOWARDS DEMOCRACY AND REPRESENTATION

> *H6: Policy priorities and the duty of representation*: Moral-minded members are the most polarised in their policy priorities, emphasising policy areas that correspond to the core of their party's ideology whilst dismissing the rest. We expect professional-minded members to be least polarised in their policy preferences.
>
> *H7: Perceptions of professionalisation*: Moral-minded members are the least likely to think of politics as a profession, whilst professional-minded members will be the most likely to be convinced of the professionalization of politics.

(6)   ON THE YOUNG PARTY MEMBER'S FUTURE

> *H5: Future of membership*: Social-minded members are the least certain of their future political activism. Moral-minded members are most likely to consider joining other organisations. Professional-minded members are least likely to do so but most likely to seek positions of responsibility or elected functions in the future.

Methods

The approach

This ambitious set of hypotheses calls for complex methodological choices. How can we test hypotheses that pertain to the past, present, and imagined future of young party members? How can we develop a research design that will allow us at the same time to test some fairly straightforward hypotheses, and to listen to every shade and nuance of long and unique personal stories? Finally, how can we study young party members as a sub-group of party members in general?

Regularly, political scientists wish to focus on a specific group and put their behaviour, perceptions, or characteristics under the spotlight – abstentionists, switching voters, extreme right supporters, and so on. In this case, we want to study a sub-group of party members, that is, *young* party members. We want to understand what drives them, the logic of the specific attitude or behaviour that makes them so interesting to us.

Studies concerning the motivations of a specific group of citizens can be conceived in two different ways. The first approach consists of isolating the population of interest, sampling it, and using quantitative or qualitative means to ask its members about their self-perceived motivations, the way they explain the logic of their own choice. This is a non-comparative approach, solely focused on the target group, which is not compared to non-group members. Thus, it is not because someone tells us that he has joined a party because he wanted to make the world a better place that a non-party member might not be equally interested in improving the world we live in. Instead, a member/non-member comparison might have revealed that the 'real' difference between those who join a party and those who do not is that the former are, say, more trusting of elites than the latter. This empathic approach is also based on self-perceptions and it shares the problems of other self-placement measures. A respondent could tell us that he has joined a party out of interest in the life of others but may well, in fact, have no interest in the lives of others at all.

The alternative model implies relying on a global survey of the population where one question discriminates between target group members and others (e.g. Whiteley, 2007), or two parallel surveys comparing two specific target groups (e.g. Cross and Young, 2008, between Canadian young party members and young advocacy group members). We can then compare the characteristics of those 'in' and 'out.' This second model, however, also has serious downsides. First, we can only compare respondents' background or attitudinal characteristics, but not their motivations (one cannot technically compare motivations to join a party to motivations that have made some people not join). Second, there are significant statistical difficulties in comparing the characteristics of members of the targeted group *vs* others within a single survey when the distribution of the membership variable is skewed (so it is easy to compare the characteristics of abstentionists to voters in an election where turnout is 50 per cent but *not* when it is 97 per cent, and party membership *is* skewed). When choosing two separate surveys, we need to assume that both can rely on similar sampling procedures, which is not always possible. There is thus no 'perfect' design for such a study. Like a vast majority of studies of party members (Hooghe et al., 2004; Seyd and Whiteley, 2004 and 1992), we choose the first solution for two main reasons. First, the existing literature simply does not tell us, as yet, how young party members explain their choice to join. This information is, as such, invaluable, requires the use of the 'empathic' method, and is arguably needed to refine any member/non-member comparative design. Second, the distribution of party membership in the population is highly skewed, and one could not possibly construct a random sample of the young partisan population.[1]

Scope of the comparison

The study thus relies on a large-scale survey of young members[2] of 15 participating parties in six countries: UK, France, Germany, Spain, Norway, and Hungary. These countries represent a variety of political and party systems.

Political systems range from old democracies (UK), to relatively (Spain) and very (Hungary) recently democratised states. France and Hungary are semi-presidential while the rest have parliamentary systems. Germany is a federal state, Spain is quasi-federal, the UK has a devolution system, and the other countries are unitary. In terms of party systems, the UK has one of the lowest effective numbers of parties in Europe, France, Spain, and Germany have multi-party systems structured around two blocks, and Norway and Hungary have larger party systems with changing coalitions. Germany and Norway have partly pillarised and corporatist organisations while the other countries do not. Hungary has a tradition of a spoils system and strong party involvement in all spheres of work and society, something the other countries do not share. Finally, the countries vary in size, wealth, and dominant ideologies.

The 15 parties also represent a broad variety of sizes and ideologies. All main party families are represented – from extreme left to extreme right via Socialist, Conservative, Liberal, Green, and Communist parties. Membership and young party membership vary considerably across the parties, from a few hundred to thousands for the youth membership, and from a few thousand for the French Greens to 540,000 for the German SPD. Some of the parties attract a large share of young members, while others openly acknowledge the ageing of their membership.

The parties included in the study ordered by country are: France: Parti Socialiste (Socialist), les Verts (Green), Parti Communiste Français (Communist), Front National (Nationalist); UK: Labour (Social Democrat), Liberal Democrats (Liberal), UK Independence Party (Eurosceptic), British National Party (Nationalist); Germany: CDU (Christian Democrat), SPD (Social Democrat), FDP (Liberal); Spain: PSOE (Socialist), PP (Conservative); Norway: Høyre (Conservative), Labour (Socialist); and Hungary: MSzP (Socialist), Fidesz (Conservative).[3]

The survey

The questionnaire was made available on the project's website in the six languages. Representative samples of branches[4] were recruited in co-operation with the parties and/or young party organisations, who circulated an invitation to participate in the study, as well as a unique pin code, to all of their members. Co-operating with the parties was necessary as party members' lists are not publicly available. It was also important because it gave some legitimacy to our appeal and, thus, undoubtedly increased response rates. The risk was that the study would be perceived as associated with the party, leading to biased answers, so all the material (invitation emails and letters, website, survey heading) insisted on the independence, academic character, and anonymity of the study. The response rate was 69 per cent across all parties[5] in a total sample of 2919 respondents. The individual pin codes were used to avoid error or manipulation by ill-intended third parties. The anonymous survey was self-completed on-line using drop-down menus and blank response fields. The survey, reproduced in the appendix, took 10 minutes to complete, and included questions on the membership, motivation, efficacy, incentives, activities, and evaluations of the young member.

The interviews

Following the survey, respondents were asked whether they would also accept to take part in an in-depth follow up interview, which would take place within a few weeks. Over 900 of the nearly 3000 survey respondents accepted this invitation, but we chose to limit our interviews to political parties where we could at least interview 20 respondents or more. The final list of parties included in the interview component of the study thus comprised of: (1) in the UK: the Labour party, the Liberal Democrats, the BNP; (2) in France: The Parti Socialiste, the Parti Communiste, Les Verts, and the Front National; (3) in Germany: the CDU, the FDP, and the SPD; (4) in Spain: The Partido Popular and the PSOE; (5) in Hungary: the MSzP, and the Fidesz, and (6) in Norway: the Høyre. A few of the volunteers were not interviewed because of a need to rationalise visits to specific cities, and so on, but overall, we conducted 519 interviews across the six countries.[6]

The interviews were semi-structured, with provisions for in-depth development, and lasted anywhere between 45 minutes and 2 hours, with an average of approximately 1 hour 10 minutes. The interviews were conducted in isolated offices within local party branches or social clubs, in cafes, or in other quiet locations available such as rental offices.

At the beginning of the interview, the interviewer would always ask the interviewee about their background (age, position, length of membership, etc) and how they ended up joining their political party or young party organisation (including questions on family heritage, role models, hesitation on which party to join, questions on when their decision to join was made and implemented, etc).

Following this introduction, the interviewer would ask the young party member about their incentives to join and mentally ascribe them to one of our three groups when possible. The other sections of the interview included questions about the interviewee's social networks within the party, what their friends and family thought of their membership, what they think of the party, its internal organisation (internal democracy, efficacy, etc), what they do and do not like about it, what they do as part of their partisan activism, how often they work for the party and for how long. Questions also targeted their perceptions of fellow members, of how democracy works in their country, on the political interest or apathy of citizens in general and young citizens in particular, its causes, and its possible solutions. Finally, the interviews also had sections on events or moments that marked the interviewee's membership, on their participation in election campaigns, and on how they saw their future. Being semi-structured, the questions varied from interview to interview but these themes were always approached systematically, and the interviewers were asked to accommodate for in-depth discussions by the respondents on the topics that seemed to inspire them most.

The interviews were conducted by the two authors in addition to one or two local interviewers in each country except in the UK. Each interviewer was fully trained and provided with an interview template, and for each of them, we conducted the firstdozen interviews together in order to ensure optimal consistency across the interviewers. The interviewers took notes during the interviews including a pre-established amount of verbatim notes, which are used for the quotes throughout the book. They translated them (interviews were conducted in the mother tongue of the interviewees) and sent them to us with a description of the interviewee's first name, age, town, and position within the party.

Confirming the moral, social, and professional members trichotomy

H1 suggests that young party members can be categorised into three broad types, corresponding to the dominant set of incentives that has led each young citizen to join a party. We defined these three member profiles as moral, social, and professional. The hypothesis has two implications: the first is the existence of three latent types of incentives, and the second the notion that every young party member has, in fact, one dominant membership drive. In order to test *H1*, we factor analyse respondents' assessment of a series of 10 possible incentives. We use principal components extraction and Varimax rotation. The factor analysis confirms the tridimensional model (Table 2.1). It shows that membership incentives load into the three predicted dimensions. The model is upheld in both the unrotated and rotated solutions. A 'moral' drive is characterised by a desire to give more meaning to one's life, to help others, to be a good citizen, and to influence politics. It broadly corresponds to the purposive incentives defined in the literature.

Table 2.1   Factor analysis of party membership incentives

Results of the factor analysis of ten-party membership incentives using varimax rotation.

2.1.1: Total Variance Explained

Component	Total unrotated	Total rotated
1	3.14	2.08
2	1.40	1.95
3	1.10	1.62
...	...	...

2.1.2: Factor Loadings – Rotated Components Matrix

Membership motivation	Component 1 – Moral	Component 2 – Social	Component 3 – Professional
Feel a good citizen	**0.77**	−0.07	0.10
Help others	**0.76**	0.28	−0.04
Meaningful life	**0.73**	0.25	0.12
Influence politics	**0.48**	0.25	0.10
Interesting people	0.13	**0.78**	0.16
Friends	0.16	**0.73**	0.18
Interesting discussions	0.23	**0.70**	−0.08
Positions and honours	0.14	0.14	**0.78**
Money and material	−0.02	−0.11	**0.73**
Become a politician	0.13	0.28	**0.60**

$N = 2919$

By contrast, the social dimension, partly overlapping solidary incentives, means that a young partisan is motivated by interesting discussions, the opportunity to meet like-minded people, and a desire to make new friends. Finally, the professional dimension revolves around a desire to achieve positions and honours, to become a politician, and to derive money or material benefits from party membership.

Of course, we included incentives theoretically, expecting them to fit our tridimensional model, but the power of the factor analysis test should not be underestimated. Indeed, the covariance-based measure does not just say something about the variables, but also about the respondents. It shows that the people who want to become politicians are *also* those who want money, positions, and honours. By contrast, those who join to help others are also those who crave policy influence. Thus, our findings go beyond the existing literature by showing that three types of young party members are driven by structured sets of incentives and not just random combination of motivations.

We then run separate factor analyses for each set of incentives to create factor scores corresponding to each dimension and compare the profiles of respondents. We need the separate factor analyses to realistically assess the correlation between moral, social, and professional dimensions without forcing orthogonality between them. The three dimensions are (predictably) positively correlated, but if the moral and social drives are strongly correlated (0.35), they remain clearly distinct. The professional dimension is not very tied with either the moral (0.18) or the social (0.16) drives.[7] These results are a first indication that young activists fall into one of the three membership types proposed, but we reassess these results with additional tests for a symptomatic differentiation between respondents' scores on the three dimensions. We find that 61.8 per cent of the respondents have a score over one standard deviation above the mean on one dimension and one standard deviation below the mean on the other two. For 26.4 per cent of respondents, scores are even two standard deviations above and below the means respectively. This strongly supports *H1* and shows that we are not just dealing with types of incentives, but with actual types of young party members, each characterised by a clear dominant membership drive.

We then look at the scores of each young party member surveyed on each of the three factors and look at the factor on which they score highest, which is then ascribed as their membership type. Table 2.2 thus shows the distribution of the three member profiles across countries and party families. Overall, 'moral minded' members dominate with 39.7 per cent of the sample. 34.2 per cent of the sample are social- minded, and 26 per cent are linked with the professional-minded category. This distribution confirms *H1a* on the imbalance between member types. Table 2.2 also highlights important differences across countries and party families. Consistently with *H1b*, Spain and France remain a privileged territory for 'moral' young activists, but most German young party members are social-minded, and a majority of Hungarian ones are professional-minded. Similarly, social-minded young members dominate the Liberal family, while moral-minded members are more numerous in Socialist and Conservative parties.

The likeliness of being a moral, social, or professional member does not vary significantly with age or the length of an activist's membership. This means that professional motivations do not 'come' after a few years of membership. Instead, we are faced with members who have truly joined a political

Table 2.2   Types of young party members

	Moral	Social	Professional
Overall	39.7	34.2	26.0
By country			
Spain	60.9	30.6	8.4
France	50.0	36.8	13.2
UK	47.5	22.5	30.0
Norway	41.5	33.1	25.4
Germany	31.1	38.4	30.5
Hungary	29.2	25.3	45.5
By party family			
Socialist	42.7	33.3	24.0
Conservative	38.1	34.3	27.7
Liberal	30.4	38.5	31.2

$N = 2919$

party for different sets of reasons. As confirmed by the interview part of the study, short of assuming that respondents change categories in equal numbers over the years (which is unlikely if one assumes the professional type to require more commitment than the other two), their typification along the moral, social, or professional trichotomy is likely to be stable over time. Finally, the difference in distribution in terms of gender is relatively small across the three member types considering current inequalities in the political personnel of most European countries: the proportion of professional-minded members is 28.2 per cent among men and 21.2 per cent among women. Conversely, moral-minded members represent 43 per cent of young female activists and 38.2 per cent of their male counterparts, with no statistically significant difference among social-minded young members. Thus, the category of 'future leaders' is only marginally male-dominated, despite the gender imbalance that has been enshrined throughout Europe for decades.

Specific incentives

Looking at specific incentives in greater details, Table 2.3 shows that two of the main professional incentives (money, and honours) come systematically at the very bottom of importance lists. However, a certain number of comparative differences are also salient. While interesting discussions are dominant in a number of countries, meeting interesting people is the first source of satisfaction for Spanish respondents, and making friends the top incentive in Hungary. Some of the main moral incentives are much stronger in some countries than in others. It is, for example, the case of the desire to influence politics in Norway (where it is ranked 3rd overall) and helping others in Spain and France, where it almost ties with the main social incentives of the list. Finally, professional incentives are not equally popular in all countries. For example, in Hungary and Norway, the prospect of becoming a politician is ranked much higher on the list than elsewhere.

Overall, however, Table 2.4 shows that moral incentives are slightly predominant over social (second) and professional (third) motivations overall. Indeed, in general, we can see that while 35.7 per cent of our respondents report predominantly moral incentives to be party members, 31.2 per cent claim to primarily benefit from social incentives, and 29.8 per cent from professional ones.

At the same time, Table 2.4 also reveals some very significant comparative differences. We find in particular that the Spanish respondents tend to fare much higher on moral incentives, while Norwegian and particularly Hungarian ones tend to be highly professionally motivated. Party family-based differences are less striking although moral incentives seem to be globally higher amongst socialist party members, and professional ones amongst conservative ones.

Table 2.3 Ranking of membership incentives by country

Germany

Incentive	Score
Interesting people	1.80
Interesting discussions	1.67
Friends	1.53
Help others	1.46
Influence politics	1.36
Feel a good citizen	1.19
Become a politician	1.09
Meaningful life	1.08
Positions and honours	0.95
Money and material	0.24

France

Incentive	Score
Interesting people	1.79
Interesting discussions	1.79
Help others	1.61
Feel a good citizen	1.40
Friends	1.39
Meaningful life	1.36
Influence politics	1.15
Become a politician	0.79
Positions and honours	0.54
Money and material	0.13

UK

Incentive	Score
Interesting discussions	1.65
Friends	1.63
Feel a good citizen	1.60
Help others	1.58
Interesting people	1.43
Meaningful life	1.40
Influence politics	1.38
Become a politician	1.20
Positions and honours	0.83
Money and material	0.45

Spain

Incentive	Score
Interesting people	1.83
Friends	1.82
Interesting discussions	1.81
Help others	1.80
Influence politics	1.55
Feel a good citizen	1.53
Meaningful life	1.52
Become a politician	1.07
Positions and honours	0.41
Money and material	0.15

Norway

Incentive	Score
Interesting discussions	1.83
Interesting people	1.82
Influence politics	1.81
Help others	1.80
Friends	1.55
Feel a good citizen	1.53
Meaningful life	1.52
Become a politician	1.07
Positions and honours	0.41
Money and material	0.15

Hungary

Incentive	Score
Friends	1.77
Interesting discussions	1.73
Interesting people	1.61
Help others	1.57
Feel a good citizen	1.47
Become a politician	1.46
Meaningful life	1.36
Influence politics	1.12
Positions and honours	1.05
Money and material	0.44

All

Incentive	Score
Interesting people	1.77
Interesting discussions	1.73
Friends	1.58
Help others	1.50
Influence politics	1.40
Feel a good citizen	1.35
Meaningful life	1.23
Become a politician	1.17
Positions and honours	0.77
Money and material	0.26

Table 2.4 Ranking of membership incentives by party family

Socialists (All)		Conservatives (All)		Liberals (All)	
Interesting people	1.79	Interesting people	1.74	Interesting people	1.77
Interesting discussions	1.74	Interesting discussions	1.72	Interesting discussions	1.70
Friends	1.62	Friends	1.55	Friends	1.49
Help others	1.62	Feel a good citizen	1.42	Influence politics	1.35
Influence politics	1.40	Influence politics	1.42	Help others	1.28
Feel a good citizen	1.33	Help others	1.37	Feel a good citizen	1.27
Meaningful life	1.29	Become a politician	1.31	Meaningful life	1.05
Become a politician	1.12	Meaningful life	1.20	Become a politician	1.07
Positions and honours	0.76	Positions and honours	0.74	Positions and honours	0.92
Money and material	0.23	Money and material	0.31	Money and material	0.25

Notes:
➤ All Incentives evaluated independently on a 0–2 scale.
➤ Global results reported in Table 2.2 for reference.

Characterisation of the three member types

After developing the conceptual model of young party members and their types and detailed the methodology that will allow us to test the hypotheses we have derived from the model, we have shown that young activists are characterised by three types of moral-, social-, and professional-minded members. We have seen how young party members are unequally divided between a large proportion of moral-minded members, a smaller proportion of social-minded young activists and a yet much smaller proportion of professional-minded young militants. We have examined the types of incentives that are archetypical of the reasons why the three categories of young party members choose to join a political party.

The existence of these different categories is largely confirmed by young party members themselves. They acknowledge the coexistence of young militants with very different reasons to join a political party, who look for diverse things and behave in different ways as exemplified by the interview excerpts that follow:

> NOCO06: People have different purposes for their membership. Some people want ideological influence. Some people participate because they want a career. Some people use it is as a social club. Personally it is a dose of the first and the last.
>
> UKLB08: The other evening, we all went out, and when I talked to my friends, it quickly became obvious that we are here for completely different reasons.
>
> HUPS08: My girlfriend is here for the friends and I really want to become a minister later.
>
> ESPS15: I do the recruitment for our branch. Most newcomers join because they are keen to fight for education or the environment, and many because they have friends here or have heard we are nice. Only a few want to really have a career in politics.

In this section, we will look into greater details at these three categories of young militants and at the types of discourses that correspond to each of them. Let us now consider them in turn:

Spotlight on the discourse of moral-minded young party members

The first category of young party members we looked at is characterised by the predominance of moral incentives in the logic of their partisan engagement. They represent 39.7 per cent of our total sample. They are particularly dominant (in numeric terms) in Spain, France, and the UK. As we have seen, these young active citizens want to give a purpose to their lives. They wish to change the lives of others, to promote specific policies which they believe in, and feel that they are better citizens. However, of course, the way they spontaneously talk about why they have joined a political party are far more subtle and diverse. Here are a few examples about what these moral-minded young party members look for in their partisan involvement:

> UKPS25: I joined Labour to change the life of millions of people who can't fight on their own.
>
> NOCO14: Ideology is salt and pepper and not much else.
>
> UKBP08: I joined the BNP to defend a certain idea of England.
>
> ESCO27: Being a member is good for you! You can learn how to work and not be too full of yourself or too selfish. You can learn that you are not anything more or anything less than anyone else. You are just working for a common end.
>
> FRCM24: I want to help others. That's why I'm here.

DELB08: One day, I suddenly realised that most people in my generation only think about short-term and materialistic things. I wanted to be different, I wanted my life to serve a real purpose.

HUPS16: I decided to become a member of MSzP because everyone in our country should have enough money to live, especially the young and the old.

HUCO12: I thought that I needed to fight to make Hungary a modern, free, and stable democracy. Everyone has a duty.

FRFN27: I believe that we all need to fight those politicians who disrespect democracy and the French people. That's why I joined the Front National.

FRGR08: I joined the Greens because the planet can't. I want to defend the environment and our future.

FRPS37: My life was empty, now it is full.

While the substance is quite straightforward, we can see that moral-minded young party members attach different images, hopes, and dreams to their political engagement and that they vary significantly from militant to militant. Some predominantly focus on the specific policy areas that got them involved in party politics, others express the desire to help others, and some decide to join because they want to give more meaning to their lives. We see that these various discourses are often associated together in an infinite number of combinations.

Dissecting the discourse of social-minded young party members

A similar interpretation can be made of the images evoked by the social-minded young party members whom we interviewed. As we saw, our survey shows that they represent 34.2 per cent of our total sample, the second largest group overall but the most numerous in Germany and quite important in France. Typically, as we have seen, social-minded young party members join to meet like-minded young people, have fun, develop a new group of friends, sometimes meet boyfriends or girlfriends, and often enjoy stimulating discussions and debates, and discover interesting people. We now put a spotlight on the nuances of the way in which they describe the logic of their political engagement and what they get from it:

ESCO14: We are all a great group of friends.

UKLB08: I have never met so many interesting people in my life.

FRCM20: I like being surrounded by honest, intelligent, and interesting people who are all willing to give up their free time for the good of others.

FRFN01: Until I came to the Front, I had never felt that much at ease with others. Perhaps because I'm still younger than most, right now, they have really become like a second family to me.

DELB16: I really like the debates and what we do.

FRPS37: I just have a great time here!

UKPS04: Some people have football or bingo and I have the party!

NOCO31: I have lots of fun, especially at UH!

ESCO03: My friends always told me the NNGG has the prettiest girls! And of course they were right!

HUPS08: I need it as a regular activity in my free time, it's important.

HUCO19: I like the stuff we do together – the parties, the chats, the people.

FRGR13: Now, I mostly come for the people, they are all my friends really.

ESPS41: I always used to feel quite different from others, now I feel normal.

On this occasion again, despite an obvious coherence of discourse across cases, we can see that the social value of membership – prime driving force amongst our social-minded young party members – can assume a multiplicity of difference stories and facets. Some particularly like the people, other the activities – be they debates or parties. Some young party members are predominantly positive in the phrasing of their motivations; others willingly admit that they used to feel that they did not fit until becoming young militants and joining their party. Many speak of 'friends', and others, even, of a new 'family.'

Understanding the discourse of professional-minded young party members

Let us now consider the last of the three groups of young party members that we have identified – that of professional-minded young militants. This third and final group only represents 26 per cent of our total sample, but is dominant in Hungary, and represents approximately 30 per cent of all the young party members whom we surveyed in Germany and the UK. The incentives of professional-minded young party members focus on the desire to get a 'job' out of politics, and to derive material benefits as well as immaterial gifts such as honours, positions of responsibility within the party, and eligible positions on party lists. Let us consider the details of the discourses that these professional-minded young activists use to explain why they have joined their party:

ESCO02: The value of my membership is the great experience that I can get by combining a professional career with a political activity.

FRPS36: I have joined the MJS and the PS to become a politician.

FRCM19: I want to be elected.

UKBP18: I have always hoped I'd be elected here in xxx.

NOCO14: I get a mobile phone and quite a bit of my travelling paid. It is not bad at all!

DELB16: I would like to run in elections.

FRPS34: I want to see my name on posters!
HUPS01: I want to become president of Hungary!
FRPS14: I could see myself as a minister and even as President.'
UKPS13: I know parties always need new politicians, so I thought 'why not me?'
DECO26: I have always wanted to work in politics.

These testimonies are symptomatic of the diverse ways in which young people can decide to 'try their luck' with party politics in order to obtain the jobs, posts, or functions of their dreams. As we will see throughout this book, (and in particular in Chapter 8), these dreams are omnipresent, and young party members often aim very high to fulfil them. Even though the category of professional-minded young party members is the least numerous of all three types, it represents an essential component of young party membership that we absolutely need to understand, that is, what brings young citizens in contemporary Europe to join political parties?

Throughout this chapter, we have seen that young party members can be typologised using a trichotomous model of moral, social, and professional young militants. We have defined and conceptualised our model, tested it empirically, but we have also given a sense of the geographical and methodological universe in which this book will navigate to better understand what are the origins, hopes, wishes, perceptions, opinions, and dreams of young party members in the UK, Germany, France, Spain, Norway, and Hungary.

It is now time to start this fascinating journey. In the next chapter, we will now consider how young citizens decide to join the party, that is, what are the origins of their political participation and their individual histories of their joining? What are their role models and sources of inspirations? Is there an apparent pattern of family socialisation that seems to explain their decision to join? and Are there catalytic 'moments' that lead them to push open the door of a party or young party organisation? Later in the book, our journey through the life, heart, and mind of a typical young party member will continue. We will investigate their activities in Chapter 4, how the party has changed their life in Chapter 5, how they perceive their own party and its internal democracy in Chapter 6 as well as their political system and national democratic institutions in Chapter 7. Finally, we will evaluate how young party members see their future in Chapter 8 before looking at the impact of our findings on what we can learn from the likely future of our democracies to conclude in Chapter 9.

3
Becoming a Young Party Member: Inheritance, Paths to Membership, and Political Socialisation

Paths to young party membership

The previous chapter enabled us to sketch and colour the 'world' of young party members – what makes them unique in terms of participation and institutional commitment – it now seems essential to understand how and why they embarked upon their road to party membership.

In this chapter, we establish three major likely paths of membership: family tradition, friends' inspiration, and union activism. We explained why we expect family tradition to be the dominant path to membership, as confirmed time and again by the literature on trans-generational inheritance. Let us define the other two possible paths of party membership. A young adult may decide to join a party that his friends belong to, and whereby a young student would get involved in student unionism before broadening his political engagement and moving on to party politics. Another important aspect of our model is the suggestion that each of the three paths to membership that we have identified could work in a 'positive' (imitation) or a 'negative' (rejection and differentiation) direction. In other words, if we expect a majority of young party members to have joined as their parents or friends have, we also suggest that a number of them will have joined because their parents or friends have not, or have joined another party, and that the young member will use party membership to differentiate himself/herself rather than reproduce a schema embraced by a role model.

In addition to the sources of inspiration to membership, it is interesting to look at the times of their joining and at the specific events or incidents that triggered their decision to join. This might be a discussion, a national or local political event which made them feel a duty to join, an appeal organised by the party or some of its members, or simply the natural continuation of a process whereby a young teenager would have wanted to join a party for a long time but had to wait to reach a specific age to be accepted as a member.

In this chapter, we want to explore exactly how the young party members 'fit' in our model of a roadmap to membership. In order to get a clear picture of the history of their membership, we use the in-depth interviews conducted with 519 young party members in the six countries included in the analysis. Towards the beginning of the interviews, each young party member was asked about how they joined without prespecification. They were also asked more directly whether anyone in their family were members of a political party, whether any of their friends were, what friends and family thought of their membership, and whether or not they were involved in any form of student or professional unionism and which of union or party membership came first. In this sense, the information we gathered on these young members is almost fully comparable.

Consequently, we first evaluate the share of the three main roads to membership that we identified analytically and assess how many young members we interviewed follow the three paths to membership we have outlined above. After identifying the weight of these three routes, we try to look into the details of individual stories. We use the interview evidence to qualitatively characterise the various ways in which our young interviewees have come to join a political party.

Membership role models – an overview

All of the 519 young party members that we interviewed were asked about the story of their joining at the beginning of their interview. As explained, in many ways, their answer to this open-ended question tells us more about incidents that triggered their joining, than about the source of inspiration of their membership. In addition, however, we also asked explicit questions about the political involvement of the young party member's family and friends, and also about the member's involvement in other organisations including unions (be they student or professional) and pressure groups. It is the distribution of these various role models or sources of inspiration that we are first interested.

The first route – family role models

In our interviews, references to 'others' proved, to say the least, frequent. In the context of family transmission, there are two very different forms that this route could assume. The first is an ideological path – whereby the young party member has continued to fight for the cause defended by another family member, who is either a member of the same party or a consistent supporter of it. The second is an organisational path, whereby a family member has inspired the decision to participate in politics via party membership regardless of whether this membership is ideologically close to that of the young party member. Ultimately, 53.4 per cent of our interviewees mentioned one or more family members who also

Table 3.1   The political involvement of young party members' families

I – 53.4% of respondents mentioned at least one family member connected with a political party including:	Of total (%)	Of I (%)
1. Both parents are/were member of the YPM's party	9.5	17.8
2. One parent is/was member of the YPM's party	8.6	16.1
3. Parents are/were members of two different parties (including one member of the YPM's party)	2.3	4.4
4. At least a grandparent is/was a member of the YPM's party	5.7	10.7
5. A brother or sister is/was a member of the YPM's party	3.7	6.9
6. Another family member (uncle, aunt, cousin, etc) is/was a member the YPM's party	2.2	4.1
7. At least one of the YPM's parents is/was employed by the YPM's party	1.2	2.2
8. Parents are members of another party than the YPM's only (ideologically close party)	2.2	4.2
9. Parents are members of another party than the YPM's only (ideologically remote party)	6.8	12.8
10. Multiple answers among 1. to 9	11.1	20.8
Total I	*53.4*	*100*
II – Among the 46.6% remaining		Of II
1. Parents are regular voters of the YPM's party even though they are not members	8.8	18.9
2. Parents are 'close' to the YPM's party	13.9	29.8
3. No expressed family connection	23.9	51.3
Total II	*46.6*	*100*

Notes: $N = 519$. The first column corresponds to proportions of total and total of all entries equals 100. Second column represents proportions of respondents who mentioned at least one party member in the family (I), and proportions of respondents who do not have a party member in the family (II).

were or had been party members, or were either directly or indirectly associated to a party (for instance, employed by it). This is of course a very high proportion, although not completely as overwhelming as the figures identified by Young and Cross (2008) in the Canadian context. The specific type of partisan involvement of family members is summarised in Table 3.1. Let us now turn to the two paths that we have identified.

The ideological path of transmission

The most obvious type of family inheritance occurs when the young person joined a political party their parents are members of. Overall, 9.5 per cent of the respondents interviewed claim that both their parents are or were members of the political party the young party member has joined, and 8.6 per cent claim that one of his/her parent are/were a member, while the other one is not involved in politics. To these figures, one should add 1.2 per cent of interviewees who claim that one parent is actually employed by the political party that they have joined. Overall, we can thus say that one in five young party member that were interviewed (19.3 per cent exactly) has followed a straightforward path of party membership, that of simply replicating parental habits.

However, the party membership 'gene' seems to be transmissible by other family members as well. 5.7 per cent stated that they have followed in the path of a grandparent even though their parents – the intermediate generation – did not join the same party. 3.7 per cent have followed in the steps of a sibling, and 2.2 per cent of another family member. This represents a total of over 1 in 9 respondents (11.6 per cent specifically) whose family partisan inheritance has been transmitted by another member other than a father or a mother.

Of course, young party members may have extended the logic of parents who are not party members themselves but have expressed strong ideological preferences throughout the youth of the young member. In particular, 8.8 per cent of the total sample explain that even though their parents have never been party members, they have always been regular voters for the political party the young members have joined. Another 13.9 per cent explain that their parents are 'close' to this party even though they might not have consistently voted for it every time. Finally, 11.1 per cent selected several answers concerning party membership in their family (e.g. parents and grandparents are party members etc).

Overall, we can thus conclude that the path to young party membership is one of strict ideological replication in approximately 64.7 per cent of the cases, including 42 per cent where the inspiration is actually a person in the family who is/was an actual member (or employee) of the same party, and 22.7 per cent where the ideological inspiration is confirmed, despite the young citizen being the first in the family to actually join the political party his family supports.

The organisational path of transmission

As explained earlier, however, another possible path of family transmission is organisational rather than ideological. After all, party membership is not only an ideological statement but also the choice of a specific – and, as seen in Chapter 2, relatively rare – mode of political participation. In this sense, it is perfectly conceivable that even if a young citizen and his family disagree politically, the family will have transmitted a certain perception of the worth of partisan politics and party membership per se. This is indeed evidenced by our findings as well.

Firstly, 2.3 per cent of our sample explain that one of their parents is/was a member of the same party as them, but that the other parent is/was a member of another political party at the same time. To this relatively small number, one has to add another 9 per cent of interviewees who tell us that their parents are members of another political party altogether. This includes 2.2 per cent who refer to membership of an 'ideologically close' party (e.g. parents are socialist and child is communist or parents are Christian democrat and child is liberal), and 6.8 per cent whose parents are members of an ideologically remote political party (e.g. parents are members of a left-wing party and child of a right-wing one or the contrary, etc). Finally, among the 11.1 per cent who provided multiple answers, 0.9 per cent included reference to at least one family member who belongs or belonged to another political party.

Altogether, it is thus no fewer than one in eight respondents (12.2 per cent exactly) who have parents who belong(ed) to another political party altogether, showing that family transmission can be organisational in a significant proportion of cases, even though this proportion is admittedly lower than in cases of ideological transmission. It illustrates the dual paths to membership provided by the family route.

Of course, ideological and organisational paths can either run in parallel, or be merged. All in all, to summarise, we can thus characterise our sample of interviewees according to the role of family role models in the following way:

- 44.3 per cent have followed a 'double' (or merged) path of family transmission along the ideological as well as the organisational route. These members have one or more family members who have also belonged to the same political party, regardless of whether other family members were not, or even belonged to other parties as well;
- 22.7 per cent have only inherited the ideological preferences of their families, but not any organisational habits. These respondents clearly continue the ideological tradition of their family and in a way further it, as they are the first (as far as they tell us) to actually join a political party they believe their parents are close to, but certainly never joined;
- 9 per cent have followed the organisation tradition of their family but departed from its ideological stance. Like some of their family members, they have decided to join a political party, but this political party is one that the rest of their family fights ideologically, whether it is relatively close or, in three out of four cases altogether far away from their parents' preferred party.

- Finally, 23.9 per cent do not refer to any form of family transmission at all. They do not remember any family member ever belonging to a political party, and the political party that they have chosen was not supported by their parents as they grew up. They are 'pioneers' within their own family, both in terms of modes of participation, and in terms of ideological choice.

The second route – follow your friends

If references to family members are dominant among the inspirations mentioned by young party members, a number of them also refer to some of their friends. In many cases, these friends already belonged to the political party that the young member has later joined. Overall, 16.4 per cent of young party members have mentioned such friends. In 9.1 per cent, these friends come in addition to one of the family influences mentioned above, in 7.3 per cent, on the other hand, these friends have been the only role models mentioned by the young party member. This time, our findings might exclude a few additional cases whereby some friends belonged to another political party than the one the respondent ultimately joined, but very few respondents spontaneously mentioned such cases in the interviews and we did not systematically asked about friends belonging to other political parties before the young citizen joined his own.

To go back to the distinction we drew between sources of ideological and organisational inspiration, we find it worth focusing on a specific and particularly interesting case. This case occurs when young friends who are members of a political party seem to organisationally 'validate' the ideological inspiration provided by parents. Among the 9.1 per cent of respondents who mentioned party members among friends even though they also mentioned a family connection to the said party, over a third (3.2 per cent) had received a 'purely ideological' party connection from their parents. That is, with parents who have been regular voters – or at least felt 'close' to a given political party, without ever joining it, meeting friends who actually belong to the same party can finally spur them to join.

In this sense, the influence of friends can be two fold. In about two thirds of the cases, it confirms and/or reinforces a pre-existing family inspiration, often prompting a young citizen to further the political allegiance of his parents by actually joining a party they have always supported, in the remaining third of the cases, with no particular family influence, friends seem to be the sole source of inspiration of membership. However, this latter case only concerns about 1 in 14 young party members overall (7.3 per cent).

The third route – From one organisation to the next

As explained earlier, our model suggests three prime routes to young party membership. A 'motorway' via family transmission, and two other

important roads via friends, and through membership in other organisations such as unions (be they trade unions or student unions) or
pressure groups. Overall, such membership in other organisations[1] is
only mentioned by 18.1 per cent of the young party members that we
interviewed. It preceded young party membership in 10.3 per cent of
the cases, and followed partisan participation in 7.8 per cent of the
cases.

Among these other memberships, one of the most interesting findings
is that party (or young party organisation) membership is more often
associated with union membership, and particularly with student union
membership, than with membership of pressure groups. This is even more
true when one only looks at organisational membership when it preceded
party (or young party organisation) membership. In short, except in very
exceptional cases (less than 1 per cent), becoming a member of a pressure
group is not a natural path to party membership.

As with friends, in a majority of cases, the 'other organisations' route
to membership seems to be particularly efficient where it reinforces a pre-
existing ideological family heritage. It is also to be noted that a number of
respondents mentioned family members who were also strongly engaged
in union politics even if they have never been members of a political party
themselves. In this sense, a combination of ideological family influence, and
organisational experience gathered from somewhere else (be it friends or
unionism) can lead a young citizen to develop his own variations in modes
of active political participation, and to further structure the ideological
family heritage he thrives on.

Overall, our three routes seem to encompass a great majority of the cases
and are largely cross-cutting. Family inspiration is important either ideologically (22.7 per cent) or organisationally (9 per cent) or both (44.3 per
cent) to over three-quarters of young party members. In most of the cases
where this inspiration is only ideological, it tends to be organisationally 'pol-
lenised' in equal proportions either by friends who are members of the party
or young party organisation parents seem sympathetic too, or by membership of a trade or student union. In about 10 per cent of the cases, party
membership seems to be *only* triggered by friends' examples or by union
experience, and in less than 1 per cent of the cases by membership to other
organisations.

This leaves approximately 12 per cent of respondents who have arrived
into party politics or young party organisations by a route not indi-
cated on our paths to membership map. They did not seem to be
particularly predisposed to become young party members by their less-
than-interested-in-politics families, none of their friends showed them the
way, and they joined a political party or a young party organisation
directly, without first stepping into the world of union politics or pressure
groups.

Individual role models and unique stories

Under this façade of relative homogeneity, however, the stories of the influence exerted on young party members by various role models are declined in an infinite number of colours by the individual stories that they narrate to us. These qualitative accounts also provide us with an essential view on the members' self perception of the specific mechanisms that have transformed family, friends, or organisational habits into sources of inspiration. We also want to look at these various 'shades' of inspirations, these various mechanisms of influence and seduction, these self-perceived accounts of how images of political involvement of others have been internalised and domesticated by teenagers who derived from them a desire to become young party members themselves.

Family stories

Let us first look at the perceptions of family role models. In an interesting way, as explained in our model, family references do not always need to be taken positively even though the majority are. Perceptions of their parents' and grandparents' political involvement can, of course, be tainted with respect, affection, or even admiration by those who choose to strictly follow in their footsteps. In other cases, parents are only perceived as having 'introduced' a youngster to a positive image of a party. Yet, in further stories, youngsters seem to have derived from their understanding of the family past a sense of family duty to replicate the political heights reached by their ancestors. In short, we identify four main distinct mechanisms identified by young party members to explain how the tradition of partisan involvement within their family has led them to join a party. We characterise these four main mechanisms as admiration, direct encouragement/pressure, exposure, and opposition.

Let us start with this first mechanism of family influence: admiration. In some cases, a family member became a prominent figurehead of local or national politics, creating a framework whereby the young party member feels a duty to either continue or even revive a family tradition of being in the political spotlight. Sometimes, this tradition seems to apply not only to one particular role model, but also to a whole family, and the interviewee mentioned it as a context whereby their political involvement was almost expected and seemed like a natural step to take. This is typically illustrated by two young French Socialist party members from a small coastal town and the centre of France:

> *FRPS06*: My dad is a former deputy mayor of Oxxx,[2] and has sat in the
> local Council for 12 years. We always discussed politics at home. My
> mother is a member of the party, but not as actively involved. My

grandfather was also in the local council. [...] My sister was the leader of the Oxxx MJS, a branch that I founded.

FRPS34: There have been three mayors on my dad's side of the family, including granddad, but all for the centrist party.

For many young party members, however, the admired family role model is a single individual who has marked the young person and paved the way to his/her involvement. This is well illustrated by the discourse of a number of our respondents including the following quotes:

NOCO14: My grandfather was Mayor in my small town and politics was a conversation subject 25 hours a day at home. I grew up in it.

HUCO03: My mother is an MP. I'm very proud of her and we very often talk about politics at home.

DEPS36: Both my parents are party functionaries in the SPD. My father was deputy head of the SPD here, and my mother the head of the SPD's women's organisation in Cologne. [...] For me, it was always very normal to take part in party events. The party was my family.

Alongside, this story of recognised 'heritage' of membership with a view to continue a family tradition perceived as prestigious and glorifying, a number of young party members whose parents have also belonged to the same party describe a different mechanism whereby 'activist' parents openly encouraged their children to join the party.

DECO21: My father always told me about his JU days and encouraged me to take part.

This is even more obvious in the case of this young French Communist who seems to have been brought into the party long before he could even join, as well as two young British and German party members:

FRCM12: My parents were communist party militants. My Dad was 'secré-taire de cellule' of the communist party and sometimes when there was no one to look after me at night I would be playing with other militants' kids at the party meetings.

UKPS13: I went campaigning for the first time with my mother in 1987, at the age of 5.

DECO09: It was my father who took me with him to the CDU.

In some cases, the parental pressure can be paradoxical, with the parents using exposure to several parties to convince a young citizen that a specific one is the best. This is explained by two young party members who highlight the pressure to join:

> NOCO28: I moved in with my aunt and uncle a couple of years ago, and my uncle is Høyre. He is active, and persuaded me to go to a Progress Party meeting – because I said I liked the party. As he expected, I discovered that I liked the social setting in Høyre better!
>
> HUPS24: If I had not joined the party when I turned 16, my Dad would have been angry and my Mum would have been upset!

The third type of mechanism of transmission described by young party members with a history of family membership is far less direct and forceful. Indeed, many young party members do not suggest that party membership was either glorified or admirable, but suggest that their parents' membership simply resulted in an obvious form of exposure and introduction into the world of the party from a young age. In this sense, a young German SPD member first questions whether his father's membership could have influenced him at all as he explains that he was never an 'active' party member, before admitting *a minima*:

> DEPS36: I guess that influenced me: that gave the SPD a positive basic image.

The young party member below describes another version of this impact of parental exposure to politics, all the more interesting is that he is one of the young party member we described as coming from a family with split political ideology:

> UKPS44: My mother is Labour and my dad is a silent Lib Dem-voter. We discussed little politics at home, but I was probably a bit influenced.

This importance of 'dinner table discussions' in politically engaged families is confirmed by this young British liberal from a large family. Interestingly enough, in the same sentence, the young member insists on political disagreement at the dinner table *and* on the fact that the entire family 'fit' in the centre right ideology:

> UKLB23: We discuss politics a lot at home. I have ten brothers and sisters! I have heard so many opinions and discussions over dinner – it lasted for hours! [...] My family are all on the centre-right though.

In the above case, the young party member explicitly furthered a perceived ideological commitment of his family by being the first to 'officialise' it organisationally by joining a political party. This is similarly true of a young Norwegian Conservative who explicitly distances himself/herself from the political passivity of a father whose ideological beliefs he/she shares:

> NOCO06: My dad is more of a 'couch-politician.' He thought about becoming a member of Høyre, but in the end he didn't.

Finally, at times this 'exposure to politics' and to a specific form of political ideology can take a vaguer and all encompassing form, as for this young British Liberal Democrat member:

> UKLB34: Everybody I know has been involved on the conservative side in politics.

Finally, the fourth mechanism of family influence that we mentioned is one of opposition. In this context, a number of young party members mention the importance of the political choices of their family, but as a source of inspiration to distance themselves from their beliefs. This can first be expressed as a generational conflict, as is the case for this young British Liberal Democrat as well as this young Hungarian Socialist in the context of family tensions

> UKLB08: My Grandma was involved with the left, Labour, like all retired people!
> HUPS16: I notice how my mother talks about things with my (12 year old) sister. I try to influence my sister in the opposite direction.

It can also be expressed as a simple form of ideological and family opposition, focused on structuring family arguments as for this young French 'Souris Verte' and this young Hungarian conservative:

> FRGR19: I like to argue with my father who is more conservative than I am.
> HUCO23: I am a capitalist. My dad, who was active when he was young, is a communist-socialist. We are a family were we discuss very much. Especially my father and I. That develops your critical thinking.

This notion was mentioned by all types of young party members, but particularly those who joined an extremist party, or some whose parents sympathise with Green politics. The case of the opposition to Green parents is interestingly exposed both by a young German Liberal and by a young French Socialist:

DELB23: My parents are Green. [...] I decided against the Green party because that party isn't close to me. It's a cultural question – I don't like the fake alternative pretension of the Greens. I also think they're quite elitist

FRPS04: My parents think it is very cool for them to have joined the Greens. For me, the Greens are a clientelistic party that focuses a lot on very few topics!

The case of opposition between extreme right and other politics is also telling, and seems to work in both directions. First, by young people who distinguished themselves from 'moderate' political families as for these two young French Front National interviewees and one British BNP member:

FRFN06: My parents vote for 'centre right' parties that have never done anything for them. I've become a member of the Front National by myself when I turned 16, it surprised everyone, family, friends, and even the FN people themselves. Many people in my family were shocked by my decision too, but at least, I make a difference.

FRFN20: My parents always told us that the left was great because it cares about people and that the right is bad because it doesn't. As I grew up, I realised this was rubbish. The FN is a far more caring party than the left.

UKBP31: All my family support Labour. They don't realise Labour doesn't support their country.

But conversely, some young party members explain how the extremist preferences of their parents have shaped their own political struggle and particularly their engagement with left-wing parties. This is the case of a young French Communist, who explained how a strong dislike of his father's political inclination towards the extreme right provoked his decision to become a Communist as did a young French Green with regard to his grandparents:

FRCM08: My dad was a supporter of the FN. When I was a kid, he left my Mum and me, and even when I came to see him, his ideology horrified me. This probably explains a lot of my decision to become a Communist. He died a few years ago.

FRGR23: As many people in the city I'm from, my grandparents vote Le Pen and when we had family meals, at the dinner table, they would explain how he is the only to propose an alternative. That has always horrified me, and pushed me to find another alternative.

Altogether, we have thus illustrated the four mechanisms depicted by young party members to explain how the political choices of their families have shaped their own partisan involvement. The first is admiration, whereby pride in the successful political career of one or several family members 'points out the way' to the young member. The second is pressure, whereby a family member encourages the young citizen to join or even take him/her to meetings. The third is exposure, whereby despite a lack of involvement on the part of the parents, the young member has the impression to have gathered a positive image of the party thanks to his parents' outlook. The fourth and final mechanism is opposition, whereby the young member's political profile has been built against the negatively connoted political choices of either some individual family members or a perceived global 'political colour' of their family as a whole. The importance of the influence of the family in becoming a young party member is so crucial, that many young party members who join from a non-politically engaged family consider themselves the exception if not an anomaly as illustrated by the following few examples:

> *DECO12*: I'm pretty atypical because my parents were not in the CDU. Usually, young people join the JU because of their parents, that's the normal way. Either that or because of someone in their environment. I'm unusual because we are not political at home.
> *DECO21*: Basically I think that there are two ways into the JU: either you're motivated through your family background or you're interested because something concerns you directly. It also helps to have friends in the party.
> *FRGR03*: It's difficult to get people to take part if they didn't grow up in a political family or have friends who are political. Then it's hard to break down the inhibitions.

My friend the party member

A second important source of inspiration for young party members can be found among their friends. Here, individual accounts provided by young party members take three dominant forms. The first is a number of stories where the young party member refers to a group of friends already being members of the political party and inspiring the young person to join. This is illustrated by the typical two stories below:

> *DECO13*: I had friends in school who were also JU members, so that's part of the reason why I joined.
> *UKPS22*: When some friends suggested I join, I decided I would try it. I went to a few meetings and then signed up.

Sometimes, this influence of friends is directly opposed to a perceived lack of influence or political apathy of family members, as below:

> *FRGR07*: My friends were quite political. My parents are not political.

By contrast, however, a greater number of young party members tend to refer to one specific friend (or a boyfriend/girlfriend) who has introduced them to the party, rather than an entire 'group' of friends already involved in the party. This is illustrated by the three following stories:

> *DEPS38*: I had also wanted to look at the Greens, but then I met someone at the SPD (who is now my employer), and through her I got to know people in the SPD. This is how I joined.
>
> *ESCO44*: One of my friends took me with her. I liked the people immediately, and they were all enthusiastic and were trying to achieve something. I realised politics isn't that boring after all. [...] it was only because my friend suggested it that I came along. [...] Having her took away my initial inhibition.
>
> *FRPS11*: I was recruited to the party by my girlfriend!

Some young party members explained to us how the decision to join is sometimes collective rather than individual. They would explain that joining a party was discussed with an equally politically interested but unaffiliated friend, and that they would both give it a try at the same time. Two stories in particular exemplify this particular form of mutual stimulation (or mutual reinforcement) to join a party:

> *DELB19*: My best friend and I were both considering going so we went to the first meeting together.
>
> *HUPS02*: My friend and I had talked about joining for a while. I think we were both waiting for the other one to take the lead, but at the same time, neither of us would have had the guts if we didn't know that the other also wanted to try.

Finally, as in the case of family influence, a few young party members insist on the strength of the stimulation offered by friends and peers one disagrees with. For instance, this is the case of young British member of the BNP:

> *UKBP32*: Lots of girls in my class were active members in Young Labour. I was provoked on a daily basis.

Politics at school

Of course, this power of political provocation on the crystallisation of one's partisan conviction is not limited to the opposition with one's friends or schoolmates. Who, indeed, would be a better person to oppose than one's teacher? Over 20 young respondents refer to their exasperation at a given teacher's 'obvious' political inclination in one way or another. In a majority of cases, this takes the form of either a right-wing or an extreme right young party member expressing anger at some leftist professor at school or university. The following four examples are very symptomatic:

FRFN20: There was a history teacher who was a Communist. He thought it was appropriate to throw his convictions in your face. He started saying that Catholicism is a rubbish religion, that it should be replaced by Islam and so on, so I stood up and left the room.
UKBP24: In fact, I was particularly turned off by the politics classes in school, where the teachers were always very Red/Green. That really annoyed me.
HUCO03: At school, I was always in opposition to my teachers.
ESCO32: My left-wing teachers really annoyed me.

Unions, pressure groups, and political parties
Finally, we mentioned that a number of young party members emphasised a path from union (either trade union or more often student unions) and party membership, or far more rarely between pressure group activism and party membership.

A number of respondents simply present a 'natural' path from student unions' membership to party politics, especially left-wing party politics, as exemplified by these three parallel accounts made by young French Socialist, Norwegian Conservative, and British Labour party members.

FRPS26: I started being involved in politics and militating at 14, in response to the 'Devaquet laws.' I demonstrated and got engaged in the College union. Then, I joined the PS as one of the 'Génération Mitterrand' people.
NOCO01: I was recruited two years ago by a friend that I got to know through the Student Council in Oslo.
UKPS23: I was engaged in school politics. I was in the students board at my school, and later became a union representative at uni and a member of the National Union of Students.

Sometimes, as in the case of this other young activist from the Spanish PSOE, unionist and partisan involvement go hand in hand to the point of becoming quasi-indistinguishable:

ESPS45: For me, politics is a social 'rapport-de-force.' So, I believe all the partisan and unionist actions are actions are all inter-twinned.

By contrast, a hypothetical path from pressure groups or labour unions to party politics is expressed far more rarely. Here are two examples from France:

> FRPS31: I became union representative (CFDT) of my company (farmers' social security), became member of the national board of the Union, and it then seemed logical to become an active socialist, and within a few months, I was elected as departmental secretary of the socialist party.'
>
> FRGR08: I had long been a Greenpeace militant, but started to want to broaden my ideological struggle. The Greens seemed to fight many battles I cared about, and not just on the environment.

In the context of people who came to politics from the world of unionism – and in fact, in particular from the world of Student unionism, mentions of a political career are particularly frequent. The following two examples are particularly telling:

> NOCO22: I became a member when the party organised a campaign at my school and I was introduced to the national organisation for pupils. That is where I discovered that I wanted to do politics.
>
> FRPS19: I had been class representative and so on, but started to be a militant when I was 18. I started with the students union (UNEF-ID) where I climbed the steps, and then the Parti and that allowed me to start at the young socialists movement very much at the top.

Finally, a few young party members, by contrast, remind us that even unionism can trigger partisan opposition, as they recall the way in which unionist pressure made them become conscious of some serious disagreements to the point that they would join a party opposed to unions politics. A young Norwegian conservative thus recalls:

> NOCO06: I received a document from SYP telling me how to argue their case against giving marks in school. I realised that it said the exact opposite of my belief.

We now have a clearer idea of the sources of inspiration that young party members mention when explaining their membership. We have not only seen the importance of three various paths – family, friends, and unionism – but we have also gained a sense of the variety of divergent and sometimes contradictory – mechanisms that they entail: admiration, pressure, exposure, affection, and opposition.

Categorising the catalyst of membership

If understanding role models and roads to membership is essential, these various sources of inspiration and paths of membership only reveal a specific part of the stories that led some young citizens to join a party. In some cases, of course, the role models and sources of inspirations that young members refer to are so strong and so obvious that they 'always' knew that they wanted to join and simply waited till they reached the official age of membership to a party of a young party organisation to formally enrol. In most cases, however, some specific incident, event, or provocation coincided with the young person deciding that they would join a party. Joining a party is a decision, a moment. Understanding the nature of this moment is undoubtedly as essential in understanding membership as is the categorisation of the types of inspirations that have made young people prone to seize it. Sometimes, this catalytic moment came very early in the life of a future young party member, sometimes it came late. This unique moment can also be positive or negative. It may be an occasion where excitement and enthusiasm is at its peak to the extent that it does away with inhibitions and leads a young citizen to join a party that truly reaches to his heart. Other times, it can be the sort of provocation, shock, or repulsion that will lead an interested but passive young member of society to feel compelled to join the ranks of a political party.

Almost all of the 519 young party members that we interviewed remembered the story of the specific catalytic moment that corresponded to their decision to join. In many cases, they remember it very well, think of it as a structuring moment in their life, and were keen on talking about it in great details. Sometimes, they mention a multiplicity of events, incidents, or coincidences that led to their joining, sometimes they only focus on one element which gave them the impetus to join, other times, they simply say that they had known for a long time that they would want to become a young party member and just needed to wait to be of age to join their organisation of choice. Finally, in a few cases, they do not mention any particular incident. We summarised the answers that we received in Table 3.2

Table 3.2 shows that, consistent with our model, elections remain a privileged time to join a party. Political parties are never as visible as in election time, their programmes, leaders, and organisations are echoed by the media, visible on the streets, and more generally appear to be at the heart of politics. Politics is also more dramatised, and parties clearly go to far greater lengths than in normal times to recruit members and sympathisers. Overall, 31 per cent of the young party members interviewed said that they joined their party around the time of an election. However, this apparently intuitive result hides a certain paradox. The efforts made by the parties to recruit and their exceptional exposure in electoral periods would principally lead one to expect a vast membership influx to occur during election campaigns.

Table 3.2 Catalyst of joining: Moments, incidents, and triggers

What triggered the young party member to join	%
Joining coincided with an election (of which:)	31
– joined following result of election	*22*
– joined during the campaign	*9*
Received party flyer/was approached by unknown activist	14
Taken by someone to a party meeting (of which:)	13
– taken by a friend	*10*
– taken by a family member	*3*
Spontaneously collected material from several parties and chose to join one	12
Shocking event (demonstration, crisis, etc)	11
Spontaneously walked in party headquarters	8
School debate / school discussion	7
Spontaneously attended a meeting	4
. . .	. . .
Always wanted to join/joined when of age	18
No particular reason mentioned	27

Note: $N = 519$, as this is gathered from qualitative interviews, several catalytic moments or incidents were mentioned by a number of respondents, hence a total well above 100. Twenty seven per cent didn't mention any particular incident or impetus explicitly.

When looking at the details of individual stories, however, we find that only 9 per cent of the respondents interviewed indeed joined during that time, while far more (22 per cent) actually joined as a reaction to the election result. In a majority of cases, this is expressed as a reaction to an unsatisfying or even shocking result: for instance, the 2002 success of the FN in France which led many young voters to join left-wing parties in France, or the severe defeat of the German SPD in 2005 in regional elections which was mentioned by several respondents, as was the 2002 defeat of the Partido Popular in Spain. In a minority of cases, by contrast, it is enthusiasm for the new victors which leads a young person to get caught up in the pioneering excitement of party politics.

In parallel, many young people explained that they were introduced into party politics in reaction to a particularly shocking event, such as a big political crisis, an extreme right demonstration, a racist attack, or a particularly antagonistic policy decision. Such defining moments were mentioned by 11 per cent of our interviewees across the six countries.

The second most frequent specific event associated with joining a party is the fact of receiving a flyer from a political party (either in election time or in another time) or being approached by an unknown party activist on the street (or in rare cases at school). This trigger was mentioned by 14 per cent of the respondents, proving the use of parties' efforts to campaign for their recruitment on a regular basis. Next to it, a large number of young people also explained how they did not wait for the parties to approach them and how, instead, they collected the manifestos from various parties, either on paper or online before choosing one (12 per cent). Incidentally, while this 'comparative' demarche is important amongst young people who knew they wanted to get involved in politics whilst hesitating between several or all parties, a number of youngsters are similarly certain enough about their future choice to directly walk into the headquarters of the party they wanted to join (8 per cent) or to spontaneously attend a meeting (be it an electoral meeting or a party branch gathering: 4 per cent).

More traditionally, as explained earlier, this initial 'walk in' more often takes the form of being taken to such a meeting by a known person. This was described as the initial introduction and joining moment by 13 per cent of the interviewees. In 10 per cent of the cases, the 'facilitator' was a boyfriend, girlfriend, friend, or colleague, and in 3 per cent of the cases a family member.

The final catalytic moment identified by an important sub-section of the sample was a school debate or discussion. This is particularly relevant in the Norwegian case where many young party members refer to officially organised debates at school during elections. In other countries, while the numbers concerned are lower, such debates are frequently organised in universities, and similarly even though partisan debates per se are not organised as a matter of routine, many respondents identified specific school discussions in history, civic education, politics, philosophy, or economy, which made them realise their own ideological stance like never before. Overall, school debates and discussions were cited by 7 per cent as the keystone to their joining.

While a majority of respondents are thus in a position to identify a specific moment that served as a milestone to their entry into the world of party politics, many others refer to a slower process or an earlier self-evidence that let them longing for several years for the day when they would be of age to join. No fewer than 18 per cent of respondents revealed that they had known that they wanted to join a political party long before they were acceptable to the parties or the young party organisations. Some explained that they realised their desire to become a party member as early as when they were 5, and many mentioned trying to walk into party headquarters when they were 14 or 15 and being asked to come back when they would have the minimum joining age (as described in Chapter 1, usually 15, 16, or rarely 18 for the young party organisations). Finally, several other young members described being accepted earlier than the required age, or at least allowed to attend meetings.

Finally, beyond these 18 per cent who declare a long foresight, 27 per cent of young party members do not specify any particular moment, incident, or event that led to their joining. They have forgotten why or when they joined, or simply think that whatever pretext made them cross the Rubicon is meaningless when compared to how natural it seemed to them to join their political party.

Alongside role models and influences, we have thus categorised the other important aspect of the decision to join, that is, the specific moment when one translates an underlying propensity to show an interest in political debate into active partisan activism. The stories we encountered revolve around elections, shocking moments, a comparative search for the best party, introduction into a party by a stranger, a friend, or a family member, school debates, or an unexplained urge to literally walk into a party's world. We will then look at the infinite variations of individual stories around these great themes, as well as the accounts of those who claimed that the story of their joining was simply one of patience.

A story of incidents? The day I joined my party

Consistently with our model, the first type of special moment that is mentioned by 31 per cent of our interviewees as the time when they decided to join a party is an election. Elections can crystallise three important types of reactions. Firstly, even at an early age, they can represent politics per se, interest and adrenalin. Secondly, they can represent the time when one fully embraces a partisan cause and decides to join. Thirdly, they can represent an electoral trauma and push a young citizen into action and into offering his energy to a party perceived as capable of fighting his newly identified enemy.

The first type of electoral stimulus is likely to occur at a relatively young age, and several young party members refer to early elections in their childhood which they directly associate with their later choice to join a political party. This is, for instance, the case of two young British party members, one from the Liberal Democrats and the other one from the Labour party:

UKLB16: I discussed politics with my father and stepmother when I was a kid. At the age of 9, I saw my first election-night on TV.
UKPS13: I went campaigning for the first time with my mother, when she ran for elections in 1987. I was 5 at the time, and thought it was so exciting!

The second type of electoral force that we describe as to do with a young citizen suddenly finding himself swallowed in an enthusiastic electoral whirlpool as he embraces the hope and promises made by a party about to win or at the very least to do better than long expected. This type of enthusiasm is described by a young member of the Norwegian Conservatives before the party were about to score their best electoral victory, by a young Hungarian Socialist before her party regained power, but also by a young member of the Front National when the party's leader achieved his qualification to the second ballot of the 2002 French Presidential election against all expectations:

> NOCO03: I became a member four days before the 2001 election. I stepped in the Høyre's office. I was met by a very nice lady who said 'Hello – you have to join us', and I just couldn't refuse. [...] The atmosphere was extraordinary.
>
> HUPS01: FIDESZ had led the country to depression, when I saw that the MSzP was about to regain power, I was so excited that I couldn't stay out of it. I had to be part of the movement.
>
> FRFN12: The idea of becoming involved with the FN clicked for me during the presidential election of 2002, in between the two rounds. I realised that this was a vote of true support and adhesion, of support for ideas as well as people.

The same discourse was held by a large number of young party members who joined just before or just after iconic party victories: the 1997 victory for British Labour, the 2004 European elections for UKIP, the 1997 legislative elections for the French Greens, or the same year for the German SPD. By contrast, an almost equally large number of young party members saw the very same elections from the eyes of traumatised potential losers. They chose these moments to offer their political stamina to defeated parties, as they realised they desperately wanted them to fight back against their new enemies. These reactions are exemplified by the following excerpts:

> DEPS09: I joined the SPD on 22 May 2005, the same night that we lost the regional election in North Rhine-Westphalia.
>
> DEPS17: I joined the SPD in May 2005, the day after the regional elections. That's what made me join.
>
> FRCM04: When I saw Le Pen's face on TV, I was horrified. I thought that he had made it there because of all the people who couldn't be bothered to get involved. Communism is the opposite of the FN's ideology, and it was a very obvious decision for me to join.
>
> HUCO16: I really thought FIDESZ would win, and if they had, I would have been happy, but I might not have joined. MSzP won again though, and Hungary was going to be sacrificed for a few more years. I thought everyone who cares should step in.

If elections are an obvious moment to join, because it dramatises politics, because their stakes are so obvious that the amount of satisfaction or anger that their results can cause may easily be enough to lead one to want to add their energy to a political movement that is perceived as strong and important, many young party members explained that their decision to join was triggered an incident that would suddenly make them feel conscious of their civic duty like never before. An event or a person that proved so antagonistic that joining a party would feel like a natural response.

As we mentioned the importance of Le Pen's second place in the first ballot of the French presidential elections for many young people who decided to join centre right or centre left party, it is not surprising that even more radical expressions of extremism are also referred to as turning points by many young party members, such as this young German Social Democrat:

> DEPS14: In a village close to mine, there had been a march of radical right-wingers. I wanted to set a clear signal that the extreme right does not belong in our area.

Many other types of 'strongly disapproved' policy decisions are mentioned by members of all political parties as a source of crystallisation of their membership decision. Here, among others, young party members from completely different party families use exactly the same formulation about issues such as the war in Iraq, Europe, social equity, and so on:

> FRFN06: One of the reasons why I am a true FN supporter and activist is that we are the only ones trying to put an end to conditions of unfairness in this country.
>
> FRCM11: For example, I remember feeling really angry about politicians 'selling' France when a referendum was organised on the Maastricht treaty. I could not vote then but would have definitely voted no.
>
> UKBP30: All the other parties are so afraid to upset small groups of angry and highly organised people that they prefer to put up with reforms, perpetuate conditions of injustice and penalise the weakest in our society.
>
> ESPS09: I have always been an angry person. […] In the winter of 2001 I had been upset about so many stupid political decisions, that I just had to become a member of a party.
>
> MULTIPLE: I joined because of the war in Iraq (mentioned by three members from the French Green and Communist parties and the UK Labour party in exactly the same formulation)
>
> ESPS45: I said 'we have to stop this government'.

Beyond the case of these young people who have joined during an election or in reaction to a particular crisis or event that strengthened their ideological convictions to the point of joining a political party, let us think again of those who have followed one of the three sign-posted routes described earlier and of those who did not know anyone in a party. In both cases, it is essential to understand the specific incidents or events that triggered their decision to join. Were they approached by a party member or received a leaflet? Did someone take them to a party meeting or did they just walk in? We showed in our overview that the first contact with the party can take multiple forms, but the stories that they encompass vary even more greatly.

First, we mentioned the story of those who 'compared offerings' by looking at various party manifestos or documentation before deciding who to join. Such accounts were more frequent than one would suspect. Let us consider four complementary narratives:

> DECO15: I got information material from all the different parties and realised that the CDU was closest to me politically.
>
> DECO18: When I fill out online programmes that give you voting recommendations (*Wahl-O-Mat*), I am always told to vote CDU.
>
> UKLB04: My parents wanted me to find out more about the parties, so I read their party programmes and thought long and hard about which party to join.
>
> NOCO15: I walked down Karl Johan [main street in Oslo] and checked out all the election booths.

These various examples emphasise the story of young people who have clearly decided to join a political party, but are waiting for a moment of crystallisation when they will understand which party is 'made' for them. They actively seek information on paper or online and try to cross examine it till it tells them where to go. A variation of a comparable story is recounted by young people who first decided to look at a party before being disappointed by its stance and firmly understanding which alternative organisation was made for them. The following two examples are provided by a young German Liberal Democrat and a young Spanish Socialist:

> DELB04: At first, I went to Cuba with the socialists and then decided that this wasn't for me – too far fetched.
>
> ESPS02: My grandfather is a Communist and I first went to the Communist party but I didn't like it. He got upset when he found out I had chosen the PSOE instead of Izquierda Unida.

Sometimes, of course, it is not the young citizen who chooses to walk in but a party which reaches out to them, occasionally, the story is successful and this is retained by the young member as what convinced them to join as in the case of a young German Social Democrat as well as a young Spanish Conservative:

> *DEPS29*: During the election campaign for the regional parliament, someone gave me a flyer for the Jusos at an event with Schröder and Kurt Beck. I went to a meeting and then decided to join.
>
> *ESCO09*: I joined because I read the leaflet I was given when leaving university one evening. I had received many leaflets before but it was the first time I read it.

By contrast, many young people expressed certainty as they describe their decision to walk into a party's headquarter or a campaign meeting to join a political party which decided was for them. The following examples are variations on the same recollections:

> *HUCO19*: In the beginning, I went along, on my own, just to see what it was like, and then I joined.
>
> *DEPS44*: I collected party paraphernalia from the SPD as a personal hobby. One day I talked to someone at an information booth, and I joined then and there.
>
> *FRGR14*: I walked passed the headquarters, I saw the logo and entered.
>
> *NOCO15*: I stepped in the Høyre's office. I was met by a very nice lady who said 'Hello – you have to join us', and I just couldn't refuse. [...] The atmosphere was extraordinary. [...] I thought – 'hell, why not get engaged?' [...] They asked: How involved do you want to be? I can probably do a lot, as long as it is not public speaking.

Of course, as we mentioned, in a number of cases, this first initiation into the world of party politics is facilitated by a friend, a colleague, or family member. In addition to the references to individual stories made earlier, let us also consider the following experiences:

> *HUPS22*: My friend was going to a campaign meeting and invited me to come along.
>
> *ESCO32*: My boyfriend seemed to enjoy his party meetings and they kept him busy. I thought the best thing for me to do was to go along.

The next moment that we have identified as key to the decision to join according to the discourse of the young party members that we interviewed is that of school debates or discussions. We already mentioned earlier the regular reference to the antagonism felt towards the view of some teacher, but more positively, school seems to play an important role in terms of civic education. Here, national differences are important and Norway stands out as a prime example of youngsters' exposure to political debate. Let us first consider the case of party exposure as a school 'exercise' for a young Norwegian Conservative and a young German Liberal Democrat:

NOCO05: We had to read all the party platforms at school. I decided UH was the right choice for me.
DELB04: We talked about the various parties in school.

Then come the reference to debates organised at school and shaping the preferences of the young voters that later became party members. Here again, Norway can be singled out as a country where such debates seem to be a regular occurrence and led to significant influx of young members, which may, in their own right, explain the country's specificity in terms of the reduced decline and limited ageing of party membership. One example among many is provided by a young Norwegian Conservative. However, similar references to more unofficial school debates are provided by a young Labour member:

NOCO23: The election debate in school had an important influence on me. I liked what the guy from Høyre said.
UKPS10: I took politics for my A-level, and the more I learnt about politics, the closer to Labour I felt.

However, as we explained, if a majority of young voters can trace their decision to join a party to a specific event, some look back at their decision to join as something deeply rooted in the earliest years of their childhood, and consider that only age restrictions prevented them from joining their political party well before they actually did. Here are a few examples of such discourse:

DEPS14: I joined the SPD in 1996, when I was 16. That's the minimum age, and I always wanted to join. My father and my mother were both in the party, and from a small age I always took part in their activities, say by celebrating after elections.
FRFN14: At the age of 9, I had my secret diary and I had my presidential programme already. My sister (5 years younger and not interested in politics at the time) was my Prime Minister, I had re-established death penalty for paedophiles and I had quite a few proposals.
FRPS23: Since 7 or 8, I was the 'Che Guevarra of the girls' [sic.] at home! Fighting for their rights and not getting anything for myself.
ESCO10: As a small girl, when they asked in school to make a drawing about a 'happy day', I drew Election Day instead of drawing Christmas or your birthday like the other kids did.

Finally, some young party members do not associate their joining with any event in particular nor with any long-held dream of getting involved in politics. It just strikes them as natural, a process of quasi-'revelation', an ideological quest that they suddenly had to embark upon because of an urge that imposed itself, as with this young German Liberal Democrat:

> *DELB23*: I was frustrated with my studies and wanted to do something that could improve the world.

In this chapter, we have looked at the sources of inspirations of party membership, and also at the specific events, incidents, and turning points that have coincided with the 'decision' to join, or at least the decision moment of young party members. We have identified three main paths to membership: family, friends/school, and unions, as well as five core mechanisms of influence: admiration, affection, pressure, exposure, and opposition. We analysed the specific 'catalytic moments' that coincided with the actual decision to join of some young people whose interest in politics had been awakened. Alongside these young people who do not think that such a moment ever occurred in their pathway to membership, and to those who think that they have really been predisposed to joining from an extremely young age, we identified several often reoccurring key moments that appear across young members' discourses. They include elections (either the campaign, or, more often, the result), antagonism to a specific policy, leader, or political event, being brought to a party by a friend, colleague, or family member, or spontaneously walking into a party's headquarters or a party meeting, as well as actively comparing the policy proposals of all competing political party, being convinced by a party leaflet or the discourse of an unknown activist, and finally exposure to school debates or discussions. It is interesting to note that there is no clear relationship between dominant 'histories of membership' and types of young party members (moral-, social-, or professional-minded).

Beyond what we have learnt about the frequencies of party members' sources of inspiration and their path to membership, the multiple shades and colours of individual stories reminds us that each party member is an individual, and that behind each new membership, there is a unique alchemy of family and social history, intellectual predisposition and interaction with the events and social realities that shape the politics of European countries. It is this unique recipe that ultimately makes the difference between a young citizen that will choose to be active outside of any party, or within a specific one. It is also likely that the resulting balance, and the coincidence between background and partisan membership choice is no stranger to the characterisation of each young party member as moral-, social-, or professional-minded according to the model that we defined in Chapter 2, as the story of one's path to membership and the nature of one's leading incentives fuse into a particular individualised shape of partisan activism.

4
24 Hours in the Life of a Young Party Member

We have seen that family, friends, and school can all have a major impact on the decision of a young person to join a political party. In turn, however, what is the effect of joining a party on the young member's relationship to his family, friends, and school or work? In fact how does joining a party impact his daily rhythm and his life altogether? As explained in Chapter 1, party membership is first and foremost a highly time consuming form of activism, which requires a high level of commitment. How does this work in practice, and what do young party members sacrifice as a result of their partisanship and their political involvement?

This chapter is precisely dedicated to a de-earthing of the daily life of young party members. What is their day like? How much time do they dedicate to their party in practice, and what activities do they undertake as part of their partisanship? Do they think of their party from the moment they wake up to the moment they rest their head, or do they hardly give it a thought at all outside of meetings and organised activities?

The chapter is based on the results of a number of survey questions on young party members' daily activities and involvement, but also on the lengthy, in-depth individual and personalised accounts that young party members recounted gave to us in the interviews, about what they do for their political party, how often, and how much time it takes them.

Because this is a unique soul searching moment when young party members offered us one of the most personal, impressionistic, and sometimes touching accounts of how they 'live' their membership; because they tried to offer us an insight into their new life, we decided to call this chapter '24 hours in the life of a young party member', trying to convey the prides, doubts, and little incidents that our interviewees recounted. The chapter starts with a general sense of the degree of involvement implied by the party membership of young people. How intense is it and how much time does membership seem to take? The second part of the chapter is dedicated to the great variety of specific activities involved. We try to convey their extreme diversity and also to evaluate the apparent tension between

66

'inward' (party-centric) and 'outward' (activities towards the population at large) activities in the practice of young party members. This is followed by a third section on the routine component of young party members – how it affects their daily social habits.

How active is active? – Faster, higher, stronger?

Measuring activism is an extremely difficult task. Are we interested in the time young party members dedicate to their party or the intensity of their activism? Is the time that matters the time a young activist spends actively engaging in partisan activities or the time (s)he spends thinking about membership? Does the time spent with fellow party members in the context of personal activities – as opposed to the political one – count as well? And does the time spent being 'politically active' but not partisan also matter? Finally, how should we deal with all the discussions, the arguments, the willingness to convince, refute, or deliberate? In fact, the vast debate on whether political activism in general starts with voting, reading newspapers, or watching tv applies – albeit more acutely yet – to the question of partisan activism.

Considering the complex nature of this debate, it is therefore not unhelpful to precede any attempt to define activism 'objectively' with a first impressionistic question about how young party members assess their degree of activism and involvement. In the survey, we therefore asked them how active they consider themselves to be. Table 4.1 provides a sense of these self-perceived levels of activism of young party members.

Table 4.1 Break down of levels of self-perceived activism by country and party family

Activism by country		Activism by party family	
Germany	3.13	Socialist	3.08
	(1.11)		(1.09)
Spain	3.11	Liberal	2.85
	(1.00)		(1.25)
Hungary	3.10	Conservative	2.64
	(0.97)		(1.34)
France	2.93		
	(1.21)		
UK	2.75		
	(1.26)		
Norway	2.39		
	(1.39)		
All		**2.91**	
		(1.21)	

Notes: Level of activism on a 0–4 scale. Standard deviations in brackets. $N = 2896$.

The question, reproduced in appendix, asked them if they perceived them-selves as very active, quite active, not very active, or not active at all, with a 'don't know' option also offered. On the resulting scale from 0 to 4, we find that the average self-perceived level of activism is 2.91 with a standard deviation of 1.21, suggesting that overall, most young party members see themselves as 'quite active.'

Comparative differences are quite interesting. The young party members who see themselves as most active are to be found in Germany (3.13), Spain (3.11), and Hungary (3.10), France is just above the whole sample's average (2.93), while British (2.75) and mostly Norwegian (2.39) young party members consider themselves far less active than their counterparts from other countries on average. In France, Norway, and the UK, activism has a high standard deviation, suggesting that some very involved members coexist alongside some rather passive ones.

Similarly interesting differences are revealed by our comparison of party families. It seems that the further left the party of membership of a young activist, the higher his/her self-perceived level of activism. In other words, young socialist party members claim an average level of activism of 3.08, young liberals of 2.85, and young conservatives of 2.64. It should be noted that young members of other smaller party families (extreme right, Greens, and Communists among others) claim higher levels of activism than mem-bers of the three main party families overall, even though we must look at their results more cautiously because of a relatively lower sample size.

Of course, we were also interested in the comparative self-perceived levels of activism of moral-, social-, and professional-minded young party mem-bers. In this context, Table 4.2 shows that consistently with hypothesis H3, professional-minded young party members claim to be the most active over-all (3.04) followed by moral-minded young activists (2.97). By contrast, consistently with our model, social-minded young party members claim far more modest levels of activism than the rest (2.64). The same results can

Table 4.2   Levels of activism by type of member – Self-perception scores

Levels of activism	Moral	Social	Professional
Not very/Not at all Active	19.7%	26.3%	17.7%
Very/Quite Active	79.3%	72.1%	80.7%
Average Index Score	2.97 (1.19)	2.76 (1.25)	3.04 (1.16)

Notes: Table 4.1 theoretical range is 0–3. Table 4.2 theoretical range of the index score is 0–4. Percentage categories total does not add up to 100 because of the don't know intermediary category.

$N = 2896$ (Table 4.1) and 2911 (Table 4.2).

be expressed as proportions of perceived active and non-active young party members. 80.7 per cent of professional-minded young party members claim to be quite or very active and only 17.7 per cent say that they are not very active or not active at all. By contrast, only 72.1 per cent of social-minded young party members claim to be quite or very active, and as much as 26.3 per cent – more than a quarter – not to be very active or not to be active at all. Amongst moral-minded young party members, these figures are 79.3 per cent and 19.7 per cent respectively.

These self-perceived figures are obviously very 'dry' on the whole. Indeed, what does being 'very', 'somewhat', or 'not really' active mean in real life? How many actual hours spent working for the party every day does it represent? What specific frequency of partisan activities does it correspond to?

Categorising the assiduity of young party members

In the interviews, we tried to explore the overall level of activism of young party members further by asking them, for instance, how often they undertake partisan activities, and how much time they tend to dedicate to them every day, week, or month on the whole. The answers vary a great deal, but clearly distinguish between four main categories of activists, according to the approximate frequency of their partisan activism and assiduity as summarised in Table 4.3.

As we can see from the table, roughly 1 in 10 young party members constitute a core of hyperactive members who come by or do something for

Table 4.3 How much time young party members dedicate to partisan activities

Frequency of activism	% of total based on self-evaluation	% of total based on evaluations of others
Core: Daily involvement in the party's activity throughout moments and circumstances	11	5
Regular: Approximately weekly involvement, more in election period	24	15
Reliable: Occasional but regular attendance (monthly on average) more in election period	38	40
Passive: Rare visits, no particular willingness to attend more in election period	27	40

Per cent based on non-representative interview answers. The first column corresponds to interviewee answers about themselves, the second column corresponds to the respondent's evaluation of the participation of others in their group to compensate self-selection effects.

the party more or less every day. These are usually either high-ranking party officials at the local, regional, or national level, or people who have become employed by the party. Sometimes, they are even high-ranking executives who cumulate their 'voluntary' position (for instance, locally) with a salaried one (for instance, regionally or nationally, or to take care of specific aspects of the party's activity such as its website or its communication). We could call this first category the *intense party-holics*. Then, there is a second tier of approximately 25 per cent of the young party members we interviewed whom we could call the *weekly activists*. They claim to dedicate themselves to partisan activities approximately once a week. In fact, most young party members told us that their party branch usually organises weekly meetings. A few branches seem to organise several events every week, especially when they are very large, and a few branches of young party organisations tend to cumulate a 'political' event (debate, meeting), and a separate 'social' one (outing, cinema, walk or party). Conversely, some smaller branches only meet less often, every other week or sometimes less regularly, but the 'weekly meeting' seems to be the pattern for the branches of approximately half of the young party members whom we interviewed. The third category of young party members could be called the *monthly visitors*. They represent a relative majority of young party members, about 40 per cent of the total we interviewed, and claim to try and attend party meetings or participate in activities regularly but less often. Some mention a monthly appearance, and others just say that they try to come 'as often as possible.' Nevertheless, these members are, let us say, apparently regular enough to be known to the rest of the branch, to be considered active, and to be relied upon during periods of intense activity such as election periods (see Chapter 5) without ever becoming core participants. Finally, the remaining 25 per cent of our interviewees could fit in a category we could formalise as one of *occasional party members*. They claim to be less regular in their presence or are less specific in their answers. These are young party members whose presence and activism may vary depending on their professional, scholarly, or familial involvement and who are unlikely to participate more intensely in the party's activities even in electoral periods despite paying their dues on a more or less regular basis. Of course, this last category is probably slightly under-represented in our interviews to the extent that participating in interviews in itself is a time-consuming act.

In order to avoid such an artificial discrepancy caused by self-selection mechanisms, we therefore asked respondents questions about the involvement of the rest of their group, and squared it with our survey data. Based on the more reliable survey data, as well as on the declaration of our interviewees when it comes to the presence of their friends, we estimate that the 'realistic' proportion of these looser young party members is nearer 40 per cent of the total, while the 'core' daily activists would be nearer 5 per cent, the 'weekly' regulars around 15 per cent, and the 'regularly-but-certainly-not-weekly' bunch who modulate their presence between election and non-election period is probably correctly evaluated at approximately 40 per cent.

Throughout the interviews, the young party members whom we talked to confirmed these various levels of commitment and contrasting amounts of time dedicated to the party's life and activities. Very often, those young activists who tend to dedicate time and attention to their party on a daily basis confess a certain pride in it. They also confirm that, as explained earlier, only those who hold leading positions of responsibility (regardless of their territorial level) or paid positions tend to become daily visitors to their party's office.

It would be wrong to assume that the question of the frequency of the activities of young party members and the strength of their involvement are simply an obsession of political scientists to categorise young party members or quantify participation. Indeed, before looking at the nature of the main activities described by young party members in the next section, it is worth noting that numerous references are made by many of our interviewees to an unexpected task, that of simply 'being there.' Very often, it seems that presence is conceived as the first duty of a young party member and that grass root members as well as leaders strongly believe that numbers matter. As a result, a large number of our interviewees seem to think of their involvement first – and sometimes foremost – in spontaneously quantitative terms. Consequently, it also seems that depending on their membership 'type' as outlined in Chapter 2, as well as on their pattern of involvement as per the four 'levels' of frequency of physical presence outlined above, young party members tend to have in mind a minimum acceptable level of attendance which they want to stick to.

Phrasing dedication – how long does membership take in the words of young party members?

A closer look at the substance and nuances of the qualitative data confirms these variations in the perceptions of how long partisan activism actually takes every week or every month. Below, we summarise some of the phrasings relating the four types of 'rhythms' of activism that we identified above.

All the time – visiting the party's 'intensive care'

Firstly, some of the testimonials focus on the notion of 'being there' as much as possible, without any preconception with regard to the frequency of the member's partisan involvement. Here are a few examples of such conceptions. We start with three typical examples of young members who confess being absorbed on a permanent basis out of choice or out of a self-established sense of duty.

FRPS37: I try to help with my time and effort in whatever is necessary. I try to be here. I think even just being here is important.

UKLB04: I want to do more and more things. I feel that what I do is never enough.

DEC026: You get more and more absorbed by it. I find myself thinking about politics all the time, I can't cut off.

Next to these cases of 'voluntary' complete absorption are the experiences of those young party members who also feel completely absorbed, but this time, rather as a result of an accepted – and conceivably approved – will of the party to use its members as much as possible. The following statements, illustrating such a perspective, are symptomatic of this interpretation. Note that two of the young party members quoted below hold relatively high level executive positions within their party and one within his young party organisation.

ESPS17: You don't really have a choice – it does take a lot of time. It is hard work but I like it.

FRPS30: They really make us work hard!

NOC003: Politics is really a 25 hour a day activity.

Finally, still to be found predominantly amongst young party members with positions of responsibility, a number of young party members rephrase this concept of permanent absorption with a connotation of acknowledged excess and, to a certain extent, displeasure, as illustrated by three young party members below.

ESPS20: My mobile phone really rings all the time. Some people call me or even approach me on a Saturday evening when I am trying to have a drink with my friends to ask me to sort out some problem that they have or to complain about some party regulation or other. Sometimes, it is really too much to take, but I am absorbed into it and I can't really leave it for now.

FRGR25: I couldn't say exactly, but I find that the activities suddenly take up a lot of my free time and it interferes too much and too often with my personal plans. That is definitely the hard part.

FRFN14: People try to get hold of me all the time. I have to keep three mobile phones, two for the party and one for everyone else.

Every day party-holics

A second type of testimonies – and, conceivably, very much a less passionate variation of the 'all the time' reference just noted, relate to a more or less daily involvement in the eyes of the members concerned. As explained, while this daily rhythm of activism is probably a little bit overestimated based on our interviews, it remains a sufficiently large number of the references that were made for us to be sure that the case is far from rare. First, for some young party members, this is really a more or less full-time job, whether paid or not, as per the testimonials of two young party members below.

> *HUPS08*: I spend 7 or 8 hours a day here, doing whatever is necessary and I get paid by the party for it.
> *ESPS33*: On average, many of us spend 6 hours a day, here, together, working on everything there is to do for the party. But it is really like a job.

For a second sub-category of 'daily activists', partisan involvement may not be a full-time job but it remains a strict and organised daily commitment, which is usually given its specific 'time slot.' The following examples of daily routines were recounted by a small selection of young party members we interviewed.

> *DEPS29*: I do some work for the party every day: at least half an hour, but often up to 3 to 5 hours.
> *DECO03*: Party work takes up a lot of my time, but either you're involved and work a lot or you're not involved at all – there's no halfway house in that. I go to lots of events in the evening, 3 or 4 during the week and 2 each weekend.
> *ESPS40*: I spend at least 3 or 4 hours on it every day. This is nothing like what I imagined from my political science studies!
> *FRGR06*: I usually come and help at the party every afternoon, after my job at the bank.
> *ESCO21*: I mostly dedicate a lot of time to the NNGG. Several hours every day.
> *ESCO29*: I'd say that we all spend on average 4 or 5 hours a day in NNGG or the PP and then some more time over the phone from home.
> *HUPS01*: I come here every day. I come here to participate in debates or just to talk about politics in our cafeteria!

Finally, a third sub-set of daily activists are, in fact, quasi-daily activists who may not strictly speaking work for their party on a daily basis but are always present several times a week and up to daily, depending on the level of 'excitement' in the party's headquarters at a specific point in time. Here again, are a few examples of this intensive involvement.

UKLB21: I don't know exactly but my membership is very demanding.
I do something for the party almost every day.

FRPS03: The huge amount of activity surprised me a lot. The truth is many
people spend lots of time and effort to organise activities, sometimes
every week, other times every day.

HUCO04: Right now, I don't go to our office every day because I am concentrating on my studies as exams are coming. But I think it is just a
phase I am in right now. I call it a phase of progression, not of calm. The
daily involvement is the more usual rhythm.

ESCO07: My main work is at the national headquarters of the NNGG.
There, the work is non-stopping. There is a new thing happening
every day.

The weekly activists

Our third category is made up of 'weekly activists', who tend to dedicate
time to the party either on a specific day every week, or between several
times a month and a couple of times a week depending on their rhythm of
work and the political context for the party. These examples were the second
most dominant in the interviews. However, in many ways, they often lack
precision and thus all tend to refer to more or less the same type of weekly
rhythms as per the excerpts reproduced below.

ESCO34: We spend part or all of every weekend here thinking or talking.

DECO21: I probably do party-related work 10 evenings a month.

ESPS04: We get together every Thursday to talk. Every month, we also
have a plenary session where everyone discusses the agenda or how
things are coming out in general.

UKPS23: I come here every week for our regular meeting.

FRPS19: Every Tuesday evening – same time, same place!

The monthly visitors

As shown earlier in Table 4.3, the largest proportion of young party members is probably the segment who attend party meetings and occasions
between 1 and 3 times a month rather than more regularly. These young
party members insist on the importance for them to be regular visitors and not to let too much time lapse between any two visits. One
of them specifically insists on the need to prove to his fellow young
members that he is 'fully' with them. While these monthly visitors are
clearly different by their level of involvement from the two categories
that we have identified as 'frequent contributors' to their party's life, in
their minds at least, they are also extremely different from the final category that we will explore, that of 'occasional' young party members.
Indeed, in terms of our model, the two could not be more different, in

that monthly visitors seem to be essentially moral-minded, while occasional members tend to be predominantly social-minded. Below are a few testimonials summarising the spirit that leads a young party member to scrupulously engage in his/her monthly meeting or party event even though he or she may never choose to become a more assiduous member of the party.

ESPS02: I am a normal affiliate. I participate as much as I can, trying to assist in demonstrations and being there in local election events or in the street whenever I can and have time. But right now, I don't have much time, so it is, maybe, a once a month thing for me.

FRGR26: There are always so many things to do. I get more or less involved depending on how much I like the issue, but the frequency of my party works ranges from weekly to monthly.

UKPS10: I'm too busy to come regularly, but I try to attend a meeting or a plenary event at least once a month.

DELB27: Some people spend their life here, but I can't do this. I attend one or two events every month.

NOCO15: It really depends on the context, like I come more when there is an election but otherwise, it can vary between once or twice a month when I am not too busy and once every other month when I really have too much work.

UKLB15: For me, it is important to show that I am part of a group so I come often enough so that the others know I'm with them completely. In practice, it means one meeting a month or so, and perhaps four or five parties or events in the year on top of it.

FRFN26: I try to make the plenary meeting every month.

The occasional young party members

In a certain way, the difference between monthly and 'occasional' young party members may have more to do with the spirit of their membership than with the actual frequency of their partisan work. As explained earlier, empirically, it seems that most monthly activists seem to fit in the 'moral minded' category of young membership defined by our typology while, by contrast, a majority of the occasional young partisans are, instead, social-minded and mostly come not to lose touch with their friends or comrades. In fact, note that in a couple of the statements below, some young party members explicitly recognise coming more often for parties and events than they do to regular administrative meetings. Among the large number of testimonials received in this category, we chose five which are symptomatic of this 'opt in' conception of party activism and come from a range of countries and party families.

ESCO22: I don't participate much in comparison with my friends. I am a bit disconnected and have no responsibilities at all.

ESPS06: It is not that I am not interested, I have to study a lot and have no time.

HUPS22: I come once in a while to see my friends here but don't have the time to come too often.

HUCO22: Last year, I probably came two or three times, mostly because I like the people but I don't really get involved in the debates all that much.

UKPS18: I have attended two parties and one meeting this year. It becomes really repetitive otherwise.

FRGR08: I have to split my time between the party and Greenpeace, so I can't come more than once a term or so.

Overall, we now have a better sense of the way in which our four types of young party members – intensive daily activists, frequent weekly participants, regular monthly visitors, and occasional young party members – understand, define, and explain their political engagement. We have a much clearer understanding of how much time young party activism can take in practice and therefore of the sacrifice that it probably represents for most young members, but what does it substantially involve? What are the activities that can keep some young party members busy for 6 or 7 hours a day? In the next section, we move on to analyse the survey results, whereby our young party members hierarchised the frequency of some of the main modes of partisan participation that have been highlighted by the political science literature, before 'fleshing out' these various components of a multi-modal activism using inspirations from the more qualitative in-depth interviews extracts.

The activities of young party members – general trends

By now, a relatively clear picture emerges as to what party membership *means* to each type of young activist. However, we must question how this translates into what they actually *do*, that is, the daily reality of their partisan activities. In this context, *H3* suggests that social-minded members will be the least active, whilst professional-minded members will be most active in the context of electoralist duties, and moral-minded members will be the most likely to engage in radical forms of participation (demonstrating, fighting other parties).

Table 4.4 fully confirms this pattern. Social-minded members seem least dedicated to their party and least willing to sacrifice time to serve it. By contrast, professional-minded members are in the front line to boost their party's electoral appeal with posters, flyers, and attempts to convince voters. They do their best to support their party as electoral machine in a Downsian

Table 4.4 Levels of activism by type of member – Types of activities

Types of activities	Moral	Social	Professional
Posters	1.68 (1.20)	*1.54 (1.09)*	**1.71 (1.08)**
Flyers	1.92 (1.05)	*1.81 (1.02)*	**1.95 (0.99)**
Convince	**2.38 (0.80)**	*2.24 (0.85)*	2.28 (0.86)
Debate	2.09 (1.00)	*2.00 (0.99)*	**2.10 (0.94)**
Demonstrate	**1.50 (1.09)**	1.25 (1.06)	*1.18 (1.02)*
Fight others	**1.23 (1.07)**	*0.94 (0.94)*	1.14 (1.01)

sense, as they tie their own fortunes to that of the party. However, the most likely activists to demonstrate or to fight other parties are moral-minded ones. They are the ones to go out of their way to engage in radical forms of participation to serve the causes they believe in.

These patterns also confirm the differences in terms of self-perceived activism that we highlighted at the beginning of the chapter. As a reminder, social-minded members claim to be the least active, and professional-minded members the most. This supports hypothesis *H3*, which claims that at this very early stage of partisan involvement, some young activists who are driven by a professional conception of their membership, already behave differently from the rest, acting in a way which they see fit for 'future leaders.'

Overall, young party members primarily engage in 'soft' forms of partisan activities, as opposed to aggressive, physical, or more direct forms of engagement. A prime favourite consists of spending time trying to convince friends and family members (2.36 on a 0–3 scale) and bringing them in line with the young member's political views. Similarly, debating remains a very regular mode of activism for most young party members (1.88) across countries and ideological families. All other activities feature significantly less predominantly in a young activist's daily life. The two main forms of electoral support to the party (handing out flyers, and sticking posters) respectively come third and fourth (1.79 and 1.57) of the list. As a reminder, a score of 1.5 corresponds to the exact average between 'rarely' and 'occasionally' on the answer scale. Finally, the two most radical and confrontational modes of activism (demonstrating and fighting other parties) are least frequent overall (1.39 and 1.27). Tables 4.5 and 4.6 elaborate on these differences of regular partisan activities and modes of participation by comparing the importance of various typical partisan duties and forms of behaviour across countries and party families.

As seen from Table 4.5, some important cross-national differences exist. Electoral activities come first for young Hungarian activists (posters top, handing out flyers second), and handing out flyers is also the second most important activity for young Norwegian party members. Demonstrations, a radical mode of participation, is the third most frequent activity for young

Table 4.5 Forms of activism by country

Country	Convince	Debate	Hand Out Flyers	Put Posters	Demonstrate	Fight Other Parties
Germany	2.22	2.29	2.02	1.71	1.24	0.90
	(0.87)	(0.86)	(0.96)	(1.16)	(1.02)	(0.93)
	2	1	3	4	5	6
Spain	2.38	2.32	2.01	2.00	**2.22**	**1.63**
	(0.80)	(0.81)	(0.95)	(1.04)	**(0.82)**	**(1.10)**
	1	2	4	5	3	6
Hungary	2.03	2.08	2.21	**2.27**	1.48	1.28
	(0.94)	(0.88)	(0.93)	**(0.88)**	(0.97)	(1.08)
	4	3	2	**1**	5	6
France	2.42	**2.70**	**2.25**	1.94	**2.22**	1.51
	(0.74)	**(0.55)**	**(1.01)**	(1.00)	**(0.87)**	(0.99)
	2	1	3	5	4	6
UK	**2.45**	2.28	1.98	1.35	1.35	1.48
	(0.82)	(0.88)	(1.00)	(1.12)	(0.89)	(0.91)
	1	2	3	5 =	5 =	4
Norway	2.44	1.41	1.44	1.06	0.74	0.98
	(0.76)	(1.05)	(1.07)	(0.98)	(0.87)	(0.95)
	1	3	2	4	6	5
ALL	*2.30*	*2.06*	*1.89*	*1.63*	*1.33*	*1.11*
	(0.84)	*(0.98)*	*(1.02)*	*(1.13)*	*(1.07)*	*(1.02)*
	1	*2*	*3*	*4*	*5*	*6*

Notes: Specific activities on a 0–3 scale. Standard deviations in brackets. Figures in bold represent the country with the highest level for each type of activity.
$N = 2896$.

Table 4.6 Forms of activism by party family

Party family	Convince	Debate	Hand out flyers	Put posters	Demonstrate	Fight other parties
Socialist	2.25	**2.24**	**1.97**	**1.75**	**1.75**	**1.28**
	(0.85)	**(0.88)**	**(0.96)**	**(1.12)**	**(0.98)**	**(1.03)**
	1	2	3	4 =	4 =	6
Liberal	2.26	2.17	1.87	1.61	0.70	0.60
	(0.88)	(0.92)	(1.04)	(1.13)	(0.79)	(0.81)
	1	2	3	4	5	4
Conserv.	**2.42**	1.69	1.74	1.44	0.83	1.00
	(0.79)	(1.08)	(1.10)	(1.12)	(0.98)	(0.99)
	1	3	2	4	6	5
ALL	*2.30*	*2.06*	*1.89*	*1.63*	*1.33*	*1.11*
	(0.84)	*(0.98)*	*(1.02)*	*(1.13)*	*(1.07)*	*(1.02)*
	1	*2*	*3*	*4*	*5*	*6*

Notes: Specific activities on a 0–3 scale. Standard deviations in brackets. Figures in bold represent the party family with the highest level for each type of activity.
$N = 2896$.

Spanish partisans, when young Norwegian and British activists are the least likely to engage in radical activities.

Table 4.6 shows that similar contrasts exist across party families. Young Socialists are far more likely than others to join demonstrations, while young Liberals and Conservatives are significantly more likely to spend time trying to convince friends and family. However, across families, the ranking of the different types of partisan activities varies remarkably little.

The routine of a young party member

Before we look at the detail of the activities that young party members engage in as part of their regular activism, let us spend a minute translating the 'rhythm' of membership discussed above into a typical routine. One of the most striking things in the discourse of many young party members is that many of them have developed a stable routine, almost a ritual, which marks their regular partisan engagement. This routine is described in various ways by a number of young party members.

First, some of them mention the way they share their work between the various types of activities organised by – or to be organised for – the party:

ESCO05: We have roundtable conferences every Tuesday, I really like them, and this regular thing is a nice way to meet regularly and bond.

ESCO37: I take part in every meeting or event organised by the party. I just try to be there, I collect signatures against the Catalan statute or attend convention days, I am there and ready to help with anything, even keeping people out of the way when our leaders need to walk out of a room.

HUPS23: So my leaders call me to tell me when and where to be and if I'm free I plan to be there.

NOCO23: I basically co-ordinate the newcomers and propose initiatives for activities. On the whole, we get together every ten days or at most once a week to plan what to do.

UKPS01: I like our roundtables every Tuesday. They are really good. Sometimes, we end up having more than 100 people coming and participating.

DECO17: I do three things as a JU member: first, there's a lot of organisational work to be done; second, I try to improve things for young people here, practical things like night buses; third, I try to make contacts and pull strings to get things done.

FRCM26: My tasks as a party member often include being responsible for campaigns and recruiting events in schools etc.

NOCO14: I have regular board meetings. It takes a lot of organising and administration.

ESPS33: I normally take care of the organic part of the movement at the provincial level during the morning. If I work on other things, it is usually during the weekend.

FRFN07: I am really just present and that's mostly it. I am one more person for the crowd, and that's it. I think that even that is important though. Not everybody has to be completely active.

Alongside this strategy of organisation of a routine by 'task' comes a second form of self-established organisation that many high-ranking young party members describe as their routine on a geographical basis. This is of course very important when they occupy positions at both the local and either regional or national levels. The following three examples are quite typical:

ESPS37: I spend most of my time in Madrid now. I don't go to La Rioja every week.

FRPS21: I go to Marseille once a week, to Paris between two and five times a month and am in Nice the rest of the time.

UKLB21: I go to London either once or twice a month.

The last form of routine described by young party members is quite different. It has to do with the balance between the 'work' and 'play' parts of their activism. To many of the young party members that we interviewed, this particular pattern is in fact essential, and many insist on the role of the latter to make the former more palatable, either for themselves as individuals, or for their group as a whole, as described in the examples below:

UKLB32: We are not always discussing politics. We also do normal young people activities like trips, eating, or drinking.

FRGR13: In my free time, I come by the office, sit here and talk or have coffee.

DECO03: Generally, there is a need to balance the fun aspects of party work with the more serious work.

ESCO47: Because I am president of the Moncloa section in central Madrid and we have 500 members, our routine is pretty comprehensive. We try to offer at least three or four and sometimes more political activities each and every week as well as a couple of entertainment activities every weekend. Usually, this may include a party or a small bullfight or a trip to the countryside.

Accounts of a varied pattern of activism

Beyond describing such patterns of routine, the interview data confirms the general tendency highlighted by the survey results in terms of the great variety of activities undertaken by young party members across the six countries included in the analysis. Indeed, the types of activities mentioned by young party members vary in seemingly infinite ways. Young party members mention the most obvious partisan activities as well as the most unpredictable ones. Yes, of course, they engage in sticking posters, handing out flyers, and demonstrating. Obviously, they regularly participate in debates, routinely join meetings with fellow activists, and often discuss politics with non-partisans or try to convince their friends and family. However, many young people also mention trips and parties, picnics and drinks (in fact, few mentions of poster sticking activities were not accompanied by references to the following drinks or meal young party members seem to particularly enjoy). Many young activists mention meetings involving experts and outsiders, a large number of them refer to the time they simply spend on the phone talking to fellow party members, and indeed, reading, writing, and forwarding the emails that relate to their partisan passion. It seems that parties are undoubtedly as touched by the current mass-mailing mania as any other sector of our societies! The other types of regular activities mentioned by young party members range from cinema outings to initiatives to support young citizens' entrepreneurship, and internal elections and auditing all the way to making films, writing articles, or meeting senior politicians and the press, not to mention some occasional references to illegal activities (such as covering other parties' posters, or even launching unproved – if 'believed to be true' rumours about opponents). Let us now try to give some shape to the great variety of activities and tasks recounted by the young party members in their interviews.

The first element that very clearly appears from the more than 500 interviews that we conducted in all six countries is that variety per se is acknowledged by an immense majority of party members. Out of 519 interviewees, literally less than a handful actually suggested that they considered their membership to be, in any way, repetitive or lacking variety. By contrast, more than 100 young members spontaneously expressed their impression that membership activities are indeed very versatile, whether they saw it as a good thing or as a less good one. Below are a few such 'positive' references to versatility whereby young party members all specify some of the at times original combinations of different activities that make their daily membership.

> UKLB20: I thought people just did a few things here. I thought many people joined to get things out of the party but I was surprised by how active people are and by the huge amount of different activities we do.
> FRPS23: In my mind, I am a street militant. I come and talk to members, see what they are doing, take posters with me to stick them in my neighbourhood, participate in demonstrations.
> NOCO20: I attend the Town Hall open sessions and follow local political developments.

ESPS27: Part of my work is directed at the outside. For instance, I deal with the press or talk on the radio about alternative ways of doing things than what the current Town Hall is doing. At the same time, in the provincial headquarters, I am co-ordinator. I oversee activities, deal with documents, and counsel our small local associations on all kinds of matters.

ESCO30: As general secretary of our party in Madrid's central district, I help co-ordinating everything – our activities, our web page, our monthly bulletin, our relations with other associations, our executive members and their activities, etc.

DELB01: As local president, I spend most of my time co-ordinating and following our local activities.

HUCO04: I check the mail, I contact the rest of the general secretaries as interlocutors of their militants, I check the press and write articles once in a while.

Similarly, these three further testimonials come from young party members who elaborate further on the essence of the diversity of young partisan action, and partly highlight the aspect of this membership which makes them, to an extent, the 'all purpose' workers of their party or young party organisation.

ESCO47: I really do a bit of everything. Everybody helps with everything.

ESPS30: I do whatever, like the rest.

UKPS23: The content of our membership and what we are asked to do seems to randomly vary by the day.

When looking further into the details of our interviewees' accounts, it is clear that the political science literature on party membership and modes of participation hardly prepares us from the amazing variety of activities, experiences, and situations, which young party members mentioned as constituting the basis of their daily business. The categories we proposed in the survey might have covered the bulk of what we normally expect to constitute the heart of partisan activism, but they need to be qualified by the infinite nuances and flesh that correspond to young party members' stories. Altogether, we can divide these descriptions of daily activities into a number of sub-categories inductively mentioned by our hundreds of interviewees when asked what they normally 'do' as members of a party or young party organisation without any further prompt or specification. These categories include providing 'manual labour' to the party, administrative duties, fellow members' mentoring, social commitments, intellectual work, public relations work and representation, democratic linkage activities, political opposition, and low-level party policy or social outreach activities.

Young party members as free labour

As explained in Chapter 1, it has long been acknowledged by the existing political science literature that one of the reasons why parties cannot survive 'without members' (Scarrow, 2000) is because these members provide a quasi unlimited supply of absolutely free and often totally dedicated manual labour. Partisans hand out flyers and other party material, stick posters, or take care of a seemingly endless list of necessary jobs which, if paid for, would end up costing the party millions of euros/dollars/pounds each year. Of course, within this context, young party members often represent the highest 'grade' of labour. They are young, valid, and strong. They often do not have young families to go back to in the evenings, and in many cases, do not have the sort of professional ties that prevent them from working for the party several hours a day. Last but not least, many young party members conceivably come across as less fearful and less picky than their elder when it comes to providing their party with manual labour.

Throughout our more than 500 interviews, young party members' references to such handy jobs and errands that save their parties a little fortune each year have been endless. Let us consider a few symptomatic examples derived from the accounts of some young party members who explain how they spend a lot of time on the street for their party sticking posters and handing out pamphlets of various sorts:

> *FRCM14*: In my daily activity, I spend a lot of time in the street, putting up posters and distributing ads everywhere or participating in demonstrations.
>
> *ESPS27*: I do different things: give away pamphlets, stick posters, write articles for our magazine or the web, organise demonstrations and political events, go to them, go to Town Hall open meetings, think of future electoral acts or campaigns, convince people in the streets and friends to join, debate and convince people that conservative policies are not good.

These manual activities whereby young party members become the arms and legs of their partisan organisation can sometimes take a lot of their time, energy, and effort, particularly, as we shall see, in electoral periods. Beyond the examples that we cited, a few young party members mentioned a wide range of other physical activities – enrolling in the party's security service to 'filter' entrance to meetings and political gatherings of all sorts, handling deliveries, moving boxes, helping the local party branch in the context of its move, and so on. A young Spanish socialist militant provides an excellent example of this multi-faceted dedication of the typical young activist:

> *ESPS30*: I have done lots of different things in here. I helped in the press departments and brought water to the meetings. I also stuck posters.

In many ways, it seems that some young party members have become used to donating their body to their party and to help with whatever technical or physical task is required at a given time, as if the party's headquarters were just another family home.

Young party members as administrators

Clearly, manual labour is not the only form of work political parties 'consume', and in addition to their body, many young party members also have to offer their minds. Indeed, an equally obvious need parties and young party organisations alike face is that of administrators. The parties' quest for administrators represents a rather paradoxical game, because the numerous administrative tasks at hand are partly fulfilled on a voluntary basis by young party members, and partly on a paid basis by other young activists who also become party employees. In the first case, the parties request a significant commitment on the part of the young activists without providing any obvious compensation, except, at times, increased positions of responsibility. In the latter case, by contrast, the party uses administrative paid work as a perk to reward some of its most committed members, and to provide them with some personal financial sustainability as the time they spend 'working' for the party may prevent them from having a normal professional activity at the same time. Of course, our interviewees' stories illustrate this dichotomy. For many of them, the unpaid administrative work of a young party member is as much a trap as its paid equivalent is a rare and desirable perk, which comes with time, luck, experience, and ladder climbing.

Let us first consider the types of administrative duties that young party members have to take care of as part of their activities. Infinite number of references were made by our interviewees to them dealing with the phone calls, the mail, and sometimes more technical aspects of a party's life like accountancy, dues collection, and party members census. Let us consider a handful of examples collected from members of various parties across the countries included in the analysis. The following excerpts give a sense of some of the types of administrative functions that young party members have to take care of on a daily basis.

> *ESPS37*: I do lots of administrative stuff like calling people and asking them to participate in meetings or protest actions, both at the regional level and here in xxx.
>
> *DEPS14*: I had to learn basic accounting and how to organise election campaigns and educational seminars.
>
> *ESCO27*: We all do whatever is necessary, even putting letters in envelopes or sticking posters, That is a pain.
>
> *DELB20*: I don't like all the administrative office work like writing minutes of meetings.
>
> *HUCO12*: I keep the census of party members. I don't like that very much.

One of the things that is very clear here is that these administrative duties are far from being the most popular in young party members' headquarters. One of the main gripes expressed by our interviewees is that it takes them an enormous amount of time, very often more so than their other tasks and duties. Here are four examples of such statements, articulated by Spanish Socialist, and French Green and socialist young party members. All either emphasise or regret the amount of time it takes them to perform their administrative tasks, and some deplore the extent to which it prevents them from accomplishing other functions which they like better.

> *ESPS37*: Almost all of my activity is internal. I make sure that the machine works.
> *FRGR20*: Most of my work is actually internal and administrative.
> *FRPS25*: I spend most of my time in meetings.
> *ESPS38*: I don't have much time to deal with real people because I generally take care of more administrative stuff all the time, like papers and letters, phone calls from members and the like.

Of course, administrative duties take an entirely different dimension in the discourse of those young party members who end up being employed by their party or young party organisation as well as remaining one of its members. In this case, young party members often tend to differentiate, in their discourse between their administrative 'job' and their substantive 'hobby.' In this sense, this makes this particular brand of young party members quite unique. Indeed, notwithstanding the fact that their party is also their employer and their 'bread and butter', they can think of their membership itself as a sort of purified and optimised quantity, devoid of the often less-glamourous administrative component that their fellow party members see as a price to pay for the intellectually more stimulating parts of the membership (see 'likes' and 'dislikes' sections later in Chapter 5). This is well illustrated by a young French Socialist militant:

> *FRPS28*: I am employed by the party as a polyvalent worker, taking care of everything from sorting the mail and answering phone calls to keeping the accounts and raising the alarm when our budget is almost spent. I am also a member and as such, participate in meetings, demonstrations and try to refocus the party in terms of policy proposals and dedication to our fundamental values.

Note the 'also' in the words of this young party member. To her, the 'party job' and the 'party membership' are two different things, which, while complementary enough to mention in the same series of sentences without any intermediary prompting, are different enough to be structured as two separate 'parts' of the story. A similar dichotomy is maintained by a young Hungarian Conservative:

> *HUCO21*: I try to keep "working" hours and "activist" hours separate, so that I can keep focusing on ideas and not only on technical details and internal organisation and co-ordination.

Once more, here, the party work quickly becomes a 'job like any other' (and not necessarily portrayed as a very lucky one to get), while the membership is seen as a rather idyllic purely intellectualised commitment, which contrasts with the far more heterogeneous stories recounted by the rest of the young party members. Few young party members who have also become employees acknowledge this as a 'privilege', but of course a few do. One of the typical comments that ensued was made by two young Spanish young party members and employees:

> *ESPS14*: I'm a strange case: a paid street militant.
> *ESCO10*: Now that I have taken a responsibility position, my job is at the same time also my political involvement.

Apart from these specific cases of activists/employees, one of the elements that come prominently in the testimony of young party members is that the administrative duties that they more or less put up with (or, at times, barely tolerate) tend to increase significantly as a young party member climbs the ladder of its internal hierarchy. It seems that the higher up one is, not only the more they do for the party, but also the more their work is refocused towards administrative duties as opposed to more outward looking ones. Here are a few descriptions of this hidden 'price' of leadership:

> *FRGR01*: I belong to the local Executive Committee, which usually means that I end up spending most of my time putting letters in envelopes! I organise communication campaigns for new members, etc.
> *ESCO30*: My becoming the local president has changed the nature of my work even more than its quantity. Before, I was mostly getting involved in outwards-looking activities, now I mostly co-ordinate the 29 people in our executive committee. Each of them has a clearly defined area of action and responsibility, but it is essential that someone is here to make sure that the whole 'machine' works efficiently.

These testimonials are quite symptomatic of the change in the nature of partisanship that many young party members associate with climbing the ladder as we shall see in Chapter 5. Meanwhile, it is also worth noting that the connotations associated with this administrative part of the work varied a lot according to the member 'profiles' that we could identify. While social-minded members and to a lesser extent, moral-minded ones seemed to resent the administrative part of the work, some of the professional-minded young party members had a much more benevolent attitude towards that part of their activism, and particularly enjoyed, in some cases, their activities of co-ordination as we shall see in the 'likes' and 'dislikes' sections in Chapter 5.

Mentoring fellow members

A particular subsection of the administrative functions of young party members has to do with their commitment to fellow young partisans, and in particular to the newer, younger recruits, which many of them claim to spend time helping, training, coaching, and ultimately integrating into the life of their new political party.

The training and integrating related activities in the life of a young party member fulfil several complementary goals and functions. From the point of view of the political party or young party organisation, these activities present the advantage of increasing the harmony and cohesion of the group, passing on knowledge, values, habits, and activist tools to new members, and ensuring a certain consistency of practice and morals across young party members. From the point of view of the young member, however, the same activities result in an increased sense of responsibility, often referred to by our interviewees as a form of hierarchical promotion, as well as an opportunity to think about their own activism in a different way, with a greater emphasis on the organisational and 'official' ideological attributes of the party as a political structure.

The specific activities undertaken by young party members as part of their 'new members coaching' tasks are varied and include answering questions, preparing activities and ideological heritage and nostalgia activities, 'taking' new members on the street for poster sticking and flyers handling, and so on. Here are a few examples and accounts provided by a number of young party members of such a mentoring role.

ESCO43: I do a lot of work to train the new party members.

ESPS14: I spend most time welcoming and 'teaching' the newcomers, talking to them about my experience.

FRGR06: I take young members with me to stick posters and try to make it fun for them; we usually go for drinks afterwards.

ESPS47: I designed a programme of activities to recover and teach Socialist history to young party members. We do round tables to analyse the role of Socialism in our transition or our welfare system. Each month, we study one character of socialism, starting with women who are less remembered.

These testimonials would be incomplete without a look at these additional impressions by two members of the German SPD, British Labour, as well as the Hungarian Conservatives from the FIDESz as to how these activities have allowed them to fulfil a new purpose and meaning through their membership.

> *UKPS31*: Education is important. It allows us to learn from errors and find alternatives.
> *DEPS29*: I particularly enjoy the internal education we do, for example a recent seminar we organised on equal opportunities.
> *HUCO21*: Since I have been asked to welcome and train our new young members, I have a different perspective on my own membership.

Social commitments

Meanwhile, after manual labour, administrative work, and 'official' training activities, young party members clearly spend a lot of time participating in social events and occasions as well. Here, it is worth remembering that in Chapter 2, we showed that the second largest contingent of young party members, social-minded activists, who represent approximately 34.2 per cent of our total sample, are motivated by their hope and desire to meet and be with like-minded young people. In this sense, it is not unreasonable to expect these particular young people to favour the types of activities whereby they would focus on social exchange and interaction rather than 'hard core' political activism. Members of a volleyball team may not just play volleyball together but may also decide to go clubbing or to the cinema together as well once in a while, and it is exactly the same for young party members. These social commitments may therefore include a great variety of 'normal' more or less regular activities that young people could choose to share with people from any group or society, but choose to experience with fellow young members instead. Such events include clubbing, cinema or film projection, plays, outdoor activities or hikes, sports, and so on. In some cases, young party members may even produce plays together or organise trips, be it to places which simply represent great tourist attractions, others which have a particular political significance for their party or its history, or again other places which 'coincide' with some major or minor partisan gathering, meeting, or summer university.

Below are a few cases that point to the types of 'simple' social activities that may represent more or less regular events on the calendar of a young party member (see, in this chapter, the section on the time partisan activities take and the routine they constitute). These particular examples are provided by two young Spanish Socialists, a young Spanish Conservative, a young German liberal, and a young French Communist party members.

ESPS47: I think of new cultural activities and organise them. We did a social movie show recently and I planned our New Year's Eve fundraising party too.

ESCO08: We have drama groups too although I'm not very much into that.

DELB19: A few weeks ago, the Julis organised an After-Work-Lounge party where we could just sit together after work and exchange views.

FRCM01: We have created a local football team together, so on top of meetings, I also spend "party time" training!

ESPS41: We also organise young people's activities like multi-adventure trips. Anything to get young people to participate and have fun.

The first testimonial is quite interesting in that it shows the degree of social integration of some young party groups. It is not a typical expectation that young party members would stick together on New Year's eve, yet, numerous interviewees mentioned similar occasions, either associated with fund-raising events, or just purely social and informal. Other young party members also mentioned similar events on Christmas eve, for other holidays, or some more or less regular Saturday evenings disco nights or Sunday afternoon picnics. Similarly, the reference to a local football team is only one of very many, not to mention basket ball, volley ball, skiing trips, and tennis tournaments. For many young party members, winning a sporting event for the party did not sound much less important than winning some elections. As mentioned, some young party members also regularly refer to slightly more ambitious or 'exceptional' social outings. Typical among them are a vast series of hikes and 'pilgrimages' as well as short or long trips. Here are a few examples provided by two young French socialists and a young French National Front member.

FRPS03: Every year, we go on a walk – almost a pilgrimage with other members on the mountain where François Mitterrand used to love walking every year himself. We bring a picnic and have a great time together.

FRPS23: Every year we go to the party's summer university in La Rochelle. We always ask who can and will go, organise a little convoy of cars, each packed with 4 or 5 of us and go together. This is a great moment, not just because La Rochelle is great fun, but because we also get to spend a lot of time together and have a shot if quite tiresome holiday.

FRFN07: Not long ago, we all went to Italy together. We met a delegation from our Italian equivalent but it was also a weekend of great fun by the beach!

All these references were in fact extremely regular throughout our interviews across countries and party families. Similar pilgrimages were mentioned in the South East of France, in the West of Germany, in the North of Spain, and so on amongst members from the whole spectrum of politicial ideologies. As for the 'convoys of local cars' which aim for party conferences and universities, they were, perhaps, even more universal. At least one person – and some times, dozens of them – from any of the 15 parties included in the analysis must have referred to such an experience at one point or another in the interviews.

In the discourse of many of the young party members we talked to, one key aspect of the importance of this social and 'leisurely' component of young party members' regular activities is to make the whole of membership more palatable. As seen in the section on the time involved in young party members' activism in this chapter, many young party members dedicate so much time to their party or young party organisation that they sacrifice much of the time most young adults would normally dedicate to their friends and hobbies. As a result, the party has to 'offer' surrogate friends and hobbies, from sports to clubbing via trips to avoid discouraging most young people from getting involved. In this sense, we are here uncovering something which is even more important for young party members than for party members in general. In order to be successful at recruiting young activists, parties and young party organisations need to somewhat 'blur' the boundary between the private and public spheres, between ideological struggle and fun, between what drives our 'moral minded' and our 'social minded' young party members.

One of the consequences of this blurring is that it may become symmetrically difficult for many young party members to decide whether some of their dreams, hopes, and passions are indeed relevant to the sphere of their partisan involvement or to that of their private life. Here are two examples provided by a young Spanish Socialist party member and a young Hungarian conservative respectively.

> *ESPS01*: One recent idea: a "hotel of laughs" where people can relax through laugh therapy! I want to work for this dream but it was difficult to decide whether to work on this in the party or outside, as an entrepreneur.
> *ESCO08*: In terms of my middle term job plans, I would like to launch a communication start up and am thinking of doing this with the party since it could be useful to them too.

In recent years, most citizens and the media across democratic countries have found it increasingly hard to tolerate what they often perceive to be unhealthy paths of permeability between public and private spheres. Such areas of permeability are sometimes clearly illegal (unlawful benefits or contracts, favouritism, nepotism, harassment, etc) but many more yet are not strictly criminal but nonetheless perceived as quite shocking by a majority of citizens (in fact, most occasions where politics seems to be mixed up with sex, money, or work are perceived as shocking by a majority of them) and have given rise to minor scandals. Here, we are simply pointing out to the fact that while many – and indeed most – of us would most probably find it shocking to see a party activist think about 'mixing' his plans to start a new private company with his party, or his political alliances with an affair, it is important to note that in the context of their lives, all of these elements may very well seem to young party members themselves to overlap naturally. Of course, they may realise that a 'border' should be kept before the overlap becomes embarrassing, but this overlap is not only real at the level of individual lives, but also to a certain extent encouraged by the very foundations of party politics, as parties do need to 'relate' activism to partisans' lives to keep them onboard. In this sense, we find the two cases mentioned above truly symptomatic because they emphasise this lack of differentiation in a way which is not morally shocking (at least in the first case) but perhaps a little bit ridiculous, stressing the way in which this blurring of intellectual and moral borders is perhaps more 'spontaneous' at times than it is 'calculated.'

Of course, an even more obvious example of such blurring is related to the intellectual side of membership activism in that it is perhaps very difficult for some young party members to differentiate between political involvement and their individual moral values. Here, the blurring is actually socially acceptable and even desirable in that most citizens want 'convinced' politicians, and indeed intellectual activities are in many ways the 'main course' of partisan involvement in the eyes of many young party members.

Intellectual work

While social commitments are predictably a highlight in the partisan engagement of social-minded young party members (see 'likes' and 'dislikes' sections in Chapter 5), the largest contingent of young party members from our sample are, in fact, moral-minded, and therefore primarily focused on the ideological and policy-related opportunities that they derive from their activism. These moral-minded young party activists represent 39.7 per cent of our total sample, and it is likely that to them, the highlight of a young partisan's week will often be associated with the intellectual work and stimulation that they derive from their partisan engagement.

Indeed, references to such intellectual work, occasions to exchange ideas, thoughts, and opinions, to agree, disagree and debate are numerous and regularly mentioned by the young party members that we interviewed. Some focus on the type of opportunities that they have to generate ideas, others on meetings and events where they can express them. Young party members provide numerous examples of both types of activities in the spontaneous words of the young party members that we talked and listened to.

For instance, the following three young party members refer to the time that they spend trying to generate or identify new ideas. As we explain later in the 'likes' and 'dislikes' sections in Chapter 5, these intellectually stimulating occasions are some of the most highly prized partisan experiences cherished by a large number of young party members across countries.

> *UKPS31*: I propose ideas. I try to be here.
> *DEPS22*: I ask how projects are going. I bring motivation.
> *ESCO33*: I survey for ideas and projects generated by my colleagues and communicate or discuss with them. I make proposals, I go to meetings and public events.

Note that the three types of references are quite different in terms of their focus, if relatively similar in the types of practical activities they probably specifically entail. The first young party member focuses on idea generation and proposition. He wants to make his mark on the party platform and reckons that he achieves that by regularly generating ideas and simply 'being there.' The second young activist, however, focuses more on motivation and interrogation. He shows his interest in what fellow young activists do, he asks how the projects are going, and generally sees his contribution as part of a more collective intellectual effort, whereby even a more secondary young party member (he does not hold any position of responsibility) has a role to play by showing his interest, availability, and solidarity to the young party members who are more systematically in the front line when it comes to implementing politics and policy. As for the third reference, it primarily focuses on intellectual co-ordination and idea formulation rather than generation. This third young party member primarily sees himself as the director of his local intellectual orchestra, trying to find talent and creativity in the hearts and minds of his fellow young partisans, and to synthesise their input to reach some sort of consensus or unity on the intellectual direction that the local party branch is following.

Similarly a whole range of connotations and ideas can be found when young party members talk about the various occasions that they have to exchange ideas and discuss preferences in a partisan context. Here are a few examples provided by a young Spanish Socialist, a young Norwegian Conservative party member, and two more young members of the Spanish and Hungarian Conservative parties as well as a young British Liberal Democrat.

> *ESPS15*: I like going to meetings often and exchanging opinions about local issues. Sometimes I take a walk around the neighbourhood to identify problems.

NOCO23: One of our main regular activities is simply to debate, meet and exchange ideas. Sometimes we agree, sometimes we disagree, but it is one of our essential functions.

HUCO03: We have branch meetings every week. We discuss everything, winning these debates is sometimes harder than winning debates against other parties but we always come out with an accepted solution.

UKLB20: We regularly debate ideas, this is one of our main activities.'

ESCO01: I try almost everything. I am still thinking about where I want to start participating. I want to debate and wait to discover my aptitudes to see where I can be more helpful. I like international issues more than purely administrative matters, but my involvement will teach me about what I am good at.

Debating is seen in all five testimonials as an essential, regular, and 'key' aspect of party membership activities. The young Spanish Socialist member is primarily focusing on debates on local issues, while his Conservative counterpart is predominantly focusing on international issues. Everyone seems to have their specific preferences and several young party members confirmed that they only or mostly choose to attend and participate in debates which have to do with issues and policy areas that they are particularly interested in. The British young Liberal Democrat member is first and foremost focusing on the importance of debates as a keystone of the party's activities, while the Norwegian and Hungarian Conservative young party members seem to insist on the fact that these debates are 'real' and involve some level of disagreement and sometimes strong ideological dissent among members. This experience, or this perception, was regularly insisted on by a large number of our interviewees, and few seemed to consider these opportunities for intellectual exchange predominantly as a 'validation' forum for the party perceptions. One small exception is provided by another young Spanish Conservative party member, who insists on the role of debates as a link between the 'centre' party and the local branch and sees her branch's regular debates as firstly a way to explain and validate the ideas sometimes generated in Madrid, and secondly an opportunity to generate local ideas that can then be forwarded to other groups. Another young socialist member this time thinks of his ambassadorial role as exactly opposite, bringing the wisdom of Albacete to Madrid:

ESCO04: We discuss things on a regular basis. We make our own campaigns or implement ideas coming from Madrid or distribute them, making sure that we reach the young.

ESPS13: I guess my main job is to work as a sort of 'ambassador' of my town's delegation to the central party office in Madrid. Whenever they need anything to be done they call me, and I do it for the Albacete's provincial group too. It doesn't take up much time and I feel useful.

Altogether, there is therefore a great emphasis on the regular chances that young party members have to either generate new ideas or discuss and debate them. As we shall see in the 'likes' and 'dislikes' sections in Chapter 5, these opportunities are more or less overwhelmingly praised as one of the great chances young party members have to engage in interesting and intellectually stimulating regular activities. In Chapter 6, however, we will see that young party members are not necessarily always convinced that these useful, enriching, and inspiring debates are really taking them anywhere in terms of efficacy.

Public relations activities and representation

While debates are usually 'private' and internal, and allow young party members to discuss ideas more or less freely amongst them, another important series of activities that a large number of young party members throughout the interviews insisted on is the representative and public relations aspects of their membership. In Chapter 1, we mentioned that part of the literature insists on the 'ambassadorial role' of party members (Martin and Cowley, 1999; Scarrow, 1996; Seyd and Whiteley, 2004). This obviously implies a certain amount of communication, activities directed towards engaging the outside world, and different initiatives to represent the party, recruit new members, or explain the parties' positions and preferences on a number of key policy issues to the public at large.

Throughout our interviews, it has been made very clear by most respondents that they feel like natural 'representatives' of their political parties and that in many ways, they are the depositaries of its image in polities which tend to be increasingly negatively predisposed towards political parties in general.

A first series of references made by young party members concern trying to convince voters that their party is the better option on a number of key policy issues. As explained in the first section of this chapter, trying to convince others is one of the most prominent activities in the life of young party members, and, in many cases, one of the types of duties that they enjoy the most. Therefore, it is unsurprising to see that in the eyes of many, public relations start at the lowest possible level by addressing the average voter on the street, at school, or in one's social circles to convince him/her that the party's positions are the right ones. Here are two examples of such consideration provided by one young socialist and one young Conservative Spanish party members:

> *ESPS13*: I like talking to people who will listen or be able to change their view.
> *ESCO12*: I do a bit of everything. I generally try to let people know what is going on, show them what options they have available here, so that they know what to choose.

Next to this very specific role of trying to convince others directly and in person, many of our interviewees preferred to refer to what they see as a more general set of public relations-related activities, including representation, public speaking, giving interviews to the press, or officially representing the party they are a member of in a number of civic occasions involving other groups, associations, pressure groups, unions, or other political parties. A young German liberal party member and a young Spanish Conservative one provide us with two typical examples of this type of activities, which are often seen as giving a sense of importance and relevance to many of the young party members who spoke to us.

> *DELB05*: There's the PR work on the one hand, and then there are also events only for the party members, which can be about building contacts but also about just having fun.
>
> *ESCO23*: I participate in meetings at all levels, organise campaigns, go to attend protest actions and take part in charity fairs and fundraising events. I also have contacts with the media and mainly organise and participate in press conferences.

A third element of the public relations and representation aspects of the work consists of trying to recruit new members – and particularly new young members – who will come to strengthen the ranks of the political party or young party organisation the young activist is a member of. From the descriptions that were made by our interviewees, affiliation and recruitment drives are often conceived as the primary responsibility of some specific executive members, particularly at the local level. However, at times, the party may require all of its members to try and bring in some new flesh and blood into the party's ranks. It was actually rather difficult to obtain very specific details from the young party members whom we interviewed as to how these recruitment and affiliation campaigns are usually organised. These young Spanish militant, British Labour member, and young activist from the French Front National gave us three of the typical and relatively general answers that were mentioned by about 10 per cent of our interviewees without necessarily providing us with much greater details.

> *ESPS20*: Beside running meetings to discuss local issues or come up with ideas, we organise affiliation campaigns.
>
> *UKSO*: The party is always looking for new recruits, and sometimes, each of us is asked to try and bring one or two new people 'in'. We usually campaign on campus to raise awareness. Some people are quite pro-active and really go out and talk to people who are just walking around. A few of us just prefer to stand there with signs and there are always enough interested new students who'll stop by and talk. You need to

get a quick sense of what is going to work with them because you don't want to waste an opportunity like that.

FRFN29: We are all on the lookout for potential new recruits. Always.

Finally, a fourth form of 'representation' that we had not thought of spontaneously when designing the questionnaire for the survey but which was mentioned by a surprisingly large number of respondents consists of simply 'being there' to give the impression that the party represents a genuine 'mass.' This part of the young party members' responsibility was actually mentioned quite often – in about 7 per cent of the cases, without any prompting at all. It seems that young party members are also, at times, expected to be present as a 'number' and part of the mass in the eyes of the rest of the world. Here again, a young Spanish Socialist militant and a young Labour member provide us with typical examples of this unusual form of participation.

ESPS06: I mostly help during punctual events and especially demonstrations. I feel it is necessary to be there, at least, to look like we are a lot.

UKPS38: Sometimes, our local secretary calls us to ask us to participate in a demonstration or in a meeting. This is particularly important when some people organise anti-government demonstrations and we need to show that it is not a majority.

Overall, whether spontaneously or because they are asked, young party members are regularly entrusted with being the depositories of the party's image, when it comes to convincing others, recruiting new members, talking to the media, or the rest of the world, or showing to the outside public that the party is in fact strong and massive. These 'representation' roles are of course very much connected to another type of outward-oriented activities, which correspond to the party's ambition to provide democratic linkage with the general population.

Democratic linkage activities

Parties have an essential role to play as representational 'links', be it in terms of policy, allocation, service, or symbolic responsiveness, as per the conceptualisation of representation of Eulau and Karps (1978). By and large, the vast body of literature on preference aggregation recognises that in this sense, the responsibility of political parties within the democratic game requires them to provide efficient linkage mechanisms between citizens and the spheres of power within a given political system. Of course, the multi-layered organisation of political parties themselves means that this linkage is likely to imply different and complementary forms of responsibility for party leaders and party members. The latter will be implicitly responsible for directly addressing citizens, both communicating them what the party thinks – as explained earlier – and fishing for ideas or improving citizens' sense of efficacy by giving them the impression that the party is actively seeking to listen to their preferences, opinions, suggestions, and policy ideas, in other words, showing them that the party actually cares about what citizens think and want. A number of our interviewees consequently referred to their individual role within this framework, not necessarily as something which they do very often or for very long periods of time, but nevertheless as a responsibility which is rather important in their view and in the eyes of the party they belong to. Three such examples are provided below.

> *ESCO12*: We do simple politics, just what we see the neighbours need or want. We ask them, they tell us, and we do it. That makes us a very good team in our district.
>
> *FRPS17*: I help organising the next electoral campaign by going around the neighbourhood and asking people what worries them.
>
> *UKBP28*: For years, we have been the voice of real citizens. I talk to people who face everyday problems on a daily basis.

Of course, a particular responsibility of young party members within this framework of democratic linkage activities consists of their soliciting the views of the citizens who conceivably feel most vividly left out of the political representation game, that is, young people. Here, two more examples are provided by a young Hungarian Socialist party member and a young French FN young party member.

> *HUPS23*: We give away pamphlets that say the party wants to hear young people's opinions.
>
> *FRFN29*: Many young people tell us that nobody really listens to them while we really go to ask them how they feel about things and take their problems onboard.

Note that in all four cases, the young party members derive a sense of use and of purpose from these democratic linkage activities. Clearly, they have the impression that they make a difference and that it makes their party different from more self-absorbed competitors. This may, in many ways justify – in the eyes of young party members themselves – the logic of a far more controversial and radical sub-element of their regular activities, those that imply a form of opposition towards other political parties, associations, or ideologies that their own organisation is fighting.

Political opposition, subversion, and demonstration

As explained by one of our young French Socialist interviewees, young party members 'are not all choirboys!' While young party members are often seen as keen to support their party, its members, its policy proposals, and of course its perceived ideals, they are also aware that their struggle occurs in a highly competitive environment. As illustrated in Chapter 7, it was the concurrent impression of all of the interviewers on this project that somehow, passion for the ideals and hopes of their party rarely seemed to quite match the passion of our interviewees vis-à-vis the parties, policies, and perceived ideological ills and flaws that they want to fight. In this sense, it is absolutely logical that a large proportion of young party members should mention, with more or less enthusiasm, opposition, subversion, and demonstration modes of participation as taking a rather prominent place in their regular activity as young party members.

The first series of opposition actions referred to by young party members primarily focus on issues rather than parties or people. They are referred to more extensively by young members of left-wing parties than by young members of centrist or right-wing parties, which is entirely consistent with the survey results analysed earlier about the relatively higher prominence of demonstrations as a form of activism amongst young Socialist party members as compared to young members of Liberal and Conservative political parties. Opposition against specific policies, issues, or social ills, however, does not only take the form of demonstrations as summarised in the following three testimonies.

DEPS14: I campaign in the streets against racism and violence.
ESCO06: But at the same time, we are concentrating in collecting signatures against the Catalan statute every day, including Saturdays and Sundays, and having debate sessions in between.
FRGR08: I regularly participate in demonstrations against new roads or railroads planned in the country, the use of nuclear energy, and GMO foods.

Note that these three examples – chosen among, quite literally, hundreds, illustrate some of the various channels of protest used by young party members to fight against what they 'don't like' in policy and issue terms. From demonstrations and street campaigns to petitions, young party members use the full range of tools available to citizens to try to stress an ideological opposition to a project, problem, or social behaviour. It is also worth noting that in the great majority of the cases, our interviewees referred to these instances of issue protesting as something that is being co-ordinated by their party or their young party organisation.

The same is true – in fact even more so – of opposition actions that do not focus so much on issues, policy proposals, or ideology as they do on other political parties. Actions of opposition against competing parties were spontaneously mentioned far less often (by about 30 per cent) by our 519 interviewees than actions relating to specific issues, but they always included references to very specific and hierarchical organisation and control of the actions. Actions against specific rival parties by young party members seem to be even more systematically party-organised than actions against individual attitudes or proposals. On average, this organisation seems to be shared by the local party branches (about two third of the cases) and the regional and national level (for the last third). Young party members with positions of responsibility seem to 'lead the way' of anti-rival actions far more than they do on demonstrations that focus on policy or ideology. Here are four examples of the most frequent forms of actions against competing parties mentioned by young party members from the Hungarian Conservatives, Spanish Socialists, and British Liberal Democrats.

HUCO01: I also think of opposition actions, such as writing pamphlets against the policy of the MSzP, calling the local press, or dealing with press conferences.

ESPS24: As secretary of the organisation in Bilbao, I do everything that is at hand. I help in campaigns, get people to participate in protests, hang posters, criticise other parties' activities and government policies.

UKLB31: In xxx, the council is Conservative and Labour is more or less non-existent, so we mostly focus on tracts, signature campaigns and demonstration against Conservative proposals while some other times, the Labour government is really the target.

ESPS17: I edit our monthly magazine to inform citizens about the bad action of the PP mayor. Everyone writes something and then we put it together, print it ourselves, and distribute it.

While these four examples are typical of 'above the table' types of protest actions against other political parties, a substantial proportion of interviewees referring to anti-party actions – about one in five of them – also referred to slightly more 'borderline' forms of actions, which they happily describe as 'subversive' or the sort of initiatives they don't inform their party hierarchy about. The types of risks or 'liberty with the party guidelines' that are taken vary from case to case. Some young members simply describe wild expeditions to stick posters on road signs while others went all the way to mentioning cases that involve what probably constitutes open cases of slander or even physical fighting with young members from other parties. Here are a few examples provided by a young Spanish Socialist, a young British Labour party member, and two young French activists, one from the Front National and the other from the Communist Party, who are, to some extent, answering each other.

ESPS11: We organise subversive opposition actions. For example, we stick "anonymous" posters where we criticise the Mayor. We don't sign these posters because they generally have to do with rumours that we cannot prove, but that we think people should know.

UKPS31: Some of the things we do, we don't even tell the party about it!

FRFN04: Many people think that we are more prone to dodgy actions than members of the other parties, but in fact, it is completely wrong. Some of the Communists or even the Socialists and the UMP are totally crazy. They spread rumours and lies, and many of them have attacked some of our members physically. Before the Presidential campaign, one of my friends in Marseille spent several days in hospital as a result, just because he was handing out pro-Le Pen pamphlets. The guideline is that none of our members ever goes alone to stick posters or hand out pamphlets, and they are trained to defend themselves, but only if attacked, which unfortunately happens quite a lot.

FRCO: Sometimes, the tension is fierce. I have never been involved in a fight but many of my friends have been. They were usually attacked by some FN members or racist kids. Some of the FNJ [young FN] are totally crazy, some of them are openly skinheads.

The last two testimonials confirm that the more violent actions that some members from all types of parties acknowledge to happen are certainly not modes of protest that they are openly proud of or easily mention to strangers. In fact, any such reference only ever came well into the interviews that we conducted, after a certain element of trust had established itself between interviewer and interviewee. It is worth noting that apart from members of more radical parties (extreme left, extreme right, etc) claiming to be more often targeted by members of other parties, there were no major differences between the perceptions members of parties from the different party families in terms of their recourse to modes of protest that would not have been fully approved by their party hierarchy. However, some comparative differences did exist with much fewer references to such actions from our young Norwegian and German interviewees, and the greatest occurrence amongst young French and Spanish party members.

None of these actions seem to be co-ordinated at the national level, only at the local level, and there seem to be great variations from branch to branch from this perspective. Strangely enough, 'hidden protest' is not only something which primarily targets the other parties, but also occasionally insiders. In that last case, the instructions often seem to come from regional or national instances instead and purely involved members with relatively high level executive positions providing information (one young party member describes it as 'espionage') or fighting 'disruptive elements' from within. Here are three further examples of such actions.

ESPS17: Beside all else, I also do espionage for the provincial Executive committee! I find out what is going on on the outside, particularly in other parties, and in fact, also, inside our own organisation, and then I tell them.

ESPS44: You have to fight the opponents from the Popular Party and the enemies inside your own party.

HUCO27: The head of my branch is someone we can't really fire because he is locally important, but he has often taken stances that went against the party's decisions. I have been asked to keep an eye on it and alert my colleagues in the national executive when something goes wrong.

In many ways, it was expected that direct action as a mode of participation – including in the form of actions of opposition towards disliked ideologies, policies, and parties – would be more frequent amongst young party members than what one could expect from party members in general (see Young and Cross, 2008). Nevertheless, while many will be surprised by the prominence of opposition actions as part of young party members' regular activities, it is worth noting that several young party members themselves are in fact surprised that opposition actions are not, instead, more obviously at the heart of party activism and membership duties. Two such examples are again provided by a young Spanish Socialist party member and a young Hungarian Conservative one.

ESPS30: Before joining, I really thought that being a party member had to do with fighting on the streets. I didn't imagine that there would be so much behind the scenes in terms of ideological work.

HUCO12: We spend too much time trying to refine our party's proposal and trying to channel suggestions from the street to dedicate any time at all to our political rivals and enemies!

By contrast, these few party members emphasise 'insiders' ideological work, which, also leads to one last category of regular young party members activities, direct policy involvement and social outreach activities.

Low-level policy and social outreach

The last type of activity frequently mentioned by young party members from all six countries throughout our interviews has to do with them actually 'doing' politics. At times, the border between members and leaders is blurred, particularly when it comes to local politics, and young party members end up getting a chance to get involved in direct low level policy making or in social outreach activities whereby they actually experience the opportunity to 'make a difference' in the lives of fellow citizens. Direct involvement is increasingly recognised as an important pillar of participation, and particularly of participation in pressure groups and civic organisations. However, similar opportunities have been described amongst young party members who, while getting involved in more abstract or intellectual activities also regularly focus on practical policy outcomes and social action.

The references made by young party members from all six countries and all party families to such elements of policy practice or social outreach have been almost infinite in their nuances and variations. In terms of policy practice, various young party members have mentioned helping youngsters, prison inmates, working mothers, the elderly, children with learning difficulties, animals, and many more. In terms of more general social outreach, they also mention collaborating with associations, unions, hospitals, schools, universities, public services providers, and many more. Below are just a few examples of such policy and social outreach activities that were mentioned by many of the young activists whom we interviewed. All mention these outreach activities either specifically or 'in passing' amidst completely different tasks.

> *ESPS36*: My duty here is to answer questions or solve doubts for my fellow affiliates in general. Basically, I spend most time in student union meetings and negotiating with people in the education ministry.
> *ESCO14*: I organise fundraising and collecting food for Western Sahara, I organise activities to educate people on AIDS too. So in fact, I am sort of in charge of the humanitarian aspect of our group. I think that in this party, it is possible to do the things any NGO would do.
> *UKPS29*: I don't really like meetings. I like the culture side of things so we have lots of activities with little kids to help working Mums. I help in whatever activity we do.
> *HUCO07*: I do all sort of things from dealing with concrete urban issues to helping to run recruitment campaigns.

As we could see, young party members do not just have 'the impression' that their activism is versatile. Far from it, as the variety of the activities embraced by young party members and described throughout their interviews illustrate a situation which in some cases borders schizophrenia, with its mixture of administrative and manual work, intellectual creativeness, social activities, policy outreach, public relations and representation, and opposition.

After getting a sense of how much time – and how often – young party members devote to their parties, we have now conducted an overview of the main types of activities that make the daily, weekly, or monthly routines of most young activists. We have also suggested that not all activists are equally likely to engage in all these modes of participation. Table 4.7 summarises how the moral-, social-, and professional-young party members identified in

Table 4.7 Membership types and dominant modes of activism

Mode of activism	Likeliness Moral-minded	Likeliness Social-minded	Likeliness Professional-minded
Manual labour	++	+	+
Administrative duties	−	−−	++
Mentoring	+	−	++
Social commitment	−	++	−
Intellectual work	++	−	+
Public relations and representation	−	+	++
Democratic linkage activities	+	−	−
Political opposition	++	−−	−−
Low level policy / social outreach	+	+	+

Note: Likeliness codes are based on the interviews. Likeliness codes range from −− (least likely) to ++ (most likely).

Chapter 2 are likely to predominantly focus on some types of activities and to desert others, as explained throughout the previous pages.

The summary glance afforded by Table 4.7 is quite telling because it shows that there is relatively little overlap in the likely main activities of the three different types of young party members. Of course, what young activists actually do is most likely to be related to what they like and what they do not like about partisan activism. Not only that, but differences in practices of activism are certain to further reinforce variations in the experience of the party that various young members will have, and thus have the effect of reinforcing the divergence between the three groups. Thus, it is not only through their diverging visions and original goals but also through their differing practices and experiences that moral-, social-, and professional-minded young party members are likely to have their lives changed by their partisan activism in very different ways. This life changing effect of young party membership, as well as the key moments that mark them will now be the object of Chapter 5.

5
How the Party Changed My Life?

In Chapter 4, we have seen what the typical day, week, or month of a young party member actually consists of. We have looked at the incredibly varied nuances of their chosen and imposed tasks, which may sometimes leave us with the impression that 'being a young party member' may mean extremely different things to different people in terms of the actual activities that it entails. However, to an even greater extent, 'being a young party member' is likely to mean even more different things when it comes to the way a young person's activism is actually lived, experienced, enjoyed, or resented. In fact, in the way in which, as a new individual experience, it may well change the life of each and every one of the young party members whom we talked to.

Does their party membership have consequences on who their friends are? On who they go out with? On what they talk about with their parents, neighbours, and co-workers? Does their entourage understand their involvement at all or does party membership implicitly cost some friendships and cause some paradoxical moments of intense loneliness? Throughout the chapter, we will get a glimpse at what partisan activities young party members like and dislike, and what they believe to be the full blown consequences of membership on their personal life.

This chapter is exactly dedicated to the way in which young party membership 'changes one's life.' We will put the manner in which party membership affects young citizens intellectually, affectively, and socially under the spotlight. How does it modify the way they interact with their peers – both within and outside of the party? How does it change their perceptions of life and activism, their ambitions, and their plans? Moreover, what are the aspects of these changes that they enjoy and that they resent? Throughout our 519 interviews, a vast majority of the young activists whom we talked to explained to us that being a young party member has indeed been a very important change in their life, and has affected who they are as young citizens and as young human beings. Sometimes, their membership affects their life first and foremost in practical terms, because of the occasionally huge commitment that it represents in terms of hours of engagement and energy, as detailed in Chapter 4. Sometimes, this effect is primarily more subtle, changing their perceived sense of their own social place, political responsibility, and moral consciousness.

In terms of how party membership affects one's life even more than in terms of how it constrains effective activities, we can, of course, expect some very significant differences between the experiences of moral-, social-, and professional-minded young party members. Firstly, we can expect moral-, social-, and professional-minded young party members to appreciate fairly different sub-parts of their activist duties. Similarly, it is most likely that they will also find different tasks within their partisan duties boring, tiresome, or even excruciating. Beyond likes and dislikes, however, this chapter is also and mostly interested in the experiences that young party members tend to single out as the most influential of their activist experience. These include the participation in elections 'from the inside', the experience of becoming a leader, and the impact of young party membership on their relationship with their friends, partners, and families, including, at times, on their perception of being marginal and marginalised.

The first two sections are dedicated to what young party members have told us about which of their main activities and modes of participation young activists seem to like and dislike. The next section is dedicated to the specific nature of two 'moments' of membership that many young party members have highlighted as the most life changing: youth activism in election time, a framework which many of our interviewees believe to be very different from the rest, and the discovery of leadership. The final section is concerned with the impact of young party membership on the broader life of individuals, that is, how it affects their relationship with (and the nature of) their family, friends, romantic partners, and co-workers.

What young party members like...

Having looked at the immense variety of activities, tasks, and opportunities that young party members experience regularly through their partisan involvement, we must now try to understand which of them they do and do not like. Indeed, the infinite array of activities referred to by young party members were most often connoted with positive or negative feelings. While these connotations were, at times, predictable, it was not always so, and it is clear that a large number of young party members sometimes seem to appreciate some tasks which most non-members would typically presume to be incredibly off putting. So what are the most popular activities of young party members, and how do they differ across countries, party families, and types of young activists?

In this section, we provide a sense of which activities young party members seem to enjoy most based on their spontaneous answers to our interview question on the enjoyable and non-enjoyable aspects of being a young party member. A large number of themes were evoked with almost similar intensity across the interviews. In fact, we grouped respondents' answers by broad types of activities or incentives and could find 12 of them which were mentioned by at least 5 per cent of our respondents. In this section, we introduce this 'top 12' of the favourite aspects of young party members, and order them from the most to the least frequently mentioned in the interviews.

Table 5.1 summarises what these 12 favourite aspects are, what proportion of our interviewees spontaneously mentioned them, and which type of young party member was most and least likely to mention them. Let us now look at these 12 aspects in greater details.

Table 5.1   Young party members' favourite aspects of membership

Activity	% mentions	Popularity Moral-minded	Popularity Social-minded	Popularity Professional-minded
Debating, arguing, formulating	14	++	−	++
Mixing with high profile politicians and celebrities	12	−−	+	++
Campaigning and elections	12	−/+	−−	++
Fun factor and socialising	10	−	++	−−
Ideological stimulation	10	++	−−	−
Micro-level democracy	9	++	+	−
Internal leadership and co-ordination	8	−	−−	++
Inclusiveness, acceptance, respect and trust	7	+	++	−
Networking	6	−	+	++
Sense of power	6	−/+	−	++
Doing things – practice as opposed to theory	5	+	+	−
Rebels and opponents	5	++	−−	−

Note: Percentages and likeliness codes are based on the interviews. Percentages represent spontaneous mentions and several categories can be mentioned by a single respondent (i.e. total superior to 100). Likeliness codes range from −− (least likely) to ++ (most likely).

Debating, arguing, and formulating

The part of young party members' activism that consistently receives the highest level of praise is made of debating, arguing, and formulating policy proposals and ideological positions, whether they end up being implemented or not. 14 per cent of our interviewees spontaneously mentioned the opportunity to debate as one of the most rewarding aspect of their membership. These references took two slightly different forms. The first had to do with the sheer stimulation of the activities of policy formulation and discussion, and ideological debate as part of the members' routine. The second has to do with some young party members thinking of arguing as something which they simply like in terms of their more general personality, and which partisan activism simply 'amplifies' and ideally fits. Here are a few examples of the first 'version' that were provided by some young party members, who all illustrate this love of partisan debates and arguments as stimulating moments in the life of a young party member.

FRPS26: What I like best is the process of elaborating ideas and arguments for the party.

FRGR10: My favourite aspect of being a member is to have an opportunity to influence the party programme and proposals. I love the serious discussions we have to refine proposals. In a way, you could say that I like the 'work' of being a party member even more than I like the 'fun'!

FRPS36: My main 'activity' is to build our ideological position and think of arguments that we will use to convince people. I am also web designer for our young party organisation's webpage, which I update regularly with news, articles, interviews, and photos.

UKBP13: My favourite part of being a party member is to participate in debates, particularly on Europe.

UKLB25: I enjoy every debate, every discussion we have, even when it is about topics I am not that passionate about.

NOCO28: I spend most of my time debating or giving presentations. I do that for the fun a lot of the time.

Note that for instance, the young British Liberal Democrat member insists on the interest of the debates and discussions held in the party even on topics he is not substantively interested in. Similarly, the young Norwegian Conservative mentions how he enjoys debating and presenting 'for the fun' of it. This naturally leads us to the second type of comment received on this particular aspect of appreciation, when some young party members suggest that debates and arguments are not so much something that they have discovered through their party membership as something that they always knew was part of their personality and that their party can help them to 'reveal', accommodate, and satisfy. The following three extracts, derived from the interviews of a young German Socialist, a young Spanish Conservative, and a young French member of the Front National illustrate this perception.

> *DEPS22*: I like to argue, so debates are great.
> *ESCO15*: My favourite part is arguing! I like defending what I believe.
> *FRFN18*: I enjoy debates incredibly. I like to fight for my ideas and convince the others to follow me rather than the guy who supports another idea. This is what politics is all about.

Throughout these testimonials, we can see that a large number of young party members particularly enjoy the debating and policy elaboration aspects of their membership. Some are mostly interested in the 'substantive' aspects of the debates and others in the 'game' of arguing and exposing their point of view or trying to 'win' a debate. Either way, debates, presentations, and arguments seem to be often seen as a prime and cherished moment of the partisan life and one when young party members can fully express themselves and become actors within a political game.

Mixing with the stars

By contrast, the second part of a young party member's life that seems to attract the highest level of praise sees them take a more secondary position to people they see as meaningful and prestigious. It is the opportunity that young party members from all countries and party families seem to enjoy to interact with high-level politicians, and more generally to 'evolve in the higher political spheres' of their town, country, and society. This was mentioned by 12 per cent of our interviewees, and is illustrated, below, by a number of testimonials by some young French Socialist party members, some young German and Norwegian Conservatives, and young British and German Liberal Democrats.

> *FRPS36*: I enjoy meeting many important politicians.
> *NOCO30*: You get to meet lots of high profile politicians, that's one of the greatest parts of the job!
> *DECO02*: The Stammtische are fun because you get to exchange views on political topics with people you would normally probably not talk to.
> *DELB10*: I like the fact that everyone can be involved in policy formulation in the FDP, for example by talking to important politicians and writing motions.
> *NOCO06*: I enjoy meeting people with whom you can discuss ideological issues and who can make a difference. I like being able to influence the direction of society.

FRPS04: What I like is interacting with and helping political leaders, sticking posters and giving away pamphlets.

UKLB26: I really enjoy the fact that we regularly meet councillors. They really ask for our advice about stuff and sometimes you have the impression that you make a real difference by advising them.

In many ways, meeting important politicians or local figures can serve as a highlight to members and play a very important role in making them feel privileged, important, or efficacious in the political and social life of their country, their region, or their village or city. This probably explains, why this particular aspect of membership activities is mentioned so often – and with so much pride – across the interviews that we conducted throughout the six countries and multiple parties included in this study.

Campaigning

Another highlight of the 'importance' of membership, however, is provided by partisan activism in times of elections, including recruitment, campaigning for issues or candidates, and increasing awareness of certain key issues and the visibility and support of the party in the member's area. Campaigning activities thus came out as the third most popular form of activity amongst our interviewees, spontaneously mentioned by approximately 12 per cent of them. Here are a few examples of such mentions from four countries.

FRPS29: I still love tracting. I love talking to people, especially those who disagree with me. I like talking and listening and trying to help them. I like the 'fieldwork' more than anything else.

HUPS02: I love having activist afternoons, when we go out to drop pamphlets in mailboxes or stick posters and have something to eat and drink all together afterwards.

UKLB26: What I really like is spontaneous actions. I love campaigning, it's great to be together in a van, going to different towns, talking to people.

ESPS45: What I like best is sticking posters. It sometimes feels a bit "borderline" or dangerous but I think it's really exciting.

As we shall see later in this chapter, campaign periods are perceived as very unique by many young party members, and in this sense, it is undoubtedly unsurprising that they are mentioned as a sub-aspect of membership that is held in particularly high esteem by so many members. They refer to the adrenalin-fuelled atmosphere, and indeed, as in the testimony of the young Spanish Socialist party member above, the 'borderline' aspect of campaigning together with the sense of camaraderie enjoyed by many contributes to the impression that they are participating in very unique hours in the life of their country.

The fun factor

If election periods represent a dramatic pinnacle for the expression of the sense of camaraderie that so many young party members describe, others also praise the more usual, low key fun that marks the party membership life of so many young activists. Indeed, next to these dramatic electoral times, we have already seen that the life of young party members is made of regular parties, outings, and other social occasions explicitly aimed at making membership 'fun' and attractive. Considering that social-minded young party members represent the second largest contingent of young activists in Europe according to our survey, it is hence naturally expected that this particular facet of membership will be highly prized. Consequently, it is unsurprising to us that it was spontaneously mentioned by many. In fact, it appears in the accounts and recollections of approximately 10 per cent of our interviewees.

> *DEPS28*: I like the more relaxing aspects of party life such as drinking a beer in the evening and singing workers' songs.
> *HUCO19*: What I like best is really what we do together as a group of friends.
> *UKPS18*: We are no different from anyone else at uni, what we enjoy best are the parties!

Ideological stimulation

While the 'fun factor' of membership is a natural reward for the social-minded section of our interviewees (bearing in mind that socially minded young party members represent approximately 34.2 per cent of the total sample according to the survey component of our study), ideological stimulation is an equally obvious element of satisfaction for moral-minded young activists, who are the largest group of all with 39.7 per cent of the total. Consistently, ideological stimulation in its various forms is indeed mentioned as a prime motive of activist satisfaction in approximately 10 per cent of the interviews that we conducted (bearing in mind that several other categories also represent natural incentives for moral-minded members!). Here are a few examples of such comments across the six countries.

> *DEPS14*: I like to feel that I'm part of a movement that wants to achieve longer-term social change.
> *FRPS23*: As a party member, you feel like you are doing something useful and that you are doing something for the good of others, at the end, that is what really matters.
> *HUCO20*: I really like participating in academic debates or conferences. The atmosphere is great with members and there is always a discussion going on about ideas.

ESPS02: Working for a common good and dealing with people is what I like best. Much better than the administrative part of the job.

No surprise here, as a natural extension to the prime incentives of moral-minded young party members, mentions of ideological stimulation and of making a difference in policy, ideology, or moral terms feature prominently in the spontaneous activity podium of many of our interviewees.

Micro-level democracy

Another variation of the same type of preferred activities is concerned with what we could label 'micro-level democracy.' In this particular instance of ideological and moral stimulation, young party members get a chance to talk to citizens whose lives they want to change. They get feedback from them or inform them and try to motivate them into political activism. There are many similar accounts that we received from the young party members that we interviewed, and overall, about 9 per cent of the young party members whom we interviewed referred to similar types of experiences, which have to do with low-level input or output democracy and representation between young party members and various types of citizens. Here are a few examples of these types of accounts.

DECO09: I particularly like being at the information stand. There, you find out what young people really want.
DEPS28: I particularly like speaking to Turkish shop owners and going to Mosques, I learn a lot and broaden my horizons. I've changed my mind on Turkey and the EU now because of that.
ESPS13: I really like managing the electoral campaigns and organising small local polls with volunteers that get out in the streets and collect the neighbours' opinions. It's like my own little social investigation.

Note the way in which a number of young party members find a form of 'specialisation' within this framework of day-to-day effort of representation. The second young party member we quote above mentions his special relationship with Turkish shop owners, but others also mention single mothers, asylum seekers, immigrants, farmers, and many other categories, which often have in common to be usually perceived as being left out of the traditional political game.

Internal leadership and co-ordination

As discussed in Chapter 4, the administrative aspects of a young party member's life are appreciated in very different ways by young party members. Administrative tasks are often seen as quite separate from membership itself by those young party members who are also employed by the party, and often seen as less-enjoyable duties by the others. Nevertheless, a significant minority of young party members specifically mention that they enjoy their various activities of leadership, co-ordination, and their service to fellow party members. Here are a few examples that illustrate a feeling spontaneously expressed by 8 per cent of our interviewees.

> *ESPS04*: I don't see anything that I don't like about my activity, I enjoy everything, but co-ordinating other members is probably the best part.
>
> *ESCO49*: What I enjoy most is liaising between militants and the party headquarters in Madrid, conveying the information and instructions back and forth. I enjoy it a lot. It is like a hobby to me!
>
> *NOCO09*: What I prefer is to be behind the scene, maybe, for instance, to assess our leaders.

Inclusiveness, acceptance, respect, and trust

Similarly, an important number of respondents refer to any type of duty or activity which highlights the overall inclusiveness of young party membership. As explained in Chapter 2, alongside the 'fun factor' of membership per se, one of the essential aspects of the incentives that are likely to motivate social-minded young party members have to do with the chance to interact with other young people who share their interests, motivations, and sometimes personality. About 7 per cent of young party members single out a range of activities, which, in their opinion, maximise this sense of inclusiveness, mutual respect, and collaboration as some of their favourite aspects of membership, as is exemplified by the following interview excerpts.

> *FRFN23*: I was really impressed by my first meeting. People were nice but very well organised; serious but friendly, very disciplined and very convincing. There was absolutely no contempt for my sport background, people were treating me like equals and everyone has got the same right to have ideas and make comments here.
>
> *NOCO22*: I feel like it frees me from the tyranny of everyday life.
>
> *ESCO20*: There are hierarchies and there are different areas, but they are mixed up somehow, so what I really like it that I find it great to work in a group. I really enjoy it.

Note that in several cases, the impression of mutual respect and collaboration seems to be paradoxically 'revealed' by the essence of the party's organisation, its hierarchy, its internal structure, and its solidity.

Networking

By contrast, about 6 per cent of our interviewees refer more directly to networking activities. They enjoy the meetings – both local and national, which explicitly enable them to meet new people, network, find friends and enlarge their social contacts over time with fellow party members. Here are a few examples of such testimonials.

DECO18: I enjoy large meetings, either regionally or nationally. There, I can make contacts and get to know people.

FRPS21: I love the meetings, especially the 'summer universities' and meeting other members from other parts of the country.

NOCO34: I have gained new friends and a different social network. We have a lot of fun aside from politics.

A sense of power

As for professional-minded young party members, it is unsurprising that quite a few of them would be primarily quite sensitive to the feeling of power that they gather from their party membership and activism, rejoicing in the activities that give them a sense of individuality making a difference. Such activities are mentioned by about 6 per cent of our interviewees spontaneously. Some of the words used by young party members to describe such feelings are incredibly candid, but they are also all quite symptomatic of one of the main ways in which probably many more than these 6 per cent of young party members spontaneously mentioning it feel that party activism has indeed changed their life.

FRPS19: I like the power that politics gives you on people, even though I don't know whether it is an engaged or manipulative power.

ESPS08: What I like most is to see an impact of our external communication campaigns, hear that they talk about us more in the news or that we are becoming more notorious amongst the young.

FRFN10: I love feeling empowered by politics, feeling in control and that I have a direct influence with what I say and what I do!

Doing things – practice vs theory

The next category of 'favourite' actions has to do with respondents who particularly enjoy 'doing' things. About 5 per cent of respondents contrast 'doing' activities to 'organising' ones, and predictably, when they do, it is often the former that they seem to enjoy more. Indeed, several respondents mention very practical fights and activities, as illustrated by the following three examples.

FRPS17: I don't like spending time organising things. What I like is to *do* things, to put into practice what we have decided. I am really active that way.

ESPS21: I like practical things, like getting the government to issue a discount transport carnet for young people.

UKLB09: I like the practical stuff, particularly when it changes the life of fellow students.

Rebels and opponents

Finally, the last type of mention made by more than 5 per cent of respondents has to do with a particular fondness for opposition activities, including fighting other political parties, demonstrations 'against' people, parties, or causes that they wish to stand up against. As mentioned in Chapter 4, these activities can represent an important part of the life of some young party members, and while many do not seem to particularly enjoy them, a few others do.

ESPS08: I like activities against the Partido Popular. Our president does some great things, but for the PP, everything he does is bad. I don't know what kind of interests move them. The PP has bad manners too.

FRPS08: I love the protests that we do here. They are quite original and creative!

UKBP02: Even being attacked by other parties is something I don't dislike, I like fighting back with better ideas than them because we know that ultimately, many people agree with us and the argument of the main parties are often very weak.

And what they dislike...

Of course, in a way that is entirely symmetric to young party members' favourite things about membership, they have, as well, varying lists of 'most hated' traits and tasks of partisan activism. These obviously vary from member to member, not only according to their individual sensitivities, but also depending on what they joined for and what they were expecting to find. Thus, a moral-minded member will be likely to be more infuriated by internal power games, while a social-minded member will be particularly put off by internal party administration and endless discussions. As for professional-minded young party members, they will be very prone to dislike what they would perceive as incompetence or lack of motivation of the grass roots. Overall, the pinnacle of young party members' most hated aspects of membership include everything that leads to the expression of personal rivalries, those activities which result in lengthy discussions and endless meetings, administrative tasks, experiences that involve aggressive interaction with other groups or parties, and, finally, time that they perceive to be wasted by incompetence, disorganisation, narrow mindedness, or lack of motivation. Let us now look at these various sub-categories in greater detail.

The personalisation of politics and power games

Internal rivalries, power games, and a conflict between egos – such is the perception that many citizens who do not belong to any political party have of partisan politics. While we will see, in Chapter 6, the extent to which this perception corresponds, in fact to young party members' view of their own parties, there is, already, no doubt that young party members often despise this potential aspect of activism and were prone to mention it most frequently as their most disliked aspect of partisan politics.

In some cases, individuals are blamed for this possible distortion of the party's political debate, while in other cases, young party members hold some specific structure responsible for it, or even some specific activities that would be particularly prone to reveal the aggressive side of – young and other – party members.

Below, we find a few examples of such complaints, articulated by young members from a variety of countries and parties:

DECO14: I don't like the importance of personal contact and all the behind-the-scenes negotiation over posts. That's what party is like sadly.
DEPS35: You always have to pay attention to the foibles and special wishes of certain people. I also don't like to justify my party work to my friends.
ESPS21: I don't like the self-campaigning part of politics which can get quite dirty.
FRPS04: I don't like it when important debates are overshadowed by personal conflicts and debates about posts.
FRGR11: Daily activity here is tiring. It's a constant conflict in the sense that you spend all day debating on things and thinking of arguments or searching for common ground or solutions.
UKLB11: What I like least is the administrative work and the problems that are created by the clashes between factions.

Note that the articulation of reproaches concerned in one way or another with the personalisation of politics varies a lot from person to person in the examples that we provide above. Some are predominantly concerned by 'corridor politics' whereby too much happens behind the scene as a result of compromises and negotiations between clans or individuals. Others are more worried about the time wasted having to listen to some continuously dissident voices within the party, which have to be 'taken into account' while agreeing on texts and policies. Others simply despise what one of our participants called 'self campaigning' and other forms of self promotion, fights for power and for position.

The circularity of meetings and internal debates

Sometimes, there is also a very fine line between young party members minding the personalisation of politics and their regretting an entire organisation of partisan activities which seems, to some of them, to leave too much space and show too much focus on internal debate and synthesis, lengthy circular debates, and a certain 'meeting mania' as described by one young French Socialist.

Below, we provide a few typical examples of these reproaches, which, as can be seen, spare members from no European country or party family:

DECO14: The conference is quite tedious at times.
DEPS18: What's frustrating about party work is navel-gazing: often, we discuss internal matters far too much. Internal disputes tire me. Working on substantive matters at a local level is also frustrating, as we waste time discussing fundamental issues which we cannot affect at the local level anyway.
UKPS34: What I don't like is all the meetings. Sometimes democracy just means that everyone wants to have a say.
FRCM01: I don't like participating in debates that much or spending much time planning things. I feel I am wasting my time that way.
ESPS17: There is one thing I detest – it's participating in our National Youth Organisation because people there don't do anything at all, so I feel I am wasting my time. The party is much much better.
ESCO17: I do much provincial co-ordination work. This is the part I like the least, but I guess that it is something that you have to do.

There was no clear winner between parties and young party organisations when it comes to figuring out which of the two is least prone to a sort of 'bureaucratic derive' of politics, whereby the organisation progressively spends an increasing proportion of the members' time dealing with internal party problems rather than the ones facing their country. Similarly, whether the worst 'waste of time' in the eye of the members takes the form of meetings, conferences, or debates remains quite unclear or at least debated, but overall, references to these lengthy meetings and increasing parochialism of the topics discussed by the party represents the second most frequent answer of our interviewees across countries when asked what they do not like about their party membership.

Bureaucratic tasks

It only makes sense from there that bureaucratic tasks themselves should also crystallise a significant sub-part of the complaints of young party members. Mailing, taking census, dealing with requests, phone calls, and accounts are, as described in Chapter 4, hardly the most exhilarating aspect of being a young party member. Here are three specific examples of the administrative tasks that turn young party members off their political engagement at times:

ESCO27: We all do whatever is necessary, even putting letters in envelopes or sticking posters, that is a pain.
DELB20: I don't like all the administrative office work like writing minutes of meetings.

In short, young party members do not want to transform into bureaucrats. Nevertheless, some do not really want to get involved in activities that seem to revolve around what they perceive as an aggressive opposition to other groups or factions either, and are particularly fear of that aspect of campaigning tasks.

The aggressive interaction with opposed groups and factions

Indeed, to a large extent, campaigning activities can prove difficult for those who prefer the search for unanimity to political struggle in democratic practice. Campaigning, trying to change people's minds, fighting competitors, and alternatives are all activities that, as we saw and will further see, stimulate some, but others see it as one of the low times of partisan activism. Below are a few examples of such distaste for 'political fights':

> FRPS07: I don't like sticking propaganda, giving away pamphlets, or going to demonstrations.
>
> DECO22: What I don't like is campaigning. It's very strenuous discussing politics with people who are aggressive. It's me who has to be on the receiving end of people's frustration even though I'm only a party member.
>
> UKLB09: I stick posters and pronounce public speeches – it goes with the job, but I am not very fond of it.
>
> ESCO19: What I don't like is the confrontation activities. It is stressful because we are always engaged in horrible fights with other associations. We just cannot talk normally and exchange views because the left-wing associations are intolerant with different ideas.

Facing ideological rigidity

Finally, after this 'dark side' of campaigning, the last issue that a significant proportion of young party members seem to resent has to do with ideological rigidity, and the impression that they can, at times, lose their freedom to criticise and think individually about various issues for which they do have to 'stand behind the party.' At times, they will blame fellow activists for the impossibility to engage in real debate. In some other contexts, they may simply think that they have to deal with incompetent people or with an ideological wall that no one in their party is willing to climb. Below are a few examples of these attitudes that epitomise what many young party members dislike about their party as an ideological machine:

> DEPS33: The grass roots are very unwilling to engage in real debate.
>
> FRCM18: I don't like all the prejudices that exist within the party. Ideas from other parties are just dismissed simply because they're from the other camp.

DELB15: I don't like people who aren't competent, but that's not just specific to Julis.

ESCO19: The hardest part of being a party member is the sense that you are completely submitted to the cause. You lose some of your freedom to criticise.

Overall, we thus find as great a variety in what young party members dislike as we did about what they like. In many ways, this can give the impression that party membership is a very individual experience for young people, and that while one may have discovered something essential in their life through internal politics, another of them will have resented it as a painful waste of time. Yet, a few privileged moments seem to mark the experience of young party members, whether they enjoy them or not. They are different, essential, and reveal something to them, not only about who they are as citizens, but also about the very nature of their political engagement. This is the object of the next section of this chapter.

Two life changing moments in the life of young party members: Experiencing campaigns and discovering leadership

Indeed, alongside the routine that marks the daily activities of young party members, a few moments represent clear 'passages' in their activism. Two of them in particular – participation in an electoral campaign, and the discovery of a young member's first positions of responsibility, have been widely described by our interviewees as life changing. Some like them, and some do not, but throughout countries and parties, they recognise that these moments in the life of a young party member are simply different and, as such, structuring of their political character.

Becoming a campaigner

As we have seen in Chapter 4 and earlier in this chapter, aspects of political campaigning represent an important aspect of the activities of young party members. Some like it because it is more exciting than the normal routine or because they like to try and convince others, while a significant minority of young party members resent the fractious and aggressive undertones that campaigning can take from time to time.

What young party members say about electoral campaigns varies a lot. Beyond liking or hating it, some look forward to them and others simply take them as a job, but the elements that transpire from our interviews reveal a certain series of patterns. First of all, a young party member's first election tends to be a life changing moment as such, one that he or she will never forget, as illustrated by the comments below:

ESCO15: I actually joined when the party was preparing the 2000 elections, so I started helping in that frantic rhythm. I will never forget it.

NOCO20: During elections, you really see what politics is all about: hectic movement, enthusiasm.

FRFN10: I joined just before the 2002 presidential elections. The 6 weeks that followed, the campaign and the vote, I will never forget.

ESPS07: Election period is a whole different story. That is where everyone takes out the best in them. We have a great time, stick posters all night, until 6 am. I was surprised when I realised the great human potential we have in the movement. It is sad to see that we don't really take advantage of it as if we used it, we would achieve great things. With every new election, however, this potential reappears on the surface.

HUPS01: When you have been involved in an election campaign, you understand some things about human dynamics that others never will.

Young party members thus insist on the role of electoral campaigns as a catalyst of their political involvement, a privileged, intense experience which they will never forget. The entire description that they make of it tends to be, in almost all cases, superlative. In some cases, these superlatives are emotionally neutral. They focus on the quantity of work, the intensity of the rhythm, and on the abnormality of the hours. In the few interview excerpts below, we can see how young party members are marked by the different rhythm represented by campaigns. The change they experience is almost physical, and so is the memory they derive from it:

UKPS14: In election period, we organise rallies to inform of the party's views. I think this is our biggest responsibility as members.

DECO03: There was a lot of work during the federal election last year, where my work for the party amounted to a part-time job.

DELB22: I led the election campaign in the last four elections. As campaign leader, I do all the organisation, such as ordering campaign material, getting permission for information stands and putting up posters. It's a very time-intensive job.

FRFN17: I am mostly very active during the electoral periods. I travel to different cities on our bus, I do it to support our leaders in their political meetings.

ESCO15: I am mostly active during the electoral periods.

FRGR14: I associate election campaigns with intense fatigue. It is worse than preparing for your exams, you simply never stop until it is over and then you collapse.

NOCO17: Militants can't forget election campaigns because campaigns don't allow them to be anything else than militants. You just don't have the time.

In most cases, however, young party members think of electoral campaigns not just as moments that are labour-intensive, days that are longer than usual, and transportation from one place to the next on a campaign bus, but also as moments they enjoy. They love the adrenaline rush that they associate with elections. They note that these moments bring members together, and make members and leaders to feel united rather than fight on programme details or personality clashes. In short, they love the fact that elections change the entire focus of their membership. Several of our interviewees stressed how elections represent a 'responsibility', how they seem to increase and highlight the importance of their membership, how they have the impression that their activism finally makes a real, genuine, difference. The excerpts below illustrate these perceptions and tell us why, a majority of over 60 per cent of the young party members that we interviewed explicitly say that they like, enjoy, or even love being involved in electoral campaigns:

> DEPS33: I loved the euphoric atmosphere during the election campaign, and the experience of the campaign gave me lots of self-confidence.
> DELB15: The election results are a positive experience; it's a confirmation of all the hard work we do.
> FRPS01: I mostly like election time. The debate is continuous and more intense.
> ESCO15: The atmosphere is so vibrant with the music, the speeches, people's enthusiasm, the shouting and the applause. I love this feeling.
> ESPS15: I campaigned very hard for the EU Constitution referendum. I found it was a difficult and tiring task, but I liked doing it.
> NOCO01: What I best like is the campaigning, the frantic aspect of it all.
> HUPS01: Election period is very tiring, it is 15 days of non-stop craziness, but I really like it!
> FRFN03: I like election time. You have to be there completely for the cause, participating in up to three meetings a day. It is a very hectic period.

What young party members like about electoral campaigns thus varies, some are into the selflessness of the experience, others about the debate, and yet more about what they get back from the public – applause, reaction, shouting, questions, any sign of enthusiasm that shows them that citizens are not indifferent to politics. Altogether, young party members tell us that campaigns – and particularly their first campaign as an activist, is thus a moment that has changed their life, and in their perception, durably so. The other 'aspect' in an activist's life that seems to be unanimously perceived as equally life changing is the learning of leadership. As young party members climb the ladder of their party's internal hierarchy, something radically evolves in their experience and in their perceptions of politics and democracy.

Becoming a leader

While virtually all young party members will, one day or another, get a chance to experience an electoral campaign from within, a more limited – if still large – proportion will have a chance, to a more or less thorough extent, to become a 'leader' within their political party or young party organisation. As seen earlier, a greater proportion of young party members get 'positions of responsibility' than would be expected of party members in general, not least because the structures are multiplied (party, young party organisation, student unions, etc) and because age limits impose a faster turnover than for older members. Moreover, the skewed age distribution of party membership and the desire of parties to 'show off some new faces' explain why ambitious and focused young members may find it easier to reach positions of responsibility.

Overall, the three types of young party members show very different propensities to take such positions of responsibility. When considering all executive positions (including small local leadership roles, and project-specific ones), the likeliness of professional-minded young party members to have held such positions is 8.1 per cent higher than for moral-minded members, and 19.1 per cent higher than for social-minded ones who prove again to be the least involved in the party's organisation. If we only consider national level positions – the most prestigious and coveted of all – the contrast is further emphasised. Professional-minded members are 4 times more likely to occupy such positions than moral-minded ones, and 5.5 times more likely than their social-minded counterparts.

Of course, 'becoming a leader' may mean very different things to different young activists. Some will merely experience junior positions in their local branch, while others will climb a full hierarchical ladder at the regional and national levels. Both these low-level leaders and these high-level ones, however, explain that experiencing leadership through their partisan activism has changed their life.

Obtaining positions of responsibility is, of course, an exciting adventure for young motivated activists, and particularly so for our professional-minded young party members. It may, however, take the form of very different experiences and individual stories, which will leave them with varying learning experiences. How young party members see their 'ascension to power' was therefore the object of highly individualised accounts throughout our interviews, but a few patterns emerged more or less clearly.

The first important aspect of becoming a leader in a party or a young party organisation is that apparently, in some cases, it mostly proved an incredibly fast, direct, and sudden – if not sometimes – unexpected ascension to some of the young party members interviewed. In the following testimonies, a number of them insist on how surprised they were by how fast they could climb the ladder.

ESCO41: My first ever activity was to stand behind a party booth during a local event. After talking to other members there, I was offered to be secretary of new technologies for the province right away, so basically, just a week after becoming active, I already had a 'leading' position!

DELB02: I was surprised how quickly I moved up the ranks. It went much faster than I thought. If you put in some effort, you can get far.

DEPS33: I moved up quickly and was quickly given responsibility.

ESPS10: When you start getting involved, things go very fast. Now, I am councillor in my town, secretary general of the young movement in the La Rioja autonomous community. I am president of the national federation of progressive students and secretary to student policies. Now, I am also working as administrative staff in the federal office in Madrid.

UKLB14: If you have strong convictions and are willing to struggle, you do climb up the ladder quickly.

ESPS46: When I joined, I never imagined that I would be where I am now. I was just working very hard for this project I believe in. Now, people have just proposed me as general secretary of the youth movement in the Basque Country, and then they voted for me.

In the extreme, the first excerpt we mention comes from a young party member who explains that he became a member of the provincial (regional) executive on the very day he came to take part in his very first activity as a young party member. All the other members quoted above express their surprise at the ease and quickness of their promotion. To a certain extent, this contrasts with the mode of pre-meditated and natural ascension that a second type of young party members refer to in the interviews. This second category of elites insist on the regular progression that they have experienced from the very bottom to the very top. In many ways, this discourse is more frequent amongst high-ranking young party elites than amongst low-ranking ones who are more likely to refer to the 'flash promotion' mentioned above:

ESPS46: I do have a position now. I've got used to it and I'll like it even more in the future. I didn't aim to run in elections, but it is logical that I do because I am here now and I'm active and that usually means that the party will need you in the future for posts of representation.

ESCO34: I started at the very bottom and now I am regional deputy secretary, in charge of electoral issues and communication. My activity is what I imagined it would be, there were no surprises.

UKBP20: I progressed step by step in the party's hierarchy. You need to gain trust and prove yourself to be offered new challenges.

FRCM22: The party is very clearly hierarchised. One knows which posts matter and which posts are not all that strategic. At first, you get offices very fast. Then, it becomes slower and slower, but more and more rewarding.

FRPS14: There are 'elites' and 'elites'. Many people get offices but are not really party leaders, and those of us who do need to work our way up slowly in a competitive environment.

Of course, regardless of how fast a young party member discovers the 'spheres of power' within his/her party or young party organisation, they all seem to agree on the price to pay. Becoming a leader takes time, it eats up one's private life, and the higher up one goes in the party's hierarchy, the more significant these sacrifices. This is widely explained by the young party members quoted below. All of them realise that one of the ways in which becoming a leader has changed their life is by implicitly making them full-time politicians:

DEPS26: I'd like to have more positions of responsibility, but every time I climb a step on the ladder, the time I dedicate to the party increases by 4 or 5 hours a week.

HUPS08: I am not surprised by my increasing level of activity. I have been open to proposals from the party ever since I joined. It has been 10 years now and I feel I have won a solid place in here in return.

NOCO02: My involvement has been progressive. I began attending meetings, and ended up joining lots of activity groups. Then, my district president asked me to help in issues related with local politics, to become more active in university politics, etc. As I climb the ladder, my activism is ending up sucking up a lot of my time.

ESCO26: I participate in the National Direction of our party. That means that I do anything. I am in campaigns and in conventions most of the time. Sometimes, the activity is ungrateful and it is always exhausting. You work a lot, give out your free time, weekends, holiday trips, friends... This is the price to pay for a high post in the party hierarchy.

Between the excitement of leadership and greater feeling of efficacy that ensues on the one hand, and the feeling that one progressively loses any right to a private life, and to an extent, right to a professional life as well, young party members have very different reactions to the way in which the discovery of leadership changed their lives. Some explain outright that the cost is too high considering the benefits they derive, and explicitly decide that the experience of leadership is one best forgotten:

FRPS06: Even with my newly gained functions, I still want to work and feel as a baseline member. I don't want to forget that power belongs to the base.

ESPS14: I prefer working behind the scenes rather than holding a representative position.

UKLB25: I prefer to help without feeling the enormous pressure of being
successful or being afraid that I'm doing everything wrong.

This explicit choice to reject the thrill of power in favour of background positions remains rare however. Less than one in ten young party members with
a position of responsibility that we interviewed suggested that they would
rather stay in the background or return to the grass roots. By contrast, the
vast majority experience, with certain delight, the new world that leadership
is opening to them. They describe their role as a leader in extremely different
ways. Some see themselves as reconciliators, others as authoritarian leaders,
a few would like to describe their main task as one of organisation, others
as one of inspiration. Below are a few of the many interpretations that our
interviewees have made of what one does and learns from becoming a young
leader in a political party or a young party organisation:

FRPS35: As secretary general of the movement in the region, I get the local
associations together to design the activities we'll organise during the
year. We generally come up with courses or debate on specific issues
with experts.

FRPS10: I usually just yell out for people to work.

ESCO28: At times, we work on reactivating the PP in the Salamanca
district of Madrid and to form our new executive committee.

UKBP07: I organise everything and sort out everyone's problems.

HUPS03: Since becoming one of the leaders in town, I have been able to
change the way in which we do politics.

NOCO09: I enjoy stimulating others, exciting them.

FRGR09: I am the fireman of the party!

All in all, experiencing electoral campaigns and the road to power and
leadership thus changes something in the lives of young party members.
Sometimes they love it, sometimes, they hate it, but few of them doubt
that what they have learnt will change their perceptions and attitudes in
a durable manner. Similarly, extremely few of the young party members that
we interviewed would doubt that joining a party has also changed their life
durably in social terms, which is the focus of the final section of this chapter.

The social impact of young activists' party membership

The social impact of partisan activism for the young party members that
we interviewed is a story of contrasts. On the one hand, party activism has
changed their life by bringing them new friends, social contacts, and sometimes partners. On the other hand, it has a cost in terms of losing time for a

non-partisan social life, and even, on occasions, is perceived as responsible for making young party members more marginalised and misunderstood by their apolitical friends and family members.

Sacrificing personal life

There is no doubt that party activism takes a lot of time. We showed how regular party activities are in Chapter 4, and the two examples above – regarding electoral campaigns and internal leadership show how, for a certain number of young party members, partisanship can become so intense and time consuming that it would take a toll on the rest of their social and personal life. This is clearly a way in which party activism changes young party members' lives. In particular, the notion of a sacrifice by young party members of their personal sphere gets declined in three principal ways: (1) a complaint about the time the party takes, (2) a difficulty to 'separate' party focus and non-partisan focus (or, at times, to 'switch modes'), and (3) an impact of partisan affiliation on career prospects, studies, and professional stability.

The complaint about the time the party takes is the most frequent here. Most young party members, however dedicated, consider that partisan activism takes 'a lot' of their time and many consider this an important sacrifice. Below are a few examples of such a complaint about young party members 'sacrificing' their time for their party:

DEPS26: Party work costs a lot of time and takes up a large part of your life.

UKPS13: Sometimes I would like to have more of a private life.

DELB18: Sometimes I don't like how much time party work costs me, which can mean that I have to neglect some of my hobbies, like sport.

NOCO2: It takes a lot of time and dedication. It takes time from other things I am involved in like running a small business.

HUCO01: The hard part of party politics is to have to give up so much of your own free time.

FRPS10: It's that simple. I have to keep my phone on 24 hours a day, be available all the time.

ESCO26: What is most difficult is dedicating so much personal time, rest time, like when you have to wake up at nine o'clock on a Saturday to go to a PP public meeting in another town. I do it to help the party and the party leaders but I get no reward for that.

UKBP10: My involvement takes too much of my personal time, and of my study time especially.

Obviously, the sheer amount of time spent on activism is a relatively easily quantifiable cost of membership for many a young party member. Others, however, are even more troubled by the fact that their partisan engagement seems to invite itself in all corners of their lives, and not only at times when they are 'supposed' to be wearing their partisan cap. This can be even more puzzling for many young party members because it can give them the impression that partisanship suffocates their private life regardless of their ability to modulate the time they actually dedicate to their party. Let us look at a few interview excerpts that summarise this uncomfortable feeling:

> *UKPS34*: Even when I'm having drinks on a weekend with my friends, we talk about politics. I talk about politics all the time.
>
> *ESCO34*: When you are in a party, when you engage in politics, it is hard to separate your engagement with your life outside the party, so it ends up being a full compromise where the party score more points all the time.
>
> *FRCM06*: Talking about politics, thinking about politics is often not really a choice. I just want to chat with friends or watch a film, but something occurs that makes me think and talk of politics.

Beyond time and the 'invasion' of young party members' minds, however, a third, even more serious aspect of partisanship may deprive young party members of their private life in their mind. Sometimes, it seems to them, rightly or wrongly, that their partisanship comes at the cost of their professional future, either because of the intensity of their engagement or because of its ideological nature. This problem, while only stressed by a small minority of the young party members that we interviewed (under 6 per cent) is somewhat acute amongst members of extremist parties and those who are quite high up in the hierarchy of their party or young party organisation, and intend to keep climbing its ladder. The following examples summarise this concern, which, to some young party members, can be extremely distressing:

> *DEPS19*: I want a 'normal' work and life for a while, to settle down, maybe to go abroad a bit but then I will start again and aim for an elected position because it's a natural path to take.
>
> *ESPS45*: I want to become a civil servant at the local level, but I know I will only be able to work in a left wing community.
>
> *FRFN16*: When you are a FN member, you can't have a normal life. You get blacklisted. This is contrary to the other parties, where instead you get preferential treatment ['pistons et passe-droits'].
>
> *UKBP01*: It's hard to make friends in the party. It's a bit hard because I'm a girl...I am not hierarchical at all but this could put some guys ill at ease. Also when you are a girl it can be misconstrued as seduction or something. I have made some friends in some other cities but it's not really friends-friends.

FRFN05: I can't say that I am a member of the FN, let alone a leader, in my football club, nor in my bank. If I did, someone would probably try to break my neck in the changing rooms or worse, and the bank would find a lousy excuse to fire me because they would be afraid to have a FN employee! And the prud'homme judges [employment tribunal] would support their decision because even this is trusted by the unions and by the world of political correctness.

FRPS21: Most people in my position can only get a job in an administration, insurance company [mutuelle], or communication company officially or unofficially affiliated with the party and that is what I will also aim for.

The fears of young party members who are slowly reaching a certain level of 'professionalism' in their political engagement are very different from the worries of those who think that the discovery of their ideological choice would alienate potential employers, teachers, or colleagues. In both cases, however, the young party members we talked to feel that they have to make a choice, and to an extent consent an essential sacrifice on part of their personal life. The other type of choices or sacrifices that need to be made by a far larger proportion of young party members has to do with their friends. Partisan involvement constrains friendships and changes them, as discussed in the next section of this chapter.

Changing friendships

Throughout the interviews, a number of the young party members whom we talked to have explained how becoming young activists has changed their friendships or forced them to manage them in a different way. The constraint on personal time that we have just established means that young party members have to reorganise their social time differently, either because they do not have time to meet fellow partisans and outside friends simultaneously or because there is an incompatibility of taste and interests between their two – partisan and non-partisan – social circles. Later in this section, we will show how party membership can make some young party members feel marginalised or cut off from their friends, but already, let us look at the friends who are kept or gained and how activism seems to affect these friendships and social relations. By and large, we can identify three main types of discourses on how young party activism affects members' friendships. The first discourse is one of *accommodation* of existing friendships, which are kept separate from the young member's partisan involvement and adapted to it. The second discourse is one of *displacement*, whereby the young party member switches his/her entire social network, including friends to the party. The third discourse is one of *fusion*, whereby the young party member tries to recruit his/her friends and partner into the party.

A first frequent element in young party members' testimonies is thus a discourse of *accommodation*. The young party member does not want to mix friendship and partisanship, but has to adapt his/her interaction with friends so that partisanship does not become an obstacle to their ties. At times, it might mean not talking too much about politics because one's friends might find it boring. Other times, it might mean avoiding clashes with friends whose own political opinions differ from the involvement of the young party member. Below are a few examples of this accommodating discourse:

UKPS17: I don't want to mix friendship and politics.

DEPS02: None of my friends are active within the SPD, but all of my friends are close to the party. So when I was still a CDU member I was ridiculed quite a bit.

HUPS09: I have friends from both sides and we get along well but when we had the Referendum (on the status of Hungarian citizens living outside of the country) I had a fight with one of my friends and we haven't spoken since then.

NOCO24: I try to avoid discussing politics with close friends, but they are involved, read the papers and follow the news. It is for my own sake that I don't discuss too much with them.

ESPS23: My political involvement resulted in my having problems with my boyfriend, but we managed to get along well with time. He is an ex-skin head of Fuerza Nueva [an extreme right groupuscule]. We met and got close because we spent hours arguing and finding counter-arguments about politics.

UKLB26: Many of my friends are more right wing or more left wing than me. We have political discussions but it doesn't affect our friendship.

ESPS16: At home, my family have no problem with my involvement, but I know that they are afraid since being in politics here means that you are a terrorist target.

ESPS23: I have friends who vote for the PP. They don't like my involvement at all, but that doesn't keep us apart as friends.

FRCM14: I discuss politics a lot with my friends but they are not politically involved. They are starting to get a bit fed up with me, but they and my family understand why I am involved.

ESCO38: I have a varied group of friends, some of them call me a fascist as a joke!

HUCO02: My friends think politics belong to the past. They are not interested.

HUPS08: My friends are into religious movements mostly, and some are nationalist or extreme left.

Note the slight variations in this discourse of accommodation. Some young party members try to avoid discussing politics to save their friendships while others try to talk about it but face a front of opposition on the part of their friends. Some see differences in ideological preferences as the main possible source of tension between them and their friends or partners, while others think that the risk of tension stems from their very political involvement regardless of its political colour.

All in all, a number of young party members choose to avoid this impression of having to tread on eggshells by slowly switching their group of friends from non-partisans to fellow young party members. We call this second attitude one of *displacement*, and it can happen either consciously or unconsciously. With the displacement discourse, young party members implicitly compare friends from within and friends from without, add some of the former to compensate for what they cannot talk about with the latter or fully replace outside friends by fellow young party members altogether. Below are some interview excerpts that typify this attitude and the impact of young party membership on a replacement of one's social network:

DEPS02: I'm in touch with the people within the party more than my friends outside of the party. I see them more often than my friends.

NOCO16: None of my friends are interested in politics, but I made really good friends here.

UKBP06: None of my friends were interested in politics but I made good friends in the party.

UKPS30: I met my girlfriend in the party, so it's fine with her as we are both members!

ESPS32: I wasn't the first one in here – many of my friends and my boyfriend were already involved in the socialist youths and they convinced me to join.

ESCO18: I have a great group of friends in NNGG so I don't mind spending my free time in there. I have no doubt my next girlfriend will be a party member too.

ESCO40: The provincial president is my friend, and it is a friend who asked me to do the provincial co-ordination for our party, so I do it for him, it is no problem.

FRFN24: The level of complicity I have with my party friends is huge, far greater than with friends outside of the party. The level of attachment between us is tremendous, so of course, my closest friends are increasingly becoming my friends from within the party.

Here again the discourse of young party members rationalises the evolution of their friendship that has been caused by their partisan involvement. Switching from 'old' friends outside the party to 'new' friends within it is seen as natural, sometimes because joining the party meant rejoining some old friends, and sometimes because the level of 'complicity' and mutual affection with fellow young party members is seen as extremely high, more so than with other friends. The same is true of lovers, and a number of young party members have naturally come to expect that their boyfriends or girlfriends would be fellow young party members. Of course, as seen in Chapter 4, the routine of young party membership means that many young party members end up spending significant amounts of time with fellow young activists. We have also seen that social-minded young party members predominantly join the party for its fun factor and the desire to socially interact with people they perceive as similar to or compatible with them. This all reinforces the impression that displacing one's social network to make it match one's partisan involvement is indeed natural.

By contrast, however, some young party members, while unwilling to share their time between inside and outside party activities do not want to lose their old friends and social networks. These people sometimes engage in a third type of approach, that of *fusion* whereby rather than having to choose between old friends and their party, they try to bring their old friends within the partisan organisation in order to retain an intact social network that will now naturally fit their partisan involvement. This type of social fusion is exemplified by the following interview excerpts:

NOCO10: My friends are becoming more aware and involved due to my involvement in UH.'
FRGR10: It can have an impact on people around you. You are in a constant recruiting and convincing mode. That can be negative.
ESPS42: I convinced my girlfriend to join.
UKBP22: I have talked several friends into joining. It is quite important when you are involved in this party because otherwise you lose people.
HUPS20: When my boyfriend complained I wasn't spending enough time with him, I explained to him that the solution was for him to join too, and we are now both much happier!

In the examples above, young party members try to rearrange their social network, and organise the compatibility between friendship and partisanship. With the first mode – that of accommodation – they do so by taming their partisan discourse in order to not lose their old friends. With the second mode – that of displacement – they choose to adapt their friendships to their partisanship by slowly changing friends, progressively ditching non-members in favour of new friends from within the party. With the third mode – that of fusion – young party members choose to bring their old friends or their girlfriends or boyfriends into the party in order to keep partisan and social circles under one roof without having to sacrifice either.

When young party members feel marginalised and misunderstood

In a way, all three modes of coping highlighted above reveal a desire to maintain or improve social networking while maintaining a partisan activity, a win-win game of sorts. Some times, however, things are not quite that easy, and young party members can experience a feeling of marginalisation and misunderstanding from their close ones. This feeling is far from rare. In our in-depth interviews, a large majority of the young party members we talked to (58 per cent) explicitly referred to such feelings. They revealed that their friends do not understand their involvement, think of them as 'weirdos', or that they do not feel able to talk about politics to anyone. Of course, these uncomfortable feelings can vary significantly in focus and intensity from member to member.

The level of gravity and the focus of this malaise can indeed range from (1) a simple impression of not being able to talk about politics to anyone, (2) having to fight stigma and prejudice on politics and feeling misunderstood, (3) feeling marginalised and not fitting with others and even (4) in extreme cases, the impression that one scares or repels others or doubting one's own involvement.

Probably the mildest form of social stigma reported by the young party members that we interviewed has to do with an impression that they cannot talk about politics with anyone they know outside of the party. Others are not interested, find them boring or exceedingly likely to preach, they do not want to listen to them and do not want to engage in political discussion. At times, this is recalled as a rather painful experience by some young party members who take it quite personally as a questioning of one of the most meaningful passions in their life by their close ones. Here are a few examples of testimonies which correspond to this particular impression that one's political involvement has made politics taboo and the unease resulting from it:

DEPS10: Even in my circle of friends, there's hardly anyone with whom I can talk about politics. I grew up in a very bourgeois area, so I don't necessarily want to discuss politics with my friends from home.
FRGR21: I can't talk about politics with any of my friends. They say 'bah, politics is for grown ups!'
ESPS16: At home, nobody likes my involvement. They think that I'm wasting my time. They say I need that time for myself, to study. They tell me they don't like politicians, that I am getting in a very difficult environment, and that no one will listen to me.
UKLB31: I never discuss politics with any of my friends, only with colleagues and rivals. I don't want to lose friends!
HUCO02: I can't talk about politics very much with my closest friends.

This impression that one cannot speak about politics to anyone – or that no one will listen, can be perceived by young party members as a blow to their ego and leaves them feeling ill fitting within their social circles, but many also resent the impression that politics in general or their party in particular is the focus of some negative prejudice. Whether a sad perception of a harsh reality or paranoid reading of others' reactions, the impression that their fight is unfairly stigmatised is again experienced as a narcissistic wound by young party members. Below are a few examples of these perceptions and how badly they are resented by a significant minority of the young party members that we interviewed:

> *UKPS17*: Being a member excludes me from certain groups of friends. People judge you.
> *DECO01*: It is difficult to get people to understand my involvement in politics, especially as the JU is seen as boring and conservative.
> *NOCO07*: General acceptance is difficult. At school I am branded as a 'right-winger', one of the goofballs walking around with UH t-shirts.
> *NOCO03*: You are sort of branded a political nerd. With UH you get a typical UH stamp on you. There is a stigma attached to the membership.
> *NOCO30*: You get some funny looks. So you are engaged in politics – you have to be strange or you are so cynical and hard because you vote Hoyre.
> *FRFN04*: If you had been playing football, it would have been obvious to everybody why it was so important ...
> *ESPS08*: I have friends who are not interested in politics at all, who tell me 'you must be gaining good money there!'
> *FRPS07*: I don't want people to think I am here to gain a position or a name.

At times, however, this impression that party members and politicians in general are prejudiced against or that their party is connoted with an unfair negative image will weigh very little as compared to the impression that the young party member, as an individual, is looked at in a strange manner by friends and family for his/her political involvement. Surprisingly enough, nearly a quarter (24 per cent) of the young party members that we interviewed spontaneously referred to the impression that some of their friends or family look down at them as weird or strange for being party members. In some cases, they laugh it off, but in other cases, they feel explicitly out of place, and derive the impression from these sarcasms that they do not fit in. Let us look at a few testimonies of young party members who, in this way, feel marginalised by the negative perception others have of their political engagement:

> *FRPS08*: I feel like an alien. I don't understand why.
> *DECO10*: To be successful as a party member, you have to change. As they say, you don't have to turn into a pig, but you have to think like a pig!
> *NOCO33*: People think there are only nerds who join.

UKLB04: I still feel like a weirdo among my friends. They all find politics extremely boring.

HUPS05: None of my friends are members. They think I'm weird for doing that.

FRCM02: When told we were members, our friends and acquaintances said that we were mad!

UKPS34: At the beginning, my friends didn't really understand what I was doing but they were asking quite a few questions about what I did. Now, they say that I'm a pain and they simply ask me to shut up!

ESPS42: My friends don't see me as a politician, only as an affiliate, so they don't reject me. However, I really don't know what would happen if I ran for office in the future!

DEPS10: For my friends, I am a weirdo!

HUCO11: My position within my group of friends is a pretty obvious one: I am the black sheep.

FRFN22: I do feel a little bit weird among my friends for being in politics. They do ask me a lot what I am doing here.

FRPS16: Well, if you want me to be honest, I haven't had a girlfriend in years!

UKBP25: More often than not, my friends just say that I am a pain!

ESCO18: I feel pretty bad. I won't tell them I am a party member.

Note the type of wordings used by young party members to describe the way that they believe they are perceived by their friends: 'weirdo', 'pig', 'nerd', 'alien', 'pain', 'black sheep.' The entire lexical choice of young party members to describe their situation resonates of impressions of marginalisation and abnormality. In the last quote we use, a Spanish young party member even claims to feel 'bad' about being a party member and not wanting to admit to it.

At times, the way young party members talk about their marginalisation gets yet further dramatised, suggesting truly painful feelings of misfit with their close friends and relatives. This is the case of the last few examples we would like to quote. An exception, only mentioned by about 3 per cent of our interviewees, but an important one because it corresponds to the discourse of people who feel that the social price to pay for their party membership is so high in terms of being rejected by others that they end up questioning the very coherence and grounding of their membership itself:

FRCM23: At times, when I see how people perceive me, I can't help crying. It usually goes after a few days.

NOCO04: They don't understand that I get so involved with the 'institution' Unge Hoyre. It is seen as boring. I am beginning to doubt the purpose of my own involvement.

NOCO33: My membership in UH entails that I am constantly bothered by people and I feel that I have to defend my membership.

FRPS16: You get really involved and that's not always good. You feel a need to defend the party at family, parties etc. You also risk being stigmatised. I have experienced that.

ESPS35: Everyone seems to hate politicians. One classmate says that we should all die.

UKBP03: My friends are afraid of me.

HUPS05: One of my friends felt so rejected that he once told me that he contemplated suicide.

FRFN08: Individually, it is hard of course. When I joined the FN I lost some friends but can you really call them friends then? I received some threats and I almost couldn't take my exams at uni because of this.

In a nutshell, while party activism can be equivalent to the opportunity to finally find new friends and like-minded people for a number of young party members, to others, it may mean unprecedented levels of loneliness, depression, and feelings of inadequacy. This is all the more true that through their activism, young party members are asked to consent some sacrifices, which, at times, they may consider to have lasting if not eternal consequences for them.

On the whole, this chapter has shown that the activism of young party members is often perceived to change their life. Some of the things that they discover through membership they will love or hate to the point that it will influence their future choices in life. Moreover, some key moments of their membership – chief among them, their first experience of an electoral campaign, and their discovery of leadership through the fulfilment of positions of responsibility – seem to change their perception of politics but also of who they are. However, quite significantly, we have also shown that while many young party members like most of the ways in which their party and their activism have changed their life, they see their membership as a cause of essential, meaningful choices and sacrifices with lasting consequences. Most young party members have to rearrange – and sometimes, in their perception, sacrifice – their personal life, be it because of the time they dedicate to their party, how it changes their way to think even outside of their party time, or even the impact of their membership on their professional opportunities and future. Most young party members also experience a lasting and severe impact of their partisan involvement on their social network and their relationship with – or the nature of – their friends. In extreme cases, however, we have also seen that the way in which the party 'changes the life' of its young members can be dramatic. Next to the many who feel more fulfilled, more connected, or more at ease with similar young people through their partisan involvement, a few feel marginalised, excluded, odd, or even depressed, at times with some extremely traumatic consequences. This is bound to affect the perception young party members have of their party. Indeed, if they consent such significant sacrifices, needless to say that, as we are now going to explore in Chapter 6, young party members will have sharp perceptions, in return, of what makes the party which has changed them so profoundly and sometimes so durably a great or not such a good place to be.

6
Young Party Members and Their Party

Becoming a young party member is no less than a change of identity. In Chapter 5, we saw how young party membership affects the daily life of young partisans, but how about the effect of membership on their outlook. One of the main consequences of identity has to do with the lens through which one looks at a given group or a given object. One can look at the family sitting at the neighbouring table as an outsider. One can criticise their screaming children and their greedy drinking with anger but without feeling any guilt or without one's perception of oneself being affected. One can admire their beautiful clothes with envy but without pride. On the other hand, when it comes to our own table, the little flaws of our own family members, as well as their little wonders will take a whole new meaning. This time, they will have a direct impact on how we feel as individuals. This is exactly the same with any other community of identification, be it a nation, a profession, a continent, town, group, or religion.

When a young individual becomes a young party member, he or she ceases to be able to look at his/her political party – and perhaps at politics in general – as the next table. The table becomes his/her own. It does not mean that the young party member loses his/her ability to be critical or to be enthusiastic. It does not even necessarily imply that the balance between ability to criticise and ability to praise will be modified in either direction, but it does mean that criticisms and praise alike are now articulated by an insider and no longer by an outsider. A further result is that the implications of these judgements in terms of the identity definition of the individual himself/herself, as well as its practical meaning will be utterly different. In this sense, we should not expect young party members to view their party as young citizens in general do. Yet, their perception of their political party, their views of what works and does not work when it comes to internal party democracy, the quality of their efficacy, their sentiment with regard to the relationship between young party members and older ones, between members and leaders are all of significant relevance and consequence for our understanding of their partisan involvement.

It is with all of these perceptions and judgements that this chapter is concerned. We start by considering the traditional model of parties' priorities summarised by Strøm (1990), which arbitrates between vote-seeking, office-seeking, and policy-seeking priorities. We want to establish how the various types of young party members that we identify situate themselves vis-à-vis this model using the survey results. We then proceed to examine the level of efficacy that young party members feel they have, evaluating how it varies across countries, party families, and types of young party members, this time, using both the evidence from our survey, and testimonials derived from the in-depth interviews that we have conducted in the six countries covered by our analysis. We then go on to dissect how young party members evaluate the relationship between party members and party leaders with an emphasis on the May's Law of curvilinear disparity, and we then look at their perception of the place of young party members specifically within the party – how their relationship with older party members unfolds, how well they are considered, and to what extent they feel heard and respected. Of course, an evaluation of the relationship between older and younger party members is only one of the many social assessments of the party's atmosphere that young members can provide – we are also interested in more general evaluations of the 'atmosphere' within the party and relationship between members, which, based on the in-depth interviews, will constitute the last section of this chapter. Throughout Chapter 6, we intersperse evidence from the survey results and in-depth qualitative accounts gathered from the comparative young party member interviews in order to obtain a more balanced account of how young party members relate to their party structure and organisation. We also try to understand what they would hope to change to it if or as they get an increasing influence on the party's dynamics.

Young party members and their party priorities

Hypothesis *H2* is concerned with which of the three 'classic' party priorities identified by Strøm (1990) – policy, vote, and office-seeking – are favoured by the three types of young party members. Moral-minded members are expected to be most likely to favour policy-seeking objectives, and professional-minded members to favour office-seeking objectives.

Table 6.1 suggests that *H2* is only partly confirmed. Whilst professional-minded members are the primary supporters of office-seeking priorities, social-minded young members seem even keener on policy objectives than moral-minded activists. Yet, this counter-intuitive result can be explained by the measurement of the variable. As we use a rank variable to establish the strength of young members' party priorities (see appendix), the scores of the four priorities are relative. As we shall see, social-minded members are the most critical of – and least involved with their party. Consequently, Table 3.1

Table 6.1   Ranking of membership objectives by type of member

Objective	Moral	Social	Professional
Vote	**2.98 (1.06)**	*2.74 (1.11)*	2.85 (1.07)
Politicians Office	**1.95 (1.29)**	*1.65 (1.22)*	1.90 (1.19)
Own Office	*1.67 (1.28)*	1.72 (1.26)	**2.42 (1.23)**
Policy	3.39 (1.08)	**3.45 (0.99)**	*3.32 (1.10)*

Notes: Bold figures represent the type of party member with the highest score, and Italic figures the type of party member with the lowest score. For example: Moral-minded members are the most vote seeking (score in bold) and social-minded members the least vote seeking (score in italic). Figures in brackets are the standard deviations attached to each coefficient.

Score represent index value on a theoretical scale of 0–4.

Respondents were asked to rank these objectives from most to least important to them, with the top choice given 4, the second choice 3, and so on. The respondents could also decide that one of the proposed objectives was not an objective at all, in which case it received a score of 0.

$N = 2878$.

unsurprisingly shows social-minded young members to be least concerned with their party's vote-seeking and leaders' office-seeking priorities. As a result, policy-seeking priorities are, by default, the *only* significant party priority of many social-minded members. By contrast, most moral-minded members also care about their party winning elections and its leaders accessing offices, particularly in countries where elections were imminent. Thus, for them, policy objectives are in competition with these two priorities for top scores. To test whether the higher policy score of social-minded members is indeed a measurement artefact, we look at the proportion of respondents who *only* rank policy priorities at the exclusion of all other priorities. This represents 0.4 per cent of professional-minded activists, 1.3 per cent of moral-minded members, but 3.8 per cent of social-minded ones. When looking at the proportion of respondents who chose policy *and* one other priority, figures become 9.1 per cent, 12.1 per cent and 17.9 per cent respectively. This clearly illustrates how the policy priority score of social-minded members is artificially inflated by their indifference to other priorities, and does not reflect a keener support for policy objectives than for moral-minded members.

Table 6.2 shows that policy-seeking objectives are the principal objective of most young party members in most of the countries included in the study. They are followed by vote-seeking objectives, the office-seeking interests of the politicians party members support, and in last position, egocentric office-seeking objectives. However, the comparative table shows that in Hungary, electoral objectives actually predominate, and that they are almost as important as policy goals in the UK and Norway. This emphasises the distinction between two competing young members' conceptions of political parties – as electoral machines on the one hand, and policy think tanks

Table 6.2 Ranking of membership objectives by country

Country	Policy Objectives	Electoral Objectives	Own Place in Party Hierarchy	Individual Allegiance
France	**3.55**	3.12	1.07	1.91
	(0.91)	(0.71)	(1.33)	(1.22)
Germany	**3.54**	2.54	2.41	1.62
	(0.94)	(1.08)	(1.11)	(1.17)
Spain	**3.48**	3.02	1.30	1.65
	(1.03)	(1.06)	(1.27)	(1.43)
Hungary	3.17	**3.31**	1.80	2.09
	(1.15)	**(1.01)**	(1.36)	(1.27)
UK	**3.15**	3.13	2.05	2.35
	(1.01)	(1.04)	(1.48)	(1.00)
Norway	**3.13**	3.09	1.50	2.17
	(1.19)	(1.02)	(1.22)	(1.16)
ALL	*3.39*	*2.86*	*1.88*	*1.83*
	(1.06)	*(1.09)*	*(1.30)*	*(1.25)*

Notes: Figures in brackets are the standard deviations attached to each coefficient.
Score represent index value on a theoretical scale of 0–4.
Respondents were asked to rank these objectives from most to least important to them, with the top choice given 4, the second choice 3, and so on. The respondents could also decide that one of the proposed objectives was not an objective at all, in which case it received a score of 0.
$N = 2878$.

on the other hand, reflecting divergent national traditions illustrated by the literature.

Table 6.3 further shows that there are also significant variations across the three main party families. In the Conservative family, electoral objectives take precedence over policy priorities, while young Liberals do not strongly hierarchise the four objectives. If getting positions of responsibility for oneself is a secondary concern across countries and party families, some important differences are noteworthy. If overall, 30.1 per cent of young party members claim that getting a position of responsibility for themselves is not an objective at all (which, incidentally, means that it *is* an objective for 69.9 per cent of them), this proportion falls to 20.5 per cent in the UK, against 47 per cent in France, where respondents seem least interested. Norway and Hungary also have low proportions of young members totally uninterested in offices (about 25 per cent in both cases). Partisan differences are even more striking, with only 8 per cent of young Liberal members claiming to have no interest at all in positions of responsibility within their party, seemingly echoing Duverger's (1954) distinction between cadre and mass parties. In Chapter 2, we also saw that the largest proportion of professional-minded members is to be found in Liberal parties, which seems to confirm this 'cadre' profile of Liberal parties.

Table 6.3   Ranking of membership objectives by party family

Party Family	Policy Objectives	Electoral Objectives	Own Place in Party Hierarchy	Individual Allegiance
Socialist	**3.50**	2.75	1.89	1.74
	(0.97)	(1.11)	(1.34)	(1.25)
Liberal	**3.46**	2.68	2.30	1.68
	(1.03)	(1.02)	(1.13)	(1.20)
Conservatives	3.15	**3.17**	1.70	2.05
	(1.19)	**(1.04)**	(1.26)	(1.23)
ALL	*3.39*	*2.86*	*1.88*	*1.83*
	(1.06)	*(1.09)*	*(1.30)*	*(1.25)*

Notes: Figures in brackets are the standard deviations attached to each coefficient.

Score represent index value on a theoretical scale of 0–4.

Respondents were asked to rank these objectives from most to least important to them, with the top choice given 4, the second choice 3, and so on. The respondents could also decide that one of the proposed objectives was not an objective at all, in which case it received a score of 0.

$N = 2878$.

Finally, while 8.2 per cent of young members rank getting positions of responsibility as their top objective, this proportion is 20.5 per cent in the UK and 11.6 per cent in Hungary, the two countries with the highest proportion of professional-minded members. Cross-party differences are also important: egocentric office-seeking goals are the top objective of 20 per cent of young Liberals, but less than 10 per cent of young Socialists and Conservatives (and less among other parties).

This emerging picture of a multi-tiered young party membership is at the very heart of our model. It highlights a sub-category of young members who are already 'leaders.' With hypothesis *H4*, we leave the realm of differences in perceptions and behaviour to pose the central question of whether some young party members – the professional-minded ones – simply think and feel like young party leaders already. Indeed, we suggest that they will be more efficacious than the rest, revealing a sense of power within the party organisation, pledge their allegiance to the party by being more positive about it than other members. By contrast, social-minded members are expected to be most critical and least efficacious. In other words, we suggest that young party members are structured around a sub-group of 'leaders' and two sub-groups of 'followers.'

Young party members' efficacy and perceptions of members – leaders relationship: An overview

Let us first look at the global trends in young party members' perceptions of their efficacy within the party and relationship to party leaders.

Table 6.4 Efficacy and democratic perceptions by type of members

	Moral	Social	Professional
Efficacy	2.51 (1.00)	*2.34** (1.05)*	**2.60** (0.95)**
May	**2.30* (1.27)**	2.20 (1.30)	*2.11* (1.30)*
Listen	**2.33** (1.26)**	*2.04** (1.26)*	*2.04* (1.25)*
Older[negative]	1.79 (1.39)	*1.77 (1.39)*	**1.83 (1.40)**
New things	**3.68** (0.71)**	*3.48** (0.90)*	3.49* (0.89)
Interesting	**3.20** (1.03)**	3.06 (1.06)	*2.94** (1.17)*

**: *ANOVA test sig < 0.01*; *: *ANOVA sig < 0.05.*

N = 2919.

Table 6.4 shows how the three types of members fare in terms of efficacy and perceptions of intra and extra-party democracy. We use an ANOVA test of differences of means to confirm that this hopeful 'leaders' group – professional-minded members – most significantly differ from the rest of the sample in their perceptions. Table 6.4 shows that professional-minded young activists are far more efficacious than average whilst social-minded members are least efficacious.

Professional-minded members are most likely to dismiss the May Law within their party by disputing the claim that members would favour more radical policies than their leaders. By contrast, moral-minded members are most likely to acknowledge such mismatch. However, the limit of this consensual approach of professional-minded members comes with their evaluation of fellow activists. They are the most likely to believe that old party members do not respect younger ones, suggesting that they consider them to be an impediment to their own progress. Social-minded members are least likely to agree and will not criticise a sub-part of their 'group.' Finally, despite their show of support for the party organisation, professional-minded members are in fact those who find intra-party discussions least interesting. By contrast, moral-minded members find them most interesting and are most likely to think that their membership teaches them new things.

A sense of power? The efficacy of young party members

Let us now look in greater details at what young party members say about their capacity to influence decision-making within their party, and their evaluation of the party's capacity to provide members with a transparent system of internal democracy. This is one of the topics that young party members quite easily talked about and which resulted in some rather contrasting statements and evaluations. As explained above, based on the survey results, there is an acute difference between the perceptions of professional-minded young party members and the other two categories of social-minded and moral-minded members.

Most of the professional-minded young party members tend to fit in the category of efficacious members both in terms of internal and external efficacy. They feel on top of the debates that their party faces, they have ideas about how they should be dealt with, and they also tend to have the impression that the party listens to them both individually and collectively – not least in terms of the relationship between the mother party and the young party organisation when there is one. Let us start with a few examples of this perceived symbiosis between mother party and young party organisation, seen through the eyes of some professional-minded members from all countries and party families.

NOCO14: The party generally asks us to write the parts of the programme related with youth.

FRPS11: I think we have a great relationship with the party. They listen, communicate with us, even include us in their electoral list.

FRGR15: We are completely autonomous.

DECO31: The youth organisation has an influence on the policies of the mother organisation as it tries to be innovative and provocative. Its mission should be to shake things up and introduce new perspectives. There are sometimes conflicts between the youth organisation and the main party, but these are about policies and issues rather than about fundamental political philosophy.

DECO20: The JU is basically just a younger version of the CDU, there is no real difference between us.

DEPS03: The Jusos are the new blood within the SPD and we are also trying to influence and move it through our criticism.

DELB31: We are effective. We are very good in university politics, and we are well-represented elsewhere too.'

UKLB17: In fact, I think that we somewhat have the power.

ESCO40: The party really listens to us. Some senators even approach us to ask us what we think.

Note that the very 'proof' of the efficacy of the young party organisation vis-à-vis the mother party takes some very different forms depending on whom you speak to. For some young members, the proof of the good relationship between the two is in the 'complete independence' or strong autonomy of the young party organisation as compared to the mother party. For some others, by contrast, evidence of the efficacy of the young party organisation within the larger party instances is, in an exactly opposite way, stemming from the complete adequacy of the preferences of the one and the other. As seen earlier, this may largely correspond to some extremely diverse tradition of institutional organisation between parties and young party organisations, with a culture of close ties, for instance for the young Spanish Conservatives of the Nuevas Generaciones NNGG, or the young Hungarian Socialists, while the young French Greens of the Souris Vertes or the young German Socialists of the JUSOS are traditionally completely autonomous. For some other groups, such as the young French Socialists from the Mouvement des Jeunes Socialistes, the level of closeness or distance from the party has often been dependent upon the personality of the leaders of the two groups. Some young party members make similar comments on the relationship between centre and periphery and the various levels of governance of the party, stressing high levels of efficacy of the local level vis-à-vis the capital. Below are four examples of such an impression.

> *ESPS27*: I know the people in the provincial office very well because they are very accessible.
> *ESCO40*: Sometime, we get ideas from Madrid, and sometimes, they come from our small towns. We try to put them into practice either way.
> *DECO20*: I was surprised at how much we can do in our town, that there are opportunities to change things here.
> *UKPS19*: We have very strong links with the whole of Scottish Labour and not just the people here.

Here again, there is a certain contrast between those who mostly stress the attentiveness of national or regional units to the thoughts of individual sections, and those who think of the local party organisation as the saving grace that allows them to have a say while the national level is harder to permeate. When this is the case, this contrasts with the third positive expression of both external and internal efficacy, which predominantly focuses on the efficacy of the individual within the party. This, again, seems to apply to professional-minded young party members more than to any other type. Expressions of this individual efficacy of young party members is particularly acute when made in reference to higher, more remote, and particularly national, parliamentary, or governmental spheres of power as illustrated by the examples below:

> *ESPS40*: When we debate, we always try to reach conclusions and push for them to be included in the next political programme.
> *HUPS23*: In the end, I think our ideas reach the top somehow.
> *DEPS04*: Some ideas get integrated into party policy, and you do have some influence as an individual member. It's motivating to see that your ideas have an influence on the party.

UKLB13: The main thing about my partisan involvement is that I feel free. In fact, we all do.

FRPS01: I don't just feel powerful, I also feel very privileged. To me, this is better than an Oscar.

FRCM12: I feel the party listens to its members. I feel I have a voice.

FRCM27: At the time I became in charge of education issues, we had a direct link with the education secretary in the government. We could express our ideas to her personally! I felt that I could really have an influence on policy.

It is worth noting, throughout these testimonials, the importance of how efficacy links into pride. Young party members do not just feel that they can change things they feel 'privileged', surprised, and proud that this be the case. They do not just have the impression that they can be heard, but that they can 'influence policy', have links with members of the government and other elites who can change and shape the future of their country. Of course, this somewhat rosy picture is not the one that is conveyed by all young party members alike, far from it. Most of the social- and moral-minded young party members that we interviewed are significantly more critical of the level of efficacy within their party.

Before looking at those who are openly critical, let us first consider the point of view of those who are more ambivalent as to the extent to which they believe that they can influence the perspective of their party. The contrasted picture that is drawn by a number of social- and moral-minded young party members usually insists on some difference between some parts of the party which are easier to 'reach' than others, or some types of policy or powers that are more willingly shared by the party elites than some other aspects of their decision-making. Below are a few examples of this message that some aspects work better than others, or that the results of trying to influence the party are inconsistent over time:

ESPS47: I would like there to be more direct interaction with party members with positions of responsibility and with councillors.

DECO04: I think there is a good relationship between the JU and the CDU, especially at the local level. The higher you get, the more potential there is for conflict.

DECO08: On a local level, the JU is separate from CDU. We're not a mini-CDU, we have our own topics and focus and do sometimes criticise the CDU.

ESPS09: I am critical, but I only criticise inside the PSOE doors, never outside. I encourage criticism too.

UKPS03: I like to see myself as an affiliate, not a sympathiser. That means that I am critical.

HUPS21: I know how difficult it is to get your voice heard, but I insist and insist until they listen.
NOCO04: I try…

As we can see, there is no simple or obvious unanimity as to which parts of European parties' internal democratic structures are more efficient or successful than others, and different members will have different understandings of what is a real impediment to young party members' true efficacy. For some members, however, still to be usually counted amongst the ranks of moral-minded and social-minded young activists, the picture is even clearer and party leaders simply show no interest in listening to the opinions, ideas, or preferences of young party members at all. This last series of perceptions, shared by roughly a third of our interviewees, draw upon the concerns and frustration that young party members experience regularly when trying to make a difference and being told (or having the impression that they are being told) that while their free-militant work in electoral campaigns is needed and in fact essential, their ideas and suggestions on how the party should be run or what policies it should advocate are certainly not. Here are a few of the testimonials that illustrate this disillusioned perception of internal party representation and democracy:

ESPSO2: Important party members don't ask or listen to us directly. This is how the party works, they have their hierarchy, their procedures.
DEPS21: The Jusos don't have much influence on the SPD, we have very little weight. We're belittled by some.
NOCO33: We have little opportunity to influence the party.
FRCM20: I usually only go to meetings to listen.
HUPS13: In the party, it is hard to climb if you are a woman. I don't like to kiss ass so I'm not sure where I will reach.
FRPSO8: What I don't like much – although I guess that it is normal – is that I don't really feel that I can make a difference on decisions or on society as I originally thought.
UKPS03: I'm not satisfied with the place the party gives to members in general and to us young people in particular. I want the party to listen to us more.
ESPSO5: Some people here are so afraid of members that they are even afraid of opening the door without knowing who it is or what it is for. Some of them are even afraid of opening the doors to new potential activists for fear that they will lose their position or their influence or will invite in new rivals. Our PSOE office doesn't keep a forum online. Guess why? Because they don't actually want any more participation!
ESCO46: We cannot just be the microphone and the speaker of our party.

Altogether, mixed or negative perceptions of the efficacy of young party members within their party account for nearly three quarters of the total accounts that we received from the in-depth interviews. We can therefore say that on the whole, the young party members that we interviewed are, consistently with our survey results, very critical of the internal democratic quality of the party and young party organisation of which they are members. The question, however, remains of who they will blame for this state of affairs. In particular, one will have noted from the comment of a young British Labour member above that some feel that *young* members are particularly ignored by their party hierarchy, even more so than members in general. One of the questions that naturally follows is how young party members perceive their status as a sub-type of activists, as well as their relationship with older members.

Getting on with other generations – young party members' perceptions of their elder

We saw in Table 6.1 that on a scale from 0 to 3 where 0 meant that they saw no problem in the way older party members treat younger ones, and 3 means that they see an acute problem in that treatment, on average, young party members 'scored' 1.79, being, in other words, a little bit more negative than indifferent, particularly when it comes to professional-minded young party members. This suggests that on the whole, young party members – and particularly professional-minded ones – do feel that the fear, contempt, or suspicion older members feel towards them is an impediment to young party members' ability to exert their influence within the party. It prevents them from promoting their ideological and organisational preferences, and even complicates their progress within the party's hierarchy, hence the particularly negative perception of professional-minded members as compared to moral- and social-minded ones.

Let us now look at the more detailed feedback provided by young party members in the context of the in-depth interviews that we conducted in the six countries. The first reaction expressed by a number of young party members when asked about that question was that young and older activists all live in a big happy family where the young respect the experience of the older, and the older praise the enthusiasm of the young and give them their chance to influence the line of the party. Below are a number of examples of these reactions.

> *FRPS37*: I spend a lot of time with older party members. I like how older party members are sometimes even more progressive and bold than us. It inspires me.
> *DELB11*: It's important to give young people the opportunity to show what they can do and to take responsibility. One example of this is the

internet, where young members can do things that the older members appreciate but can't do themselves.

FRPS24: The older people are very nice to me. A bit paternal/maternal at times, but nice and helpful and they listen to me I think.

ESPS26: Older party members do take us into account. We have an office in the building where the party is and they usually pass by to talk and ask what we think.

ESCO46: On the whole, I think old members listen to young people more and more, at least here in Andalucia. Now, what we ask the veterans in the party is to allow for more renovation and dynamism, new ideas and more space for young people participation.

All of the above quoted young party members describe a situation of harmony and denounce the notion of a tension between older and young party members as nothing more than a mere myth. Nevertheless, it is fair to say that such a positive and optimistic set of reactions represented the exception rather than the norm in the interview feedback. Far more numerous were the young party members who, while claiming not to have a general problem with older members tended to nuance their answer by insisting on the difference across levels of government, branches, or individuals. Let us now look at these more ambiguous accounts which tend to suggest that the relationship between older and younger members is not necessarily uniformly horrible but that tension and rivalries are not unheard of either.

DELB06: The Julis are important to the FDP, because the older members need the impulses coming from the younger ones. It's quite good when people think outside the box and don't stick to what is well-known.

HUPS21: There is a very old generation (over 60) who are not active. The majority of people are between 40 and 45, if we have any idea, they support it.

NOCO07: Our relationship with older party members is generally good. Ordinary members do not really understand the importance of what Unge Hoyre does.

ESCO24: Here in xxx, the older members are interested in listening to the younger generations. In the province and at the national level it is quite different.

FRCM22: You can't compete with veteran politicians, but I don't necessarily feel rejected as a result as they give me an opportunity to put fresh ideas on the table, and also the young ones are generally more qualified and educated so they are interested in our ideas, at least at the provincial level.

ESPS31: In the Merida provice, 50% of the party's executive organ is under 30 years of age. At the local level it depends on the personality of whoever is in charge.

ESPS44: Right now, relationship with the older members of the PSOE are good, but it has not always been like that in other times. It really all depends on the attitudes of the local leaders.

ESCO31: The relationship between young and old party members is directly related to the relationship between the PP and the NNGG. We help the party to do the job that the older members cannot do because they have their own professions and jobs and they have no time. Also, young people tend to like better these kinds of 'risky' activities such as sticking posters on the walls, giving out flyers, or more generally being on the street. So altogether, this means that this way of sharing the work is quite ok and so is our relationship.

ESCO39: On the whole, recently, it has become clear that a political meeting without NNGG members is really bad. We bring all of the enthusiasm. The PP is therefore counting more and more on its young members.

As can be seen, these contrasted accounts vary from 'mostly good' to 'mostly bad', but in a few cases, some young party members try to rationalise the hesitation of some older party members to fully take into account the preferences or recommendations of younger activists as exemplified below:

DELB30: The Julis are the fountain of youth of the FDP. We're the radical ones. Many of our ideas aren't fully formed but that's normal.

Finally, approximately a third of our interviewees denounced some outright tension between young party members and older activists, even though they might view the reasons behind such misunderstandings through varying lenses. Some predominantly think that older activists do not take them seriously, others that younger and older party members simply disagree on the substance of their ideological and policy positions, to the point that they cannot be reconciled or reach a consensus on a given party line. Below are a few examples of young party members who express such frustration at the way older members treat them on the whole:

FRCM05: I was in the list for local elections, but I was last and the only young one.

DEPS21: We are seen as children, who sometimes make good suggestions but often need to be ignored.

DELB24: When I joined in 2000, I was surprised that the Jusos members were all quite old, and also overqualified in my opinion. There was a long period of time when there were very few young people involved in the party.

HUPS01: There are one or two old people who like the young ones. They are jealous, they don't want to pay attention to them but some of us are there to help them.

HUCO01: If the older ones step aside, there would be bigger influence for the younger ones.

UKPS14: Doors are closed to us by older members in many ways.

FRPS31: Older politicians? Their first reaction when I talk or bring up an idea is 'who are you to say this?' or 'how old are you?'

NOCO09: Unfortunately, they don't let young people with strong will get high enough.

HUPS08: There is a huge generation gap. We wouldn't want to exterminate the old generation, of course, their experience is valuable. It's just that I would like them to accept our energy!

ESPS27: Our relationship with older members and in particular with the local party office is very bad. They avoid us, never approach us to ask us what we think about anything or more generally show any interest whatsoever in what we do. It is only in election time, when they need a hell of a lot of help that they suddenly remember that we exist. Then, they ask us for a lot of work on activities such as handing out pamphlets and going to knock on voters' doors. By that time, we are not willing to co-operate with them at all in that way.

FRPS01: Older party members do not seem to like us at all!

ESCO39: We get tired of seeing always the same old people.

As can be seen from this variety of conclusions, while many young party members think that 'there is a problem' between them and those older than them, the scope of the problem and its main forms of expression are perceived quite differently by many young activists. Some think that the problem is one of respect, others one of ideology, others, yet, one of structure. Similarly, some young party members are merely amused by the lack of willingness of older members to fully take them into account, others resent older members, or, occasionally, downright hate these older activists. Of course, sympathy or resentment towards older members may only be the tip of an iceberg which, in the eyes of young party members, represents the atmosphere of the party as a whole. Some love this atmosphere, some rather dislike it or dislike some of the fellow members that they interact with on a quasi permanent basis.

Feeling good – when young party members find a new family

As seen in Chapter 2, the second largest of our three groups of young party members consists of social-minded members, who are predominantly driven to join a political party in order to enjoy what they see as a positive social atmosphere and interaction with people they have an a priori sympathy for. Short of finding that party membership is 'disappointing', we should therefore find that a large number of young party members see the party as a new family, a group of friends, which projects a sense of gratifying interaction and sense of belonging for its members.

Indeed, a number of young party members stress the positive atmosphere within their party and all that it means to them in terms of personal development and intellectual, human, and social fulfilment. Below are a few examples, all drawn from our in-depth interviews, of such positive experience of party life for young activists across the six countries. Overall, we can classify these praises for the atmosphere of the party into three main categories: young party members who predominantly enjoy the impression of solidarity in work and shared intellectual experience, those who have a predominantly affective relationship to fellow young party members, and finally, those who enjoy the stimulation of networking and learning from the party.

The following examples all correspond to the first category of praise, that which relates to the impression of young party members that through party membership they 'share experiences', stick together with people who have the same goal as them, in short that together, within their partisan organisation, young party members build something together and create the atmosphere that makes them feel as though they were commonly constructing something important. The following testimonies all express this perception in a number of different ways:

UKPS12: It's great to be with people that have the same interest, worries or ideas, with whom I can talk about the things I like.

UKLB17: Just like if I was fond of football I would join a football team.

NOCO15: It is enriching to discuss politics and to be engaged in current affairs and societal issues.

HUPS06: There are lots of hard-working people here, people with a lot of charisma.

HUCO14: What I love about our youth movement is all that enthusiasm.

ESPS01: There is always a good atmosphere here, and there are always discussions. I think it's good. Nobody keeps quiet here, everyone says what they think.

DECO04: I love working in a group. I enjoy it. I have a good time with the other members.

ESCO39: Really, we all help each other with anything when we don't have too much work in our area.

UKBP23: We generally agree what we need or have to do.

ESCO03: I like the passion I see floating in the atmosphere, It is contagious and provides the strength to change things.

FRFN31: I became very active immediately. I loved the great atmosphere, it trapped me in this completely.

Throughout the accounts summarised above, young party members praise a sense of mutual solidarity, shared goals, shared experiences, and intellectual stimulation. By contrast, a second category of young party members predominantly see their party as a human group, a 'bunch of friends', and have a predominantly affective perception of what makes this group such a nice place to be, blessed with the greatly positive atmosphere that they describe. The following few examples testify of this particular alternative 'angle' to describe the great atmosphere within the party:

DECO04: I am well integrated into the group, even though I am one of the youngest and one of the newest members.
DEPS01: It is all very amicable, almost family-like.
HUPS22: Now we are having Christmas dinner coming and I'm really looking forward to it!
ESPS16: I have a sentimental relationship with the Youth organisation. I feel I love being here, even though I give a lot and receive little in return.
ESCO02: I feel so great in my local delegation. I think the party is listening to young people much more lately. I feel great, even loved and missed.
NOCO16: Honestly, I was surprised to see so many normal young people, all with different interests.
DECO27: Most young Liberals are quiet types, not people I would usually hang out with, but unlike most of my friends they are interested in politics, which is something I value.
UKPS12: In a way, you grow up with the other party members. That's a real bond.

A third 'vision' of the great atmosphere within the party predominantly focuses on the impression that one 'learns politics' from it. This perception, most likely to be shared by professional-minded young party members involves descriptions of exciting networking, stimulating debates, and what one young party member below describes, quite simply, as 'playing politicians.' Here are just three examples of this third 'take' on what makes the atmosphere of a party a great one:

HUPS13: It is a kind of education. You establish a network professionally and personally.
NOCO32: It is maybe the best school of life you can go through.
FRPS27: I love the atmosphere. It's like playing politicians!

Finally, a small number of young party members love the atmosphere of their party for a mixture of the three types of dimensions mentioned above as in the following three cases:

> *ESCO14*: The relationship with other members in the local headquarters is great and mostly friendly. At the provincial level, though, it is often tense but also more interesting.
>
> *UKPS02*: We work hard and have lots of fun too.
>
> *UKBP15*: The party is all at once a place to have fun, a place to learn, and a place to meet great inspirational leaders.

The good, the bad, and the ugly – criticising others, a tale of three stories

While a large number of young party members praise the good atmosphere within their party, almost all of them also have some gripes with some aspect of the partisan atmosphere or with some particular sub-types of members who, in their opinion, tend to damage an otherwise great institution. This will be the last section of this chapter, and we will start by trying to understand what young party members dislike about partisan atmosphere (in a more holistic perspective) before looking at two particular types of fellow young party members that they dislike and hold responsible for this bad atmosphere: ambitious ones and lazy ones.

When the atmosphere is bad

'A bad atmosphere'... One of the most amazing patterns of our interviews is that over 85 per cent of our interviewees mentioned that in some branches of the party, the atmosphere is extremely unpleasant. In a majority of cases, the young party members point their finger at someone else's branch – that of a neighbour, a friend, or a rival. In short, almost everyone seems to see bad atmosphere somewhere, but the differences occur when it comes to understanding how they read it or ascribe it to specific sources of problems or types of issues.

First, a number of young party members blame the atmosphere of politics in their country in general. Politics tempted them before, but once they started getting mixed up with it through their partisan involvement, they got turned off it rather quickly, realised that the 'popular perception' that it is unglamorous, aggressive and petty is by and large real, and matched by their own experience. The following three testimonies represent a small cross section of such comments:

HUCO11: Once you start getting deeper into politics, you start disliking it.
FRPS03: I don't like the way politics is done here. I find it boring, aggressive, and I think it lacks the ability to generate enthusiasm. I don't feel attracted by it any more.
ESPS13: Politics is a nasty world. You can pass from having all to having nothing in a few hours. It depends on who's in charge and on whether he or she trusts you.

If some young party members blame politics in general for the atmosphere that they consider unpleasant, by contrast, some other young activists believe that the reasons for the bad atmosphere that they resent is to be found closer to home, and in particular in the internal structures of their own party. They blame the party structures for a certain rigidity, inherent conservatism and resistance to change and initiative, or, more simply, an inevitable and continuous break down in communication between members and leaders or between various spheres of power. The following five excerpts from the interviews illustrate this uncomfortable feeling that many young members perceived in their party structure:

DECO08: I think it's a problem that the structures of the CDU are very hierarchical and closed.
DEPS10: I was disappointed with the party at first. I had high hopes when I was 15 and quickly saw that everything takes a long time.
HUPS13: I don't like people in the party who try to block our initiatives. A lot of people only want to conserve the status quo.
FRPS29: There is a gap between militants and leaders in the party.
ESPS10: I only go to the meetings in xxx because I don't like the atmosphere in the provincial and regional bodies.

A particular variation on this theme has to do with a problem of atmosphere and lack of friendliness between the mother party and the young party organisation. Of course, we already mentioned the fact that many young party members contrast their experiences with the party and the young party organisation and seem to like one of the two (not always the same) significantly more than the other. Below are a few examples of young party members who ascribe the bad atmosphere they experience to some permanent tension between these two competing structures:

HUCO11: We don't get enough recognition for the work we do.
DEPS27: We're the thorn in the side of the SPD. I feel that the SPD can't live without us but doesn't really like us either.

FRGR01: The atmosphere between the Souris and les Verts is often tensed, and I find it tiresome. I don't have a particular preference between the two but wish they would stop fighting all the time.

ESPS19: There is a huge difference between the atmosphere in the party and in the young party organisation. The former is very bad, the latter quite good.

FRPS13: Relationships with other Youth organisation members are perfect, but inside the party, you have to move carefully.

A perhaps more interesting reproach that was articulated, in one form or another, by approximately 1 in 10 young party members has to do with the impression that party politics leads to intellectual or ideological rigidity and indoctrination, and the impression that parties and their members live in what one of the young party members called their own 'glass bubble.' What makes this negative assessment particularly interesting to look at is that it corresponds to a widespread conception that is held by many citizens about party politics and partisanship. The following examples illustrate this impression that the party prevents members from feeling free rather than emancipate them, that it conveys a sense of narrow mindedness and indoctrination:

FRPS07: Sometimes the party seems like a sect to me, that is very negative.

NOCO02: You tend to end up a bit too indoctrinated. You don't see criticisms. It's a glass bubble.

DEPS06: I dislike the fact that the SPD has to be very politically correct concerning women, but at least we don't have a quota.

DEPS11: The camps are very clear, for example, the left, the employee wing and the women.

UKBP27: There are things you simply can't say within the party because then, you're accused of being a monster. At times, this is tiresome.

FRFN19: Nobody will tell you that, but freedom of speech within all parties is rather minimal. For instance, among us, no one can ever openly criticise Le Pen, and if the UMP tell you it is not the same with Sarkozy or the Socialists with their own elephants, they are just liars.

Another form of rigidity of political parties that can put off young party members has to do with the transformation of political parties from mass membership organisations into electoral machines. In many ways, this is a change that has been noted and analysed by political scientists for over 30 years. However, perhaps precisely because young party members are new to party politics, and because, as detailed in Chapter 3, many seem to have been brought to political parties on the basis of the mythical memory of the former glory of mass partisanship experienced by their parents and grandparents, a significant proportion of them seem to believe that this is a new development and one that surprises them. In short, many young party members believe that parties value votes more than members, have forgotten about the 'human factor', and by and large despise their grass roots. A few typical expressions of this unease are presented below:

> *ESPS10*: Parties care too much about elections and don't realise that it is the human capital that counts.
> *UKPS15*: Unfortunately, parties don't care enough about their members. An educated member is more convinced of what he says because he has analysed and understood it and therefore can persuade others more easily.
> *FRCM06*: Many politicians are absurd, foolish, or just distant.
> *FRPS02*: Right now, people in the party only see votes, they don't see people.

It is worth noting that unlike most of the other complaints summarised before and after, this regret with regard to the transformation of member parties into electoral machines seems particularly acute amongst left-wing young party members rather than among right-wing ones. This may well reflect the fact that, as explained in Chapter 1, the tradition of 'mass parties' in Europe (Duverger, 1954) was predominantly a left-wing tradition, while a larger number of cadre parties were to be found towards the centre and right of national ideological spectra.

We have now read about those who blame politics for the bad atmosphere within their party, as well as those who blame the internal organisation and structure of the party, the relationship between mother party and young party organisation, ideological rigidity, factions, and the transformation of mass parties into electoral machines. However, the largest proportion of those who criticise the atmosphere of party politics blame it on people, the 'human factor' and the difficulty in managing human relationships between large numbers of individuals with different preferences, perceptions, and personalities. Some young party members just believe that by the nature of things, too much time, energy, and effort needs to be spent trying to sort out personality clashes, to the point that some doubt if, if they were not joined together by a common cause, young party members would want to do anything together at all. Below are a few typical excerpts from our interviews that illustrate this impression that human incompatibility and a tendency to clash all the time as well as permanent internal rivalries explain what is less than desirable about the atmosphere of their party and their political activism:

> *ESPS04*: There are bad moments like in any organisation integrated by humans. Dealing with people can be hard.

FRPS05: I spend much of my time mediating between members in dispute for personal reasons. It's natural for personal clashes between members emerge, being together for more than six hours a day.

FRCM14: There are clashes between people although most of the time, it is not too bad.

ESCO45: Sometimes, it is really hard to deal with people you don't like or respect that much, especially when you have to run an activity together.

UKLB30: Human relationships are really complicated. They take up a lot of emotional effort sometimes.

ESPS11: I'm usually in for most things, but sometimes I don't do it because I don't like the person in charge of a particular initiative or I don't like his way to work or his attitude.

DEPS20: If we weren't in Jusos, we wouldn't do anything together. There's no real feeling of community.

When social and moral-minded members resent professional-minded ones

Of course, there is only a very small step from blaming the bad atmosphere within a party on a sense of permanent rivalry and disagreement to blaming the people that are seen as responsible for that bad atmosphere. A very large proportion of young party members, mostly moral-minded and social-minded ones, explicitly target those fellow young activists who are, in their opinion, predominantly characterised by obscene levels of ambition and shark-like behaviour. In their eyes, they are the ones who only come for honours and positions, who want all the power, and who fail to play as a team because the only 'cause' that interests them is their own.

In some cases, young party members primarily target the blame at some politicians rather than members in their midst. 'Professional politicians' in particular come, as we shall see in Chapter 7, as a prime target for moral-minded young party members. Below are a few examples of how at times, politicians are seen as the prime cause of bad atmosphere within the party:

ESCO45: There are many professional politicians who would do anything, including betraying their colleagues, to survive.

HUCO05: I only trust those politicians that I know least.

ESPS21: People who are high up on the ladder generally lose their sense of reality.

For a majority of young party members, however, ambition, individualism, and careerism are not the privilege of established politicians but also the desire of many members. Some are first perceived as likely to cause division in names of personality clashes and factional fighting, as illustrated in the few testimonies below:

> *ESCO16*: What I find most difficult to endure are the internal fights. Especially when the fights have to do with a clash of personalities.
>
> *FRPS06*: I don't like all the rivalries between the factions. When there is a fight for positions or personal clashes, I leave the room, I can't stand them.
>
> *ESPS35*: I really don't like to see all the people who join the PSOE to get applauses or to have authority in their district. There are lots of people like that.
>
> *HUCO05*: I really don't like the personal clashes and the fights for positions, but I guess that this is inevitable in politics.
>
> *UKPS21*: At first, it unnerved me to see people who didn't co-operate and came just for the credit. Now, I don't care.
>
> *FRFN25*: Some members are plain crazy!

Next to this impression that many of the people who 'cause trouble' within the party do so out of an aggressive personality (or indeed, outright personality disorder!) a yet far larger proportion of young party members mostly blame personal ambition and careerism for problems within the party. Below are a few of many similar comments made about those young party members who only come 'to make a career' and betray the spirit and objectives of their own party. Such comments were extremely rare amongst professional-minded young party members, and extremely frequent amongst moral- and social-minded young activists:

> *ESPS34*: Many young members are extremely ambitious. They just strive for a position, think of other members as rivals and criticise them all the time.
>
> *FRPS13*: There is cannibalism in politics within the party. People keep eating each other for positions and they lie all the time.
>
> *NOCO11*: Many people, especially women, are very competitive, which I don't like.
>
> *HUCO18*: The relationships are tensed because too many people only care about power. They don't understand that a baseline member is as important as a minister.
>
> *DEPS23*: Everybody wants to be something, and there's a lot of secrecy and underhand dealing.
>
> *DECO30*: I don't like people who only care about their careers and just want to get ahead. Some people don't stop at anything to move up in the party or to keep their nice posts. Some people just join the JU to have something nice on their CV and to get good contacts for their later careers.

DECO25: Your career can't be the most important motivation for joining. I really don't like that, and sometimes I have considered leaving the party because of that.

DEPS08: I don't like the rule that you can't go past people who have been active for a long time. It seems that just having been around for long gives someone the right to have an important say or a veto in everything.

DEPS15: I don't want to be a professional politician, and I don't like people who aim to be one. The best politicians are those who have had a different job before. It's not good to be dependent on the party, especially financially.

UKPS21: I was surprised that some people really are in the party to get somewhere, I didn't know it was really like that.

FRFN30: I don't like it that lots of people are very career-conscious. Some people try to gain a high profile by exploiting the work of others.

DELB25: I don't like careerists, who only want a post to have the prestige that comes along with it.

HUPS12: There are many individual players around, they put their own interest first ahead of the community's (MSzP) interest and aims. The party's hierarchy is important, they step forward very fast through manipulation.

UKLB02: I don't like seeing lots of people coming here to get benefits or climb the ladder. It's sad.

NOCO26: There are intrigues within the party. There are struggles for power. It can destroy friendships. I have seen some friends become enemies.

NOCO17: The social setting is not very healthy. People get obsessed with positions and power even in a tiny organisation. Many people have lost friends in UH.

ESPS34: When I see all these people coming here to fulfil their ambitions, it makes me feel as if my grandfather gave away his life for nothing.

UKPS06: There are lots of people who approach politics with an obvious interest to climb the ladder, but eventually, they get tired soon and leave.

FRPS17: Of course, being in this party means that there are many things about politics and about politicians that actually disgust me.

ESCO16: I think that some young people here want to be politicians right away. I don't like this at all.

As can be seen, such reproaches addressed to ambitious careerists, who only militate to climb the ladder, fulfil their ambition, and in a word, rule, come in a seemingly infinite range of variations. The feelings they generate amongst our interviewees range from 'dislike' to 'sadness' and from 'disgust' through to 'anger.' What is more, in the opinion of some, this inappropriate level of ambition, careerism, and strategic behaviour of some is further aggravated by the hypocrisy that it implicitly encourages:

ESCO35: There is so much falseness in here.
HUPS07: I don't like falseness. Too many people try to be very nice to get support or just to climb up positions.
FRGR02: There are so many hypocrites within the party that when someone smiles at me, I start wondering what they want.
UKBP11: Too many hypocrites!

Fighting free-riders

In short, many young party members direct their blame for an unpalatable party atmosphere on what they perceive as professional-minded young party members devoid of true public spirit and consciousness. By contrast, many of these professional-minded young party members themselves think, instead, that the people who make the party a not so great place to be are predominantly those lazy free-riders who hope to come to the party without ever making any sacrifice for it. This opinion also seems to be shared by a meaningful proportion of moral-minded young activists but only by extremely few social-minded young party members. The phrasing of the criticism is exemplified in the few typical statements below, once again, all derived from our in-depth interviews:

FRPS16: I want to delegate functions but no one wants to assume any responsibility.
DEPS10: I feel that I have to do everything myself, for example, there's little enthusiasm to set up an information booth outside of election campaigns so often I have to do that on my own.
DEPS12: Some are phlegmatic. Some are hard to motivate to do something. Most of the work is done by a small group of people.
HUCO26: I can't stand acquiescence, and people here often accept too easily things that they are told cannot be changed.
NOCO20: The problem with most active young party members is that they are active in a utopia, not in a real political project.
ESCO42: On the whole, there are very few people who are really in to help or to take a serious compromise.
UKPS05: In the typical youth party organisation, only 20% of members are more or less active.

As we can see, the reproaches articulated by young party members here are quite different from those targeted at their ambitious counterparts. To those who hate the young party members who only care about their own personal power and future answer those – less numerous but still important – who criticise the activists who 'live in utopia' or are unwilling to work for their party.

Such a misunderstanding between sub-groups of young party members motivated by vastly different types of incentives is typical of the contrasted view of their party that young party members express. Throughout the chapter, we have shown that on the whole, young party members tend to be quite critical of their parties, but for different reasons. In particular, in terms of perceptions of their own party, young party members seem almost entirely split between professional-minded young activists on the one hand, and social and moral-minded young party members on the other hand. Thus, while a majority of young party members across all three types claim to be predominantly policy seeking, we could see that they vary significantly in terms of their other priorities, and particularly in terms of their office seeking preferences. We saw that differences also exist in terms of country and party families.

Similarly, we showed that the three main types of young party members have very different discourses when it comes to their level of efficacy, and to a lesser extent, their perception of the relationship between leaders and members, and between older and younger party members, with a certain sense of unease that remains with regard to both. While many have a certain fondness for their party for intellectual or affective reasons, a majority of young party members are also rather critical of the atmosphere within their party. However, here again, we have seen that the great variety of reproaches addressed to the party atmosphere in general or to specific fellow activists, in particular, vary significantly, with many professional-minded young party members blaming lazy, utopian free riders at the very same time that they are themselves targeted by many moral- and social-minded young partisans for their apparent ambition, careerism, and hypocrisy.

Is the party a good place to be? Yes and no. Young party members like it on the whole, but remain underwhelmed by its internal democratic structure and their exposure to relatively frequent elements of tension, rivalry, or misunderstanding between members. Do they plan on reforming things in the long term? Some think that they have already found a solution in the form of young party organisations, which are often perceived to be rather friendlier than their mother party counterparts, and many of the others seem to have given up on any great chance to change the way things work within the rigid structure of the partisan organisation. However, it is also possible that the truth of the matter is that many young party members prefer to focus their energy on changing democracy in their country rather than democracy in their party. The element of 'freshness' brought by many young party members has to do with the fact that many seem aware and critical of the tendency of political parties to 'derive' towards an excessive concern with their own structure and problems, rather than those that face their nation. A very large number of young party members stressed this so significantly in the interviews that it is, therefore, not entirely absurd to expect that most of their creative thinking will target a reform of democracy rather than a reform of their party. This is what Chapter 7 will now investigate.

7
Young Party Members and Their Democracy

In Chapter 6, we have seen how young party members perceive the internal structure of the party they are members of, how they see the relationship between leaders and members, the priorities that the party should follow, and the relationship between younger and older party members. However, regardless of his/her main incentives, one rarely joins a political party for the sole purpose of influencing the structure of the internal organisation. A far bigger – and presumably far more stimulating challenge – consists of trying to influence the specific way that society is organised, of completing a representational duty, towards society and citizens in general.

The work of Miller and Stokes (1963) significantly influenced our understanding of the process of representation between an elected representative and his/her constituents. The authors focused on the dynamics of a process whereby a politically 'responsible' individual will tailor his/her vote on a given bill according to a mixture of his/her own real preferences on an issue and his/her perception of the preferences of his/her constituents. However, we must also consider the insights of Eulau and Karps (1978) who distinguish between four pillars of representation: policy, allocation, service, and symbolic responsiveness.

Policy responsiveness consists of the capacity of an individual or an institution to fairly implement the policy preferences of the citizens that are represented in a context of representative (indirect) democracy. In the context of young party members, we would thus expect them to try and improve representation by trying to defend the policy preferences that they believe voters to hold (especially, of course, if they are consistent with their own priorities).

Allocation responsiveness, in the context of relatively well-defined districts consists of trying to support the financial, infrastructural, or technical interests of the specific communities a politician has been elected to represent. In the context of young party members, this would take the form of a certain interest or involvement in local political debates and of an attempt to publicise and defend the needs of the specific communities the young party member emerges from, including, in a demographic and social rather than geographical way, the interests of young people at large.

Service responsiveness corresponds to the representative process, and in particular to the ability of an elected member of parliament to be reachable by and available to his constituents. Service responsiveness includes the willingness to hold surgeries, listen to citizens' concerns, communicate with them on the political life of the country, reach out to members of various boards, circles, and associations, and so on. When it comes to young party members, we also expect them to be concerned with the representative process within their political system, to improve communication between political parties and citizens – particularly young citizens, fully play the 'ambassadorial role' highlighted in Chapter 2, and reconcile 21st-century politics with 21st-century technology by caring about the visibility of their party on the internet, blogs, television programmes, social and virtual networks, and so on.

Finally, symbolic responsiveness is conceived solely at the societal level and consists of a certain match between the 'face' of a representative institution, such as a legislature, and the make up of the civic body of a community. In Eulau and Karps' vision, this means that a legislature should leave some room to representatives from various under-represented social and demographic groups (women, young people, ethnic or religious minorities, less-privileged social groups, etc). In this sense, young party members are, by nature, at the heart of an important sub-component of symbolic representation. The whole challenge of symbolic responsiveness, is that the discrepancy between the make up of a representative body – and thus, ultimately of a political elite – and that of the citizenry of a political system should not become so vast that citizens would feel entirely at odds with their political leaders. In this sense, young people play a crucial role in brokering a potential link between young citizens who, as shown in Chapter 1, seem to feel increasingly alienated from politics in contemporary democracies, and a political world which seems to be losing citizens' trust, respect, and confidence by the day. These young party members – particularly professional-minded ones, are thus the only way for ageing parties to avoid being accused of a lethal demographic gap between old leaders and young voters.

Now that we have sketched the potential value and the responsibilities of young party members as new entrants in the world of partisan politics from the point of view of the theory of political representation, it is important to understand how they themselves perceive their responsibility towards fellow citizens in general, and disaffected and young citizens in particular. How do they conceive their own added value, no longer from the point of view of the party but from the point of view of democracy and their citizenry? Which policy priorities do they try to support? And do they see themselves as the primary advocates of globally underestimated policy challenges, of their parties' traditional agendas, or of the sectorial and specific policy inter-ests of young voters? How do they believe that they can renew, reshape, and rearrange the democratic link between voters and leaders? How would they like to 'change' politics? Do they perceive it as a profession or as a broader civic duty? Do they want to 'do politics' differently from current party lead-ers and how? These are the numerous challenges that we want to tackle in this chapter.

In other words, we want to understand if young party members see them-selves as a 'new democratic blood' and how they propose to change things. We want to uncover their own analysis of the current crises of democracy and party politics as well as identify the solutions that they intend to propose or slowly put together as their own influence increases within their parties. In this chapter, we thus start by questioning whether young party members see politics as a profession. We then analyse their support for various pol-icy priorities. We then proceed to present the results of their vision of what constitute some of the main current challenges to and problems of contem-porary democracies, chief among them the place of young people in politics, what is problematic with political apathy, and what is understandable with political dissatisfaction. Finally, we explore some of the potential avenues that they have identified or thought of in order to improve the quality of democracy and representation in their political systems. In other words how, as a generation of new young militants and/or leaders, young party mem-bers want to change how democracy works. Throughout the chapter, the evidence provided is drawn from a mixture of the data extracted from our comparative survey, and testimonials and thoughts drawn from the series of in-depth interviews.

Politics as a profession: Old practice or new thought?

In traditional democratic theory political charges are everything but profes-sional. In Ancient Athens, public representatives and political leaders were simply randomly drawn from the list of citizens and asked to perform their representative duty for a limited period of time until a new draw was organ-ised. With direct democracy, for instance in Switzerland, citizens even vote directly on given bills through the organisation of referenda on important questions (in Switzerland, 'votations') where they can directly express their preferences without relying on the decision of any intermediary. With the reinvention of representative democracy in the 18th century, however, and its progress throughout the 19th and 20th centuries, things changed quite significantly. The notion of representative democracy relies on the idea that a 'miniature' representation of society can be elected by the citizens of a political system to take decisions in their name.

Officially, within this context, politics is a public charge and not a profes-sion, as a professionalisation of public duties, which would imply hurdles and limits to the effective ability of all citizens to have an equal chance to access power would result in an implicit form of oligarchy. Indeed, the instauration of financial compensations for elected representatives was seen as a key to prevent the tying of public charges to pre-existing wealth and, therefore, an implicit limit to this equal opportunities of access to political functions. Nevertheless, a vast literature has been devoted by political scientists to the continuous professionalisation of politics (Squire, 1997) since the beginning of the 20th century. This literature shows that financial compensations have implicitly become salaries, that the knowledge and commitment required by public duties have implied a form of necessary professional selection, and that rates of re-election and lengthy terms have implicitly resulted in many political offices, particularly at the national level, becoming de facto professional and therefore coveted by political 'workers.'

Overview

There is, therefore a tension between a democratic theory, which implies an absence of professionalisation of politics, and a practice empirically identified as increasingly professional in both its requirements and its outcomes. The fact that one of our three categories of young party members is characterised as being 'professional minded' is hardly a coincidence and highlights the potential professional 'charm' of what remains officially 'not a job.' We therefore asked our respondents across the six countries targeted by our mass survey whether or not they believe that politics is, indeed, a profession. Later in this chapter, we will also analyse respondents' answers in in-depth qualitative interviews as to whether politics *should be* a profession, a different but intimately related query.

The results are hardly surprising. On the whole, on a scale from 0 to 4 where 0 means that respondents do not agree at all that politics is a profession and 4 means that they agree strongly that it is, respondents provided an average answer of 2.60 (Table 7.1), meaning that they globally agree with the statement.

The difference is predictably quite striking when it comes to comparing the propensity of our three major types of young party members to think of politics as a profession. Professional-minded members largely embrace this perception, with an average score of 2.83, very near the 'agree to some extent' mark. By contrast, moral-minded members are far less

Table 7.1 Attitudes towards professional politics by type of members

Agree that	Moral	Social	Professional
Politics is a profession	2.50** (1.40)	2.55 (1.37)	2.83** (1.28)

**: *ANOVA test sig < 0.01; *: ANOVA sig < 0.05; N = 2919*

convinced with an average score of 2.50, exactly half way between neutral uncertainty and this moderate agreement. Social-minded members are very close to them with an average score of 2.55. In short, while moral-minded and social-minded members are only a slight majority that agree with the statement suggesting that politics is a profession, professional-minded members are quite sure that it is. We can also note that the standard deviation for the answers provided to this question is quite a bit lower for professional-minded members than for moral- and social-minded ones, suggesting a significantly more homogenous set of beliefs for professional-oriented activists than, particularly, for moral-minded ones who are more widely spread between supporters and opponents of a professionalisation theory of political functions.

The qualitative evidence derived from the mass survey provides us with important elements of further information with regard to how young party members specifically feel about the general notion of professional politics and the impression that professionalisation is indeed more and more a reality in most European democracies. Altogether, we can divide the attitudes that emerge from the in-depth interviews into a few distinct categories within the obvious dichotomy between those who think that politics is not a profession and those who think that it is. In the former category, we can differentiate between those who base their vision on non-professional politics on a militant experience and preference of politics as a hobby, and those who base it on their perception of citizens' needs and on a certain conception of democratic theory. Among those who think that politics is a profession, we can differentiate between negative, ambiguous, and positive attitudes.

The non-professional vision of politics

A significant minority of our interviewees suggested that in their opinion, politics is indeed not a profession but a hobby or a passion. A first variation of this conception is expressed by those young party members who refer to their own experience of politics quite directly and to a certain extent quite candidly, to explain how, in their view, politics is and remains a hobby. This attitude is exemplified by the few testimonies reported here:

DEPS31: I don't have the right character to be a professional politician. There's a lot of competition, sometimes bitter, from a certain level upwards.

DEPS25: I don't want to become a professional politician. You become a public personality, and it's a risky job. If you're unlucky, you lose your job security.

NOCO08: I don't see myself as a politician.

ESPS09: I want politics to continue to be a hobby, although you get more and more involved until it absorbs you completely.

FRGR16: I am partisan, but for me, politics is not professional, and parties are just here to defend ideas, it shouldn't be about the people.
UKLB07: To me politics is not a profession but a way of life.
ESCO35: Politics is vocational to me, not a profession.
ESPS39: Politics shouldn't be a profession, but it's inevitable to get more and more involved as you climb the ladder. I think it's normal to become absorbed.

By contrast to these direct personal experiences, a number of young party members believe that politics is not a profession but justify it in a more theoretical manner by a certain conception of democratic politics and representation that they hold. Here are a few examples of this other variation on the theme of non-professional politics:

HUCO05: Politics is not a profession. I think that a good politician is someone who has achieved something in his profession and then turned to politics to be able to help the people.
HUPS01: You should have a calling to be in politics. It's for special people.
HUPS03: It is a lifestyle not really a profession. There is no school that teaches you to become a politician. He has to take care and represent the interest of the majority. He has to be obsessed.
NOCO19: Politics needs to be an addition to something else. Personally I believe that the so-called political broiler who hasn't done anything else has a very limited perspective. Other experiences make you a better politician. Input from people outside the system is valuable.
ESPS26: I don't know if politics is a profession but I'd say everyone is a politician in Spain!
FRFN09: Politics should not be a profession, because it has become a job-creating machine this way, and it makes politicians too attached to their positions. It should be a hobby done with pleasure.
UKLB18: Every politician should have their professional activity outside the party.
DEPS07: Politics is an ideal, it should be guided by society's feelings but we often forget them in favour of individual desires and ambitions.
ESCO42: Politics is a passion, not a profession.
FRCM17: Many very capable people don't get in this because it is not profitable. A good politician does not have to be a professional politician but he or she has to familiarise with the subject in question.

By contrast to the first version of the amateur politics argument, supporters of this second version tend to be a little bit more prescriptive and a little bit more abstract. In many ways, they consider that politics is not a profession because it should not be so. To a certain extent, this makes them not all that dissimilar to those other young party members who believe that politics should not be a profession but has implicitly become one anyway.

Criticising the professionalisation of politics

While only a small minority of young party members believe that politics is not a profession at all, a large minority of them believe that while it has implicitly become a profession in recent years, this does not go without problems. What these 'problems' are varies a lot in the discourse of the young party members that we interviewed. Some think that it is a problem of inspiration, others of corruption, some think that it is a problem for the politicians themselves and others, instead, for citizens or for party activists. In short, while nearly 30 per cent of the young party members that we interviewed think that there is something wrong with the way politics has progressively become professionalised in Europe over the past few decades, they do not necessarily elaborate on what this wrong thing is. Below are a few interpretations of the problem of professionalised politics as perceived by the young party members in our interview sample:

ESPS42: When politicians reach the top, they become bourgeoisie and forget what they were there for!

DECO30: I don't like people who see politics as a job. I know them from my work as a civil servant: they decide something up there without knowing how things work on the ground.

DEPS34: Some professional politicians don't know what the little people need. They don't know about normal life, for example of a construction worker and his money problems.

UKPS24: With professional politicians, I miss the idealism. In politics, you should fight for your ideals.

HUCO24: Lots of professional politicians are just in it for the money. They may have had some goals at the beginning but lost those with the arrival of money and power.

DELB09: Many people in the Bundestag have only ever been politicians, and that's bad.

FRGR19: The biggest problem with professional politicians is that they become dull after a while – they lose their spark.

NOCO11: People don't respect politicians because they argue dirty rather than seriously.

ESPS47: Professional politics is a cancer.

UKLB22: Professional politics has a very strong ingredient of commitment with power that it is hard to detach from. I don't like that.

ESCO47: Politics is too professionalised already. People should not be in politics all their lives, like Zapatero and other socialist leaders.

The argument against a professionalisation of politics that is considered a fact by a majority of young party members is therefore strongly expressed from a range of different perspectives. However, the majority of young activists are more positive about it, either treating it ambiguously as a natural development with good and evil, or frankly supporting it as a necessity.

Begrudgingly – or frankly – supporting the professionalisation of politics

On the whole, a majority of young party members believe that politics is now a profession and that either, whether you want it or not, it is not such a horrible thing, or that it is quite a good thing altogether. These two attitudes are of course different. In many ways, only the in-depth qualitative interviews can allow us to partly distinguish between what is merely the acknowledgement of a situation that young party members are best placed to spot thanks to their close observation of political processes within their party, and what is a genuine enthusiasm for a system that will implicitly multiply the creation of potential 'jobs' for many of them. Once again, it is not unimportant to stress the importance of our trichotomous model of young party members with regard to the professionalisation of politics. Indeed, professional-minded young activists have reasons to directly benefit from a process, which, by contrast, could well continue to limit the power and influence of moral-minded young party members more.

A first sub-part of those young party members who acknowledge and legitimise the professionalisation of politics is thus rather unenthusiastic about it. These young activists mostly see it as a fact of life, a tendency which is here to stay, and while not necessarily a great improvement as such, is not necessarily a necessary deterioration either. The connotations of this ambiguous support vary a lot, from those who think of professionalisation as a 'necessary evil' to those, more positive, who think that politics is 'what you make of it.' Another interesting element which largely differentiates these ambiguous activists from the ones, described earlier, who think of the professionalisation of politics as a bad thing is that on the whole, many of them suggest that this process of professionalisation, however questionable in philosophical terms, really proceeds from an explicit or implicit preference of citizens. Symmetrically, some suggest that professional politicians are not the winners of this process of professionalisation, but that, instead, they do dedicate and sacrifice a lot to work for their country even when it is a 'job.' Let us now look at the details of the arguments that make a significant sub-part of young party members consider the progressive rooting of professional politics in European democracies as something one can and should accept and adapt to:

> *ESPS33*: Politics is what you make of it. If you want to make it your profession, then it is a profession.
>
> *DECO07*: Politicians who see politics as a job are a necessary evil. The problem is that they lose touch with the street.
>
> *DECO34*: I think politicians who treat their work as a job is something new, they didn't exist in the 60s and 70s. Today they are all very similar.
>
> *DELB26*: I don't want to just restate that young people just go into politics in order to have a career because it's not true of all of us.
>
> *FRGR22*: Precisely because there are professional politicians, people let them do the job, as if it was a professional cleaning business.
>
> *ESPS18*: Politics is not a profession but many people take it as such. I do realise that at a higher level it becomes a profession because it's too much work otherwise and requires full dedication.
>
> *ESCO36*: The professionalisation of politics is not without problems. Politicians have a reputation of being lazy and dishonest people. People don't know much about politics and hold the wrong conception because we only see the dark side on TV.

Next to these rather nuanced accounts, which account for about a third of the interviews that we conducted, a smaller proportion of the young activists whom we talked to are more unilaterally positive about the necessity for politics to become increasingly professional. The arguments that they develop are quite different from those mentioned by the previous group of 'accepting' militants. This time, these enthusiastic young party members suggest that the qualities that make good politicians push them to be professional. They believe that politics should not only be professionalised but should indeed be better paid as a highly qualified work, and that the sacrifices consented by professional politicians would be beyond the tolerance threshold of a vast majority of citizens. Let us look at these arguments in greater detail:

> *UKPS11*: Any politician would gain much more money in a private company than in politics, people should see that they sacrifice their lives to serve the public and society.
>
> *FRPS36*: This profession should be better viewed. Corruption and nepotism would lessen if politicians had better salaries like in Scandinavia.
>
> *DECO07*: You need to be career-conscious and be tenacious; idealism is not enough on its own. You need to be professional to make it.
>
> *DELB12*: I have nothing against professional politicians. I respect them. They have to give up a lot: time, their family ... even when they're on holiday, they have to do a lot for the party. They don't have a lot of freedom.

HUPS13: I think that if you are passionate about it, you can make a living out of politics.

NOCO29: I think power only corrupts people who are not honest to begin with.

Therefore, there remains a strong contrast between young party members who believe that politics has become professional and those who do not think so, and between those who support a professionalisation of politics and those who reprove it. All in all, a majority of 63 per cent of the young party members that we interviewed therefore believe that politics is now a profession, although they are split between a significant minority who believe that this is a bad thing, and a small majority who, on the contrary, take this to be an acceptable or a good thing. As was noted when it came to the survey results, the type of party member one talks to has a strong effect on their likeliness to be positive or negative about professionalisation. But what are the consequences of these perceptions in terms of other democratic priorities? One of the most logical implications of a disapproval of professional politics, particularly amongst those, numerous, who argued that professional political personnel lose touch with the needs and priorities of 'real people' should be the perception of a gap between the policy priorities of our elites and those of the young party members themselves. In the next section, we will precisely evaluate these policy priorities and compare them across types of members, countries, and party families.

Deconstructing the policy priorities of young party members

As explained earlier, since Miller and Stokes (1963), policy congruence has always been deemed to be the cornerstone of the process of political representation of citizens by their elites. In this sense, one would expect young party members who claim to be more in tune with citizens than their elder to use policy priorities to bring their party's agenda in line with that of voters, and to demonstrate their greater natural harmony with the everyday concerns of disengaging citizens. On the face of it, and when asked about their main priorities in general terms, we have seen that despite some differences, most young party members claim to be keenest on the policy-seeking objectives of their party. However, hypothesis *H3* claimed that when it would come to the specifics, moral members would be the most intense in their specific policy preferences. At the same time, we suggested that professional-minded members would put the least emphasis on specific policy priorities because of a desire to keep their party attractive to the electorate. Table 7.2 shows that the contrast between the two types of members is, as expected, very significant. Overall, moral-minded members tend to give higher policy importance scores than their social and professional counterparts in all areas except lowering taxes. At the same time, professional-minded members give the lowest importance scores to the same five areas and the greatest emphasis

Table 7.2   Policy priorities by type of member

Policy priority	Moral	Social	Professional
Unemployment	3.55	3.47	3.45
	(0.66)	(0.77)	(0.74)
	1	1	1
Taxes	2.25	2.34	2.48
	(1.33)	(1.25)	(1.24)
	6	6	6
Environment	3.11	2.93	2.83
	(0.87)	(0.90)	(0.95)
	3	2	2=
Europe	2.90	2.83	2.74
	(1.00)	(0.99)	(1.03)
	5	5	4
Crime	3.00	2.86	2.83
	(0.95)	(0.94)	(0.91)
	4	3	2=
Inequalities	3.12	2.84	2.62
	(1.13)	(1.22)	(1.27)
	2	4	5

$N = 2903$.

on the electorally attractive question of lowering taxes. Differences are again confirmed when it comes to the ranking of policy priorities by each type of member. Moral-minded members put inequality second out of six, and crime 4th, whilst professional-minded members put fighting crime second, and inequalities fifth. Professional-minded members are also rank European issues higher than social and moral-minded members. Finally, types of members are also characterised by different levels of disparity between their policy priorities. The difference between the top and lowest policy priority scores for moral-minded members is 1.30, but it is of 1.13 for social-minded members and only of 0.97 for professional-minded members, who obviously find it harder to decide whether any policy area should be sacrificed over another.

The same variety of policy priorities is reproduced across countries and party families. In Table 7.3, significant cross-national variations are immediately evident. In France, fighting inequalities tops the respondents' list, while in the UK it is the protection of the environment, which is deemed most essential. In line with the overall average, young party members in Spain and Hungary first and foremost want to fight unemployment, while in Norway, unemployment is no more a priority than fighting crime. Europe is given a relatively high priority in France (3rd), the environment in the UK and Hungary (1st and 2nd), and tax reductions fare better in Hungary and Norway (4th) than elsewhere.

Table 7.3 Policy priorities by country

Country	Unemployment	Environment	Crime	Inequalities	Europe	Taxes
France	3.70	3.22	2.63	3.73	3.28	1.28
	(0.72)	(1.01)	(0.90)	(0.71)	(0.78)	(1.15)
	2	4	5	1	3	6
Spain	3.70	3.28	3.29	3.66	3.04	2.10
	(0.55)	(0.78)	(0.87)	(0.71)	(0.83)	(1.17)
	1	4	3	2	5	6
Germany	3.59	2.84	2.54	2.87	2.84	2.12
	(0.71)	(0.89)	(0.95)	(1.20)	(0.98)	(1.24)
	1	3 =	5	2	3 =	6
Hungary	3.45	3.26	3.15	2.88	2.32	3.13
	(0.73)	(0.75)	(0.83)	(1.01)	(1.03)	(0.84)
	1	2	3	5	6	4
Norway	3.24	2.88	3.24	2.35	2.80	2.79
	(0.74)	(0.96)	(0.75)	(1.30)	(1.09)	(1.30)
	1 =	3	1 =	6	4	5
UK	2.95	3.20	2.85	2.95	2.53	1.83
	(0.88)	(1.02)	(0.80)	(1.11)	(1.13)	(1.28)
	2 =	1	4	2 =	5	6
ALL	*3.50*	*2.98*	*2.91*	*2.90*	*2.83*	*2.34*
	(0.72)	*(0.91)*	*(0.94)*	*(1.21)*	*(1.01)*	*(1.28)*
	1	*2*	*3*	*4*	*5*	*6*

Similar differences can be observed across party families. Reducing inequalities is an overall favourite amongst young Socialists with unemployment in second place, but crime, followed by taxes, are dominant amongst their Conservative counterparts. Young Liberals get the gold medal of post-materialism by primarily focusing on the environment, followed by inequalities (Table 7.4). It is also worth noting that altogether, Liberals are the most adverse to tax reduction (more so than young Socialists) echoing signals of an evolution towards political – rather than economic – liberalism amongst young European Liberals.

Finally, Table 7.5 looks at the results of the open-ended question on other top policy priorities. It shows that a number of 'favourites' emerge across countries and party families that attest of the importance of 'young people's topics', such as education, and their living conditions, which are spontaneously mentioned by respondents in a majority of cases. Beyond this, young party members follow the idiosyncrasies of national political debates. Access to accommodation is most often cited across the spectrum by young party members in Spain, which has experienced one of the highest levels of real estate inflation in recent years. Similarly, in Germany, the question of family is mentioned by Social Democrat and Christian Democrat young members alike, echoing the same important national debates on opposite

Table 7.4 Policy priorities by party family

Party Family	Unemployment	Environment	Crime	Inequalities	Europe	Taxes
Socialist	3.60	3.15	2.78	3.51	2.90	1.71
	(0.64)	(0.84)	(0.96)	(0.81)	(0.94)	(1.15)
	1	3	5	2	4	6
Liberal	3.49	2.67	2.52	2.06	2.67	3.00
	(0.81)	(0.88)	(0.85)	(1.33)	(1.04)	(1.04)
	1	3 =	5	6	3 =	2
Conservatives	3.31	2.80	3.34	2.16	2.78	3.20
	(0.79)	(0.97)	(0.79)	(1.15)	(1.11)	(0.88)
	2	4	1	6	5	3
ALL	*3.50*	*2.98*	*2.91*	*2.90*	*2.83*	*2.34*
	(0.72)	*(0.91)*	*(0.94)*	*(1.21)*	*(1.01)*	*(1.28)*
	1	*2*	*3*	*4*	*5*	*6*

Note: All items on a 0–4 scale. Third entry is the rank out of six pre-proposed categories.
$N = 2903$.

Table 7.5 Main other objectives by country and party family

Country	Socialist	Liberal	Conservative
France	Education Racism		
Spain	Housing Living Conditions Immigration		Housing Immigration Terrorism & Regionalism
Germany	Family Gender Equality Education	Civil Liberties Bureaucracy Education	Patriotism Family Education
Hungary	Education Youth		Education Youth Freedom
Norway	Education International Solidarity Poverty		Education Freedom
UK		Rights Freedom	

Answers to the open-ended 'other' question were pooled when very similar (e.g. education and universities, or war in Iraq and foreign policy). Answers are reported when they were spontaneously mentioned by at least three per cent of any given cell.

sides of the ideological spectrum. Overall, national patterns tend to be far more salient than party family ones, with the exception of the importance of freedom and individual rights for a number of Liberal and Conservative young party members across countries.

On the whole, it is therefore clear that beyond national and ideological divisions, young party members share a certain number of big priorities, which differentiate them from the rest, not least, when looking at the answer to the open-ended question, policy areas of particular interest to the young people in their country. This interest in young people politics, from education to accommodation and family policy, could alternatively be seen as 'corporatist' or 'representative.' As explained at the beginning of the chapter the question of how to 'correct' the failure of our political systems to represent the young be it in terms of policy, service, allocation, or symbolic responsiveness to use the categories of Eulau and Karps (1978) again is at the heart of the role that many young party members claim to want to play in their democracies. In the next section, we put the spotlight on how these young party members intend to address the young in their country and to sort out the perception many of them share that they are left out of the political game.

Addressing the young

As explained in Chapter 1, there is no doubt that across European democracies, young people increasingly feel left out of politics. Later on in this chapter, we will look at the way young party members interpret this sense of apathy in their democracies and whether they blame citizens for it or find it justified. But already, let us consider the ways in which young party members expect to use their special positions as politically involved youth to re-establish a certain linkage with young citizens in general. Overall, about 32 per cent of the young party members that we interviewed claim that they want to play a special role in the representation of young people, while the rest tend to see themselves as working equally for the benefits of all citizens.

When it comes to understanding how these young party members intend to play a special role in the linkage between the political system and young citizens, it is first important to understand how they analyse young people's disaffection. A first crucial element is that a majority of those who want to use their profile to re-establish the link between young people and politics tend to think that young people are, in fact, really interested in politics. This contrasts with the interpretation of many of the other young party members who, as we will see later in this chapter, believe that there is a certain form of apathy amongst the population in general and young people in particular. In fact, many of these wannabe young citizens' representatives tend to say that young people are, if anything, more political than ever, as well as more politicised than others. Here are a few examples of young party members holding this particular perception about the level of political interest of their contemporaries:

> *DEPS12*: Yes, young people are interested in politics. Everything is political, where you shop, the economy, the culture. You can't help but be political.
>
> *HUPS19*: The youth are interested in politics. The division of parties into two blocks is not good for the youth. There is also a problem with teachers, if they are right-wing they don't like it if you are left-wing.
>
> *UKLB01*: Young people are far more interested in politics than people think. In my area, they have an opinion about things, they watch the news, and if there is frustration, it is for us, the young people in politics, to actually get politics in tune with young voters.
>
> *ESCO38*: I think young people are getting more and more interested in politics. They do discuss the issues that affect them, at least, that is what I see among the young people that I know. But politics itself, in this country, needs another 20 years to reach maturity and catch up with the evolution of voters and society who are not all about being divided in the way that it used to be during the civil war.

Once this interest in politics of young people is established a priori instead of the competing hypothesis of apathy, the question remains of how young party members intend to play a role to 'reveal' an interest that is, so far, not transformed into actual active behaviour. The first series of answers provided by many young party members is that while young people are globally interested in politics and politicised in 'abstract' terms, they need to be brought back to *party* politics. Indeed, a number of the young activists whom we interviewed suggest that currently, young citizens overestimate the efficaciousness of other channels of participation, such as lobbying and direct action, but need to be brought back to the realm of party politics. The following few quotes summarise this feeling:

> *DECO06*: How to get young people to their first political meeting? Now that's the million dollar question.
>
> *DEPS32*: Young people are politically interested, but they are not close to parties. We need to re-educate young people.
>
> *FRPS20*: Young people are more likely to join groups such as ATTAC and Greenpeace.
>
> *DELB14*: Young people are active, just not in parties. They join organisations like ATTAC or churches, or even locally active groups. They also participate in university politics and school student groups that take part in school administration.

NOCO11: Many young people think you have to be particularly intelligent to be involved in politics – all potential members of Mensa. But that's not true. . . .

Next to this insistence on party politics, however, a larger number of young party members prefer to explain that so far parties have failed to find the right way to address young people and that they, as young – and politically active – citizens themselves can remedy this. They insist on the fact that they understand young people in a way that older adults do not. They stress the fact that bringing young citizens back to politics is their prime duty and responsibility, and they make more or less specific proposals to sort out the broken link between young people and politics. These ideas include more young representatives, focusing on issues that interest the young (perceived to include education, the environment, new technologies, Europe, etc), and changing the very vocabulary of politics. Here are a few variations on these ways in which young party members want to assume responsibility for an improved linkage and representation of young people in politics, and how they intend to succeed in bringing young people back to politics in that way:

FRPS10: I understand the young.

UKLB19: They need to see that there are things going on, actions being taken that affect them or where they can take part. We members have that responsibility.

ESPS39: I think young people are ready to participate. The problem is we haven't reached their emotional part. We have to serve as a link between young people and politics more effectively.

ESCO25: I express the problems that affect us, young people. I think I am the best placed to do that.' I make environmental campaigns fun to attract new people, and we campaigned for Europe and for the spread of new technologies.

HUPS06: Politics uses terms that young people are not familiar with. The two main parties are always fighting and throwing mud at each other, they hear the same at home.

NOCO13: The parties, they do politics *for* young people, but they do not do politics *with* them.

ESPS22: We need to address teenagers because they are going backwards in all respects. The girls don't respect themselves, they let the boys treat them roughly. The only solution is education, education, education.

FRCM05: We need more young people *in* politics to convince other young people to like politics. Right now, when the young want to change things, they go to NGOs. They don't want to be part of a group where they don't like the leaders, so they don't join the parties. This would be different if leaders were younger.

ESPS05: Every young person is by nature a rebel. This is what we can relate too, because otherwise, parties don't encourage them or include them.

DECO06: All young people talk a lot about politics nowadays [...] but they talk about issues, about what is happening. This is a great opportunity for us to take young people one step forward, to work on a better involvement of young people in the problems of our society.

FRFN21: I think young people – and people in general – are not really represented. Millions of them are being represented which creates an obvious deficit of democracy. This is what undoubtedly leads to widespread abstention.

ESCO48: Many people are worried about apathy, but I don't see much apathy. What worries me is the radicalisation of young people holding undemocratic views and being aggressive. I see a huge problem amongst the young which older people do not see. Everybody wants a degree, everybody wants a job, and there are not enough jobs for everyone with a university degree. That creates frustration, forces people to depend on their parents to survive, to live at their parents when they are adults, over 30 year old, and so they end up behaving in childish ways.

As we can see, young party members have very different interpretations of how to bring their contemporaries back to politics, and of what is missing in the discourse and actions of politicians to properly 'reach' young people and what young party members themselves can do about it. Of course, in a way, there is only a small difference between considering young citizens as interested in politics but left on the side of political life, and thinking of them as apathetic for specific reasons that could and should be remedied by politicians themselves. Similarly, while a relatively large proportion of young party members want to specifically represent the young, as we saw, many of the others may simply think that the problems the young have with politics are just not specifically applicable to the young, but also to the vast majority of citizens.

This naturally leads us to the question of apathy, and of the perception that citizens have lost touch with politics. The interpretation that citizens in general and young citizens in particular are more apathetic today than they were 30 years ago has a large resounding in the political science literature and in the mass media. Do many young party members share this impression that many citizens are apathetic? And if so, do they blame politics for losing them on the way, or do they blame what is often seen as an increasing sense of egoism and self-centredness in European societies? Let us now turn to these questions.

Dealing with apathy – the case for the defence

The vast majority of young party members who believe that the public shows signs of political apathy is almost split half and half between those who claim to approve and understand this apathy, and those, on the contrary, who tend to condemn citizens for their disinterest or perceived selfishness.

Of course, among those who say that they understand the rise of political apathy, the types of explanations that are provided vary quite a lot. First, they vary in terms of what or who is perceived as culprit for this apathy, starting from the assumption, of course, that this cause is always to be found outside of citizens. In a nutshell, some blame external factors and an environment which is more propitious to de-participation or participation through non-partisan channels, others blame the media and its way to tarnish the image of politics in the opinion, a third category blame the political system as a whole or the very way our democracies are conceived, and which is supposed to have reached its limits, and fourthly, some criticise politicians. Among this last group, two main sub-types of criticisms tend to re-occur: the first has to do with the notion of politicians who are out-of-touch with citizens, do not listen to them, and are simply power thirsty, the second, by contrast, focuses on the perceived tendency of politicians to keep on fighting and insulting each other. Let us now look at all of these types of arguments in defence of political apathy in turn.

Accusing a changing world and the alternatives to party politics

The first type of discourse that we got in the interviews from those who say that they understand citizens' tendency to become apathetic attributes this growing apathy to external elements. These interpretations include the perception that we live in a pacifying world where citizens do not have to fight for their lives or for 'big causes' anymore through politics, and, quite importantly, the notion that party politics now has to face the more appealing competition provided by a number of pressure groups, radical movements, and organised direct action. Here are a few examples from those of our interviewees who believe in this thesis that apathy is justified by a changing world and political environment:

FRPS08: Nowadays, there are fewer public objectives to fulfil or dreams to pursue, that leads to detachment.

ESPS12: Nowadays, young people are like asleep because they don't have anything big to fight for. They have more comfortable lives, the get money to go for drinks, they have mobile phones. Our parents have given us everything because they didn't want us to suffer like them. But at least, young people do vote. I have only one friend who doesn't vote.

FRGR08: We are not offering the right incentives to people to participate in politics, and many choose other social organisations. I understand them.

ESCO11: Some people – many people – think that their voice will be heard better if they get out on the streets and shout out rather than go out to vote. That's a mistake, because elections are the basis of democracy, but

it is largely the fault of past governments to have conveyed that feeling
to the people.

NOCO16: Politics is less important than it used to be, because there are so
many alternative ways to influence society. Politics as the only route to
change society has been weakened.

UKLB19: Nobody wakes up in the morning with political interests. Interest is provoked.

This first, external interpretation of the decline of citizens' political interest is one of the least dramatically exposed on the whole. The young party
members who believe in this explanation tend to think (with some exception, as for the case of the last quote) that not much can be done against a
changing world environment, and that the spontaneous appeal of pressure
groups and direct action is, by nature, very hard to fight. A particular variation on this theme of external causes of apathy has to do with those young
party members who principally blame the mass media for damaging the
image of politics and, implicitly, accelerating the exodus of citizens towards
other channels of participation. In such cases, the discourse of young party
members tends to become more aggressive and flamboyant. The following
excerpts from our in-depth interviews stress this impression that progressively, the mass media has stopped acting as a constructive counter power to
willingly try to damage the image of party politics, either to support its own
power, or to favour other alternatives to partisan activism:

ESCO11: There is a lot of disenchantment because people get an image
of politicians that doesn't correspond to the truth. They hear from the
media that politics is something bad but it isn't.

HUPS15: I think that it is undeniable that political apathy is mostly fuelled
by the media. For years, they were repressed by the party, so now, they
want their revenge on the new parties as well.

FRGRO4: Apathy is something that some big media groups have willingly generated because they think that if people don't really believe
in democracy anymore, then the big media groups will have even more
power.

Of course, journalists are a very specific brand of 'external factors' simply
because, as pointed out by the last young party member quoted above,
they may have specific incentives to see apathy increase or decrease. Indeed,
while the young French Green member's argument probably makes sense, an
equally plausible argument could be developed to suggest that when apathy
and cynicism gain ground, the media are likely to be the very next target of
citizens' criticisms after the political elite. In this sense, the media partly represent an 'external context', but partly represent an aspect of a system. Many

young party members, more generally, think that their political system as a whole is responsible for the growing apathy.

Accusing a decaying political system

The question of what constitutes the analytical 'borders' of a system is, of course, bound to always be controversial, but some young party members – in fact many of them – believe that the progress of political apathy in recent years is due to a combination of systemic factors that have depreciated politics in the eyes of citizens. These may include the ideological convergence of political parties (or a catch-all version of them, à la Kirchheimer), which thus appear too close to each other in the eyes of voters to justify their involvement, the types of power sharing agreements and corporatist politics that have led to repetitive coalitions in many European countries, or, indeed, decaying conceptions of democracy and public service or a tendency to corruption, which some authors point out in some political systems. All these elements are largely mobilised by young party members in their analysis of the causes of increasing apathy among the masses, as illustrated by the following examples:

NOCO06: There is a perception that the differences between parties is so small it doesn't matter to vote. There is no heaven and hell in Norway.

DEPS24: In general, politics is becoming farther away from normal people. I also worry about corruption in politics.

HUPS01: When young people tell me that politicians are corrupt, I tell them that corruption is everywhere, not just in politics.

FRFN15: Democracy is only a name in this country, all the elites come from the same mould. The elites are completely disconnected from the people.

ESCO13: Young people don't participate because they don't like how politics works. In many ways, I think that their lack of participation is a form of protest I think.

ESPS23: Elections sometimes create a form of apathy. People think we only remember them every four years and sometimes, I realise that they are right!

Note that some of the accusations made by a number of the young party members that we interviewed are rather serious. Some believe that democracy has been emptied of its substance (although this interpretation is almost exclusively found amongst young members of radical parties from the extreme right as well as the extreme left). Others suggest that corruption still affects politics (since saying that corruption does not only exist in politics does amount to admitting that politics is not devoid of it), and more that politics has become disconnected from the preoccupations of regular citizens in their daily lives. In this sense, we can easily see that accusations against the system almost implicitly contain, as well, some attacks on the way politicians themselves use it.

Accusing fractious politicians

Indeed, politicians themselves are, to a certain extent, a particular sub-element of the political system, and one of the core aspects that associates systemic elements and personal elements corresponding to the quality of a country's politicians has to do with the 'way' that the political debate is conceived in a given nation. Indeed, in this case, while the system may be held accountable for part of a reality of aggressive political debates and arguments, it is not doubtful that the bulk of the blame – on the part of citizens of course, but also on the part of the young party members who believe in the hypothesis that fractious and aggressive political debate causes apathy. This is indeed reflected by their discourse, and the brutality of some of the accusations formulated against politicians and a conception of politics alike may surprise some. Indeed, it is worth noting that extremely few professional-minded young party members seem to share this interpretation of what leads citizens to become apathetic. For the rest, here are some of the typical comments that young party members put together across the interviews that we conducted to explain how, why, and what citizens see of the political debate naturally drives them away from political involvement and diminishes their respect for party politics:

> *HUPS06*: They don't like politics because all they see is fighting. They don't see the meaning of it.
> *ESPS16*: Young people are not interested in politics. They vote with no enthusiasm. They turn the tv on, see two politicians insulting each other, and they turn the tv back off.
> *UKLB03*: Public debates are filled with insults and people don't feel like listening.
> *HUCO24*: Politics in the high spheres has a lot to do with insulting.
> *FRPS13*: By just confronting each other, parties weaken politics.
> *ESPS19*: Politicians are just mad!: They are throwing politics to each other's face as if it were knives that they could use to destroy each other.

It is worth noting that these attacks against politicians are often quite violent, and often stem from a number of moral-minded and even more often, social-minded young party members who also tend to be quite frontal, in the same interviews, in their attacks against those fellow young party members who they judge to be overly ambitious and divisive. The reproaches that these young party members address to politicians, however, are not limited to an aggressive style.

Accusing bad politicians

Indeed, in the eyes of some social- and moral-minded young party members, modern politicians are clearly the black sheep of parties, and bear some serious responsibility in the disaffection of European citizens for party politics and the traditional democratic process. Many young party members accuse them of an entire string of evils: they are considered to be mediocre or altogether bad, untrustworthy, likely to forget their promises, only interested in people's votes, and even to be 'idiots'!

UKLB03: I think politicians don't know how to listen to people.

FRPS15: Politicians often forget what they have promised.

ESPS08: I understand why the young distrust politicians because of the way politics is done here in Spain.

DECO12: One reason why young people aren't interested in politics is because politicians are so terrible, they're all idiots.

DECO18: There are no role models in politics anymore not like when Kohl was in power. Good people become business people, they don't go into politics.

DELB29: Lots of politicians are bad role models. In that sense, it's understandable that young people aren't interested.

NOCO21: Young people are not apathetic, they just don't trust politicians.

ESPS11: Young people perceive politicians as distant, unfair people who do not inspire trust, but they do vote anyway.

FRFN28: Because our politicians are the way they are, young people feel their vote goes to the garbage bin, so it's logical that they don't vote.

ESPS10: I understand the lack of interest of the young. Politics' bad image is justified. It is only my own high interest in high politics that makes me stay here, but personally I wouldn't believe in any politician if I wasn't here now.

FRCM09: Apathy is mostly an effect of the mistakes of our ruling class.

ESPS21: I understand disenchantment. I feel disenchanted myself sometimes. To be honest, the way politicians behave is sometimes absurd, so it is hard to say that you are in politics and have people identify you with a liar and a dishonest person who is just willing to do anything just to seek power.

UKBP05: Young people are just bored by politics. Politicians don't really address our problems and we have many.

ESCO13: I actually think that politicians have earned their bad image. Most of them seek to be close to power, to increase or maintain their money, and some get into politics to build profitable social relations. Here, I mean politicians at the top, not base line activists.

HUPS11: I think politics has degraded a lot. It is everybody's fault.

UKPS33: I think that parliamentary debates are mediocre here. There are no great speakers like before. That may well explain why.
ESCO47: I think that our political elite, here in Spain are mediocre.

Stop the shooting! In the eyes of so many young party members (but unsurprisingly, almost none amongst the professional-minded ones) politicians seem to be held wholly responsible for everything that is going wrong with politics in their country, and ultimately for growing levels of political apathy. Is it therefore the case that citizens are just the fair and innocent victims of devious power-hungry, incompetent and dishonest professional politicians who alienate them? For approximately half of the young party members that we interviewed, certainly not. Because on average, for every single young activist who claims to understand the sources of political apathy and sympathise with citizens, another one blames the same citizens for a disinterest attributed to their selfishness, self-centredness, and lack of social consciousness. Let us thus consider the 'case for the prosecution' of those young party members who simply do not believe that political apathy is caused by anyone else but citizens themselves.

Dealing with apathy – the case for the prosecution

On the whole, half of the young party members who believe in the concept of contemporary political apathy blame citizens for it. The types of reproaches thrown at our apathetic, disinterested, and cynical citizens vary as much as those addressed to politicians by other young activists. As we will see in this section, they are in turn accused of being ignorant, uninterested in anything that does not gratify them with immediate pleasure, selfish, and only interested in always complaining.

Before we look at the detail of these attacks, a first important point is that those young party members who accuse citizens of being responsible for their own lack of involvement in politics find this situation utterly worrying, and sometimes accuse citizens of endangering and even betraying democracy as such. Let us try to understand the way young party members define what is at stake with citizens' lack of involvement in politics:

DEPS07: Frustration with politics is poison and undermines democracy. It's a problem with young people.
FRCM16: I find it terrible that young people don't vote.
UKLB12: Apathy frustrates me.
ESPS06: I try to get my friends to get involved but it's useless!
ESPS13: Apathy is *en vogue*!
HUCO08: Young people's disenchantment worries me. People don't react, nothing seems to move them. Participation rates in university are unbelievably low too.

DEPS30: If you compare today's young people with those in the 60s and 70s, you have to think today's youth are apolitical, lazy and contented. They don't participate in politics and just accept decisions as given. They think individuals can't make a difference.

So apathy is abundant, it is 'en vogue', and it is worrying. In the perception of many young party members, citizens in general and young citizens in particular fail to react or get involved in anything political, and it is, largely, their fault. But how do these critical young party members explain and characterise the failure of citizens to prove worthy of their democratic systems?

Blaming ignorance

A first very frequent argument in the discourse of many young party members suggests that they consider most citizens (and indeed, often, in particular their fellow young citizens) to be completely and happily ignorant about politics. They reproach them not to understand or want to understand anything about ideology, institutions, or democracy in general. This reproach is dominantly expressed in the interviews by some young party members whom we would characterise as moral-minded. Let us look at the heart of their accusation of political illiteracy:

ESPS10: I sometimes feel that my struggle is against people's ignorance.
UKLB35: We all give opinions about everything and pretend to have all the answers, but we are all ignorant so it's a disaster!
HUPS18: I see very little capacity in young people to form their opinions and argue or defend their ideas or be critical.
DECO28: With young people, I'm shocked at how little they tend to know about politics. I mean, some people don't know who the President or the Chancellor are at the moment.
FRPS29: People don't care about politics. It is ignorance. They don't know how much fun it is to participate in politics.
NOCO21: Politics has no ideological meaning for about 90% of the nation those who know nothing about politics but politics has an enormous impact on these people in the long run.

A significant proportion of young party members perceive their fellow citizens as political ignoramini. Nine per cent refer to the lack of knowledge (and absence of desire to learn) of citizens spontaneously at one point or another in the interviews. They have the impression that this lack of knowledge is cultivated, and that citizens feel no shame about it and certainly no humility. Quite the contrary, according to many young party members, this ignorance is in fact happy, and doubled by some pure interest in shallow hedonistic pleasures and a focus on materialism and consumption.

Blaming hedonism and materialism

The notion that citizens are increasingly hedonistic and materialist is of course widely spread by parts of the mass media, and somehow, it seems to have convinced a significant proportion of young party members. They are most severe against fellow youngsters, which many of them see as only interested in 'drinking, dancing, clothing, and sex.' A number of young party members express a same concern in different ways. They seem to believe that political apathy is the result of spoilt citizens who have it all too easy. Since they do not really experience any problem, they do not feel any particular reason to get involved. In the eyes of these young activists, many citizens, and particularly young ones, are completely absorbed by their shallow problems and incapable of projecting themselves into intellectually and socially more challenging questions. Let us consider the following interview excerpts which characterise this relatively widespread impression:

ESPS19: I am worried about the young teens, 15 year old and below. They are completely indifferent to everything except drinking, dancing, clothing, and sex.

NOCO24: Life is too comfortable here in Norway. You can adopt a passive attitude.

HUPS18: There are so many other things for young people to be interested in like TV, computers etc. The youth is open for the extremes.

FRCM16: Young people aren't active in general. They take everything for granted.

UKPS35: The young seem to think that they have what they need mostly, so why bother. This is selfish and irresponsible.

DECO05: Apathy is generalised. It is not only political, and it is not only amongst the young. Young people only think of drinking and having fun nowadays. Yes, it is true that politics has a bad image at the moment, but young people don't care about their country anyway.

ESCO10: I am very worried about apathy. There is a total lack of interest in fighting for a social cause. It would be very sad if my generation only fought for better ways of having fun.

The attacks may sound severe, but it is clear that many citizens in general and young citizens in particular are thus too 'spoilt' to realise that some things are 'more important' than drinking and partying. It sounds rather paradoxical at times, because this type of discourse is also what a few young party members reproached older members to unfairly propagate in Chapter 6. However, this belief that many young citizens have the 'wrong focus' in life seems to be deeply rooted and quite widely held by many young activists. Of course, from saying that young citizens are self-centred hedonists who only care about sex, drinks, and shopping to saying that they

entirely selfish and devoid of any form of public consciousness and interest for others, there is only a small gap to bridge, and many young party
members cross that new line quite happily.

Blaming selfishness and the absence of public spirit

Indeed, there is, nearly half of young party members across all three types
(moral-, social-, and professional-minded) who seem to share the impression that a large proportion of citizens are indeed selfish, and totally lacking
a sense of public spirit and willingness to spend time, energy, and effort – if
only through thinking – for the benefit of others. These young party members blame apathy on a lack of solidarity and responsibility. In fact, many
of them, particularly in recent democracies, such as Spain and Hungary, and
even Germany, go so far as to blame citizens for betraying the efforts of their
parents and grandparents to establish or restore democracy in their country.
The accusation is quite radical, but again, corresponds to perceptions largely
diffused by some of the mass media and clearly shared by parts of the young
party members that we interviewed. We present below a few examples of the
ways in which they formulate these accusations and read the consequences
of what they perceive to be citizens' selfishness, disinterest, and absence of
solidarity and of public and civic spirit:

ESPS19: The young people who are completely disaffected are lacking
    respect for their past generations, as many in those generations died
    for us to be able to vote at all.
ESPS12: I see the youth in our country as a big mass in grey, with the
    slogan 'I don't take any stance' or 'I'm cool' written all over them. I think
    that is really selfishness, or maybe it means that I am really becoming
    an adult!
HUCO17: Young people just don't want to give up their free time for
    anything. They find politics boring too, I really don't know why.
ESCO10: When I began university, our student association was huge, and
    it had a lot of life. Now, there are fewer and fewer people joining. It is a
    pity and I am really worried about the effects that this apathy will have
    on society in the future. People are becoming increasingly selfish and
    self-centered.
DELB13: Young people don't seem to realise that it is our duty to maintain
    and strengthen democracy.
FRPS02: I just think that young people don't care about politics. In
    general, they are not interested.

Once again, young people are perceived to be even more selfish and disinterested in others and in politics than older citizens. This seems to stress
how 'different' many young party members – particularly amongst moral-
minded ones – seem to consider themselves from their peers. They see their

own involvement as one which is largely sociotropic, and as a result, the impression they hold that by contrast, many other young people are selfish and egocentric proves both painful and disillusioned. Many young party members accompanied the criticism of their peers or of citizens in general with comments about how difficult it is for them to understand this perceived selfishness. Another attitude which many young activists claim to have noticed amongst citizens and to not only disapprove but fail to understand is what they portray as a tendency to always criticise while never doing anything to sort things out.

Criticising and destroying

This, to many young party members, is the final stroke. Many of them express bewilderment, disillusion, and often anger at what they believe to be a tendency of modern citizens to always criticise things and even try to destroy systems without being willing to participate or to devote any thinking, time, or energy for others and for society. This impression is largely conveyed by a significant number of young party members across countries and party families. It is particularly vivid amongst moral-minded young activists but also, to a lesser extent, amongst professional-minded ones. Some young party members openly talk of laziness on the part of citizens, accuse them of hypocrisy and of choosing a solution of facility by always being critical but never constructive – let alone involved. The following excerpts from our in-depth interviews convey the scope of the anger and annoyance that many young party members feel towards what they do not only perceive as damaging democracy and representation but also as unfair to the 'political personnel' that they feel implicitly or explicitly part of in a variety of ways:

> NOCO08: People are lazy. They don't understand what they really want. They just complain and complain. They have given up the right to complain. It is idiocy and laziness and political ignorance.
> UKPS29: It is so easy to criticise everything, to be destructive.
> ESPS34: My friends don't care about politics. They do talk about it and criticise it but they don't do anything about it.
> FRGR05: One can't be 'apolitical' because that doesn't exist. When you complain because the subway is late, you are talking about politics. So I don't understand young people who say they are apolitical.
> ESCO06: On the whole, political apathy is huge within the young. People are generally uninterested and only speak to criticise. They criticise everything, and at the same time, they are not willing to contribute to anything.

In many ways, these criticisms are the most severe of all. Unlike those young party members who accused politicians of betraying citizens and generating apathy, the young activists who focus their criticism on those citizens who they see as perpetual critiques with no constructive will and who make no effort to improve things see these very citizens as betraying democracy. There is no doubt that by projection or by fusion, these young party members feel directly targeted by these uber critical citizens and react in consequence. Altogether, however, we have seen that young party members' perceptions of apathy are highly contrasted. Some see citizens as really interested in politics but are let down by the system, some see the system, politicians, or external factors as responsible of a growing sense of cynicism and apathy. By contrast, some think that modern citizens simply do not show that they appreciate and deserve their democracies because they are too selfish, too materialistic, too ignorant, too stupid, or too lazy to get involved and try to participate in the collective good and shared destiny of their community. One thing that young party members seem to have in common regardless of their interpretation of these ills of democracy, however, is that they do seem to agree that something needs to be done, changed, or transformed, and that currently, democracy in European countries functions in less than satisfactory ways. However, what do we know about what these young party members intend to do to change things? Do they believe that their generational contribution can be different to that of older party members and leaders? This question is the object of the last section of this chapter, which focuses on how young party members intend to 'change things.'

How young party members plan to change the world

How do young party members intend to change their world and their democracies? In the rest of the chapter, we have seen that young activist often pass severe judgement on the state of their democracy, regardless of whether they predominantly blame a system, a world, politicians, or citizens for the problems that they denounce.

Overall, when directly asked within the context of the interviews whether they think that their generation will be able to change the way politics and democracy work, 87 per cent of the over 500 people we talked to said that they think they can. When looking at the details of their suggestions, however, it remains quite clear that most of the suggestions made by young party members are not significantly different from those of more experienced politicians. Some believe that their contribution in terms of renovation will be natural because they represent 'new faces', others suggest that their main success will be to bring political parties back to the genuine preoccupations of citizens – both in terms of substance and of style, some insist on rediscovering political pedagogy and improving the communication flow between citizens and party elites. Finally, some look for the reinvention of politics in the reconstruction of their political system. Let us now look at these various options elaborated upon by young party members.

Bringing new faces into politics

Some of the young party members whom we interviewed believe that the main reason why political parties have lost touch with citizens is because they always try to recycle more of the same. To them, their contribution to the re-invention of representativeness and democracy will be quite natural because they represent new faces, a new way to talk, and globally speaking, a new image of politics. In their perception, more rejuvenation is what the people want and what they can bring if they win in their ambition to get more power from older party members. The following testimonies summarise this perception:

> *HUCO10*: Politics needs new faces, we need young educated people. That is a problem in this party, there are no educated youth in the party.
> *HUPS17*: Community space should be established, where young people can get together. They should create this community, programmes, hierarchy by themselves. If the MSzP helps in this their ideology will be turned towards the MSzP.
> *DEPS03*: We need a better exchange of views between the generations, and why should a young party member not go up against an older one from time to time?
> *ESPS28*: I don't like veteran politicians very much. I think they follow their private interests too much. They are not sincere and they are not interested in real problems. Among young people party members, this doesn't and won't happen.
> *FRGR17*: I guess I just believe that people, or society, have to be more active in politics, that's all. And our generation of activists can certainly do something about it.
> *UKLB05*: I – and most of the other young ones – would like to fight for a renovation.

Of course, the notion that rejuvenation will naturally lead to renovation is perhaps, in itself, rather optimistic. However, many of the young party members whom we talked to went further in their analysis explaining that the rejuvenation of their country's political personnel would not only result in a 'change of faces' but also in a better effort to interest citizens and talk about their true preoccupations.

Regaining citizens' interest

Indeed, the interpretation made by many young party members is that on the whole, they are better in touch with the daily preoccupations of their fellow citizens than more experienced party members and politicians. It is not always completely clear whether this perceived added proximity comes from the age of the young party members (closer to the age of the most demobilised segments of the population) or their freshness and newness in the political game (source of a lower 'bias' related to the internal preoccupations of within party politics). On the whole, however, many young party members promised that when they get the chance, they will regain the interest of their fellow citizens, convey their 'contagious' enthusiasm for public questions, and re-introduce common sense and down to earth preoccupations into the political spheres which have forgotten these values for too long. Below are some examples of the type of discourse held by those young party members who, indeed, want to embody this change of perspective and reconnection with citizens' daily preoccupations:

> *HUCO15*: We have to find things that interest them. Something that really moves them and then I think they will care more.
> *FRGRO5*: We have to be active and enthusiastic because it is contagious.
> *ESPS28*: There is a lack of common sense and perspective among politicians.
> *DECO19*: To get people interested, you have to mix parties and serious work. The mix is important, especially for the CDU, as it is has such an old-fashioned image.
> *UKLB10*: We need to show people that we're like them, normal young people.
> *DECO17*: Sometimes parents tell their children that they shouldn't join a party. We need to change this, it is their responsibility to get them interested in politics.
> *DELB20*: We could improve levels of interest by encouraging discussion of politics at home and at school.
> *ESPS25*: Young people are not apathetic, we just need to insist on their priorities. That is, for instance, they demonstrate more and more and sending ETA the message that they are sick with them.

Note that the recipes proposed by enthusiastic young party members to bring citizens' hearts back to the political sphere are quite varied. Some think that it is a question of changing the policy priorities of their parties, some think that it is a question of style, image, or lost enthusiasm, and some think that it is a question of motivating discussion at an early age. In all cases, however, motivation is what young party members promise to re-introduce in the political world.

Being pedagogical

For some, however, the problem is not so much one relating to regaining politics' place into citizens' hearts, but one of explaining it better to citizens. A small number of the young activists whom we interviewed think, indeed, that citizens' lost link with politics is due to it being poorly explained, politicians lacking pedagogy and explaining things in simple terms, and them being able to convey a sense to citizens of the purpose of public action, public good, and social justice. The following interview excerpts summarise these attitudes:

> *DELB21*: To get people to participate, you have to present them with a clear problem to solve.
>
> *ESPS33*: We need to do political pedagogy. Pedagogy means explaining to people what is going on in a clear way, even on the blackboard.
>
> *UKPS36*: I want to explain to people why we do what we do. I want to contribute in a specific way to have justice made. That's what moves me to participate in politics.
>
> *NOCO20*: I feel the responsibility of doing what young people are not willing to do.

The search for political pedagogy, and for a better sense of what politics and partisan action is all about is thus an important part of what many young party members want to change in politics. Nevertheless, relatively few would claim that politics is working perfectly well and simply misunderstood. A greater proportion of them have ideas in mind to change the way their political systems operate.

Reforming democratic political systems

In the minds of young party members, current politicians have shaped national political systems that corresponded to an 'old' conception of politics, which is no longer relevant. Consequently, many of them aim to reform political systems in line with the way in which they want to make this conception of democratic linkage evolve. Of course, few of them agree on the priorities in this architectural reform of their institutions, and most even disagree on what to keep and what to change. Altogether, the aims of young party members seem to focus on a need for more efficiency, more transparency, less fighting, and by and large, the abolition of processes of political opposition which many believe to have been inherited from entirely different contexts. Their proposed reforms vary a lot. Some think that the parties are 'too distant' and others think that they are 'too close.' Some think that their political system gives too much room for lengthy debate, others not enough for real negotiation. Often, these differences are related to the history of the nations in which young party members live (the party system often seems to be seen as too aggressively divided in Spain and Hungary, as not sufficiently differentiated in Britain and Norway, and a mix of the two in France and Germany), the party families they belong to (left-wing activists seem keener on greater differentiation, except in Norway). Below are a few ideas thrown in by various interviewees as to how they will change democratic practice in their country and their political system in general:

DELB27: The political system needs to change, more needs to be decided and there are fewer logjams.

ESPS15: We need to change the way things are. I don't like politics' obsession with votes nowadays. Anything, even a terrorist attack, is used to grab votes.

FRPS17: What are centre politics? You are either left wing or right wing. I don't understand centre parties, they are incoherent.

NOCO27: People don't see the big differences between parties. It is too woolly. One possible answer is to reduce the number of parties, especially getting rid of the small parties that draw a lot of votes but not enough to achieve representation.

DELB30: Young people have to understand that parties are necessary.

FRPS37: Right now, politics is too far away from the ordinary citizen. But what is worse is that parties are too far away from each other. The politicians of now have had to deal with the very difficult things of the transition at a time they were inexperienced, that's how they came into politics. Now, the time of transition is over.

DEPS18: Sometimes, I feel that our Youth movement is here to launder the image of the party or of high politics in general.

ESCO06: If I am given the chance, I would like to do politics differently. It would be nice to be able to have a talk with every citizen. I would invite them over the watch us work.

At stake, in the minds of many young party members is the survival of modern democracy, and this is why many find it essential to go even further, and more than reforming their political systems, think of an entire way of thinking about and doing politics.

Throughout this chapter, we have seen that young party members are often critical and even severe towards the current state of their democracies. They are split on the notion of professional politics, rather predictably – and not so differently from others – when it comes to their policy priorities, albeit with a greater focus on the policies that particularly affect young people. However, they are mostly concerned and slightly lost as to what is wrong with the current state of politics and what they can do about it. Most agree that there is a 'crisis' of politics and of democracy, regardless of their country and ideological preference, but they find it hard to agree on its cause. To some young party members, citizens in general and young people in particular are really interested in politics but have to be regained, for some they have become apathetic because of a systemic failure of democratic institutions or bad politicians, and yet for others, citizens have simply become spoilt and selfish and incapable of being interested in anything else than their own little comfort. The same split occurs when young party members are asked what they can do to bring young citizens back into politics and whether this is a priority, and a certain hesitation is noticeable when it comes to the details of how young party members intend to do politics differently.

Interestingly enough, in this context, the difference between the general and the specifics is striking. An extremely large majority of young party members believe that they can and will do politics differently and that rejuvenation will change things dramatically. However, at the same time, their propositions on how they will change things, as we have highlighted in the last section of this chapter, are far from revolutionary or greatly original. In fact, many of them simply reproduce the traditional and somehow predictable basics of politicians' discourses on democratic reinvention for the past 30 years. In this sense, we could say that for many young party members, the future of their democracies looks problematic and they know that they want to change it. But how about their own future, and what role do they specifically and individually intend to play in this forthcoming fight? This is the main object of Chapter 8, which will look at how young party members perceive their own future.

8
Young Party Members and Their Future

In Chapter 7, we have seen how young party members view the 'crisis of democracy' faced by their political systems, how they analyse their causes and symptoms, and how some of them intend and expect to make a real significant difference in the life of their contemporaries and of their nations over the coming decades. They want to re-emphasise policy areas that citizens care about but which, in their opinions, have been over-looked by political parties and incumbent politicians. They believe that they can streamline representation, improve the sense of efficacy of their con-temporaries, and rejuvenate the entire world of politics and representative democracy in Europe. However, we have also confirmed that to a certain extent, young party members continue to fuel a certain derivation of rep-resentative democracy towards a professionalisation of politics. At the same time, young party members are rather straightforward in their interpretation of what is wrong with current politics and are enthusiastic with regard to their willingness to change the way politics and representation are organ-ised across our countries, but that they are not necessarily in a position to formulate very specific solutions to the ills of European democracies, let alone agree on such a common solution as a 'new generation' of politically involved citizens. Last but not least, we have seen that in the context of the re-invention of contemporary Western democracy, young party mem-bers differ very significantly along the three prototypes of young activists that we have identified in Chapter 2: moral-minded, social-minded, and professional-minded.

This tells us something about the multiple ways in which young party members envisage the future of our democracies, but what about their own futures. Obviously, there is an enormous difference between hoping for a change in the way one's political system is organised and being willing to play a role in this forthcoming transformation. Even more obviously, the role one can play in the rejuvenation of a state's democratic structures, and representative linkages can vary a great deal, as can the types of tools and channels which one identifies to efficiently facilitate such a desired evolution over time.

Let us now consider some of the scenarios that could be envisaged by young party members willing to enact such a modernisation of representative democracy in their own country and in Europe. Firstly, it is not inconceivable at all that a young party member, disappointed by his/her experience in a political party – and we saw in Chapter 6 that many have negative things to say about the way their political party functions and is organised – could decide that they have done their duty and are not interested in taking any further part in active politics. In other words, a young party member could expect to not remain an activist in his/her party in the middle term or take any active role in any other political or quasi-political organisation. On the other hand, a young party member could be happy with his/her current participation in the active world of democratic politics and see himself/herself as continuing to play the same role – no more, no less – in the medium term. Thirdly, the same party member could instead see partisan politics as an ascending slope rather than be satisfied with the status quo and hope to progressively take further positions of responsibility within the party's organisation. Fourthly, this increasing political activism could be conceived not within the party's internal structures but, rather, within the context of electoral politics at large. After all, one of the main characteristics we attribute to professional-minded young party members in Chapter 2 is their willingness to 'work' through politics and to achieve power through it, not least via prime-elected positions. Finally, a young party member could well be willing to give more to society but decide that political parties are not necessarily the most effective channel to achieve the best results with their increasing motivation and effort. As shown by Cross and Young (2008) and as discussed in Chapter 1, in the eyes of a large number of young politically active citizens, political parties are in perpetual competition with other structures such as pressure groups and associative networks when it comes to finding the best 'location' for one's activism. In this sense, even a young citizen who has chosen to join a political party may or may not currently be, and envisage to remain or become, in the future, a member of such a pressure group.

This leaves us with a vast array of possibilities that this chapter tackles in turn. How do young party members see themselves in the near future? In the next ten years, do they believe that they will still be party members? That they will have taken positions of responsibility within their parties or will have run in competitive elections? Do they expect to be members of non-partisan political organisations such as pressure groups and political associations either, instead of, or in addition to their party membership? And how do they look at the detail of their future involvement? Beside the evidence derived from our mass survey, it is perhaps when it came to asking them questions about their perceived future that young party members became the most personal and elaborative in their answers. Our model suggests that young people join political parties to fulfil three main types of goals, and in many ways, what they aim to achieve is most obviously likely to influence how they imagine the future of their involvement and what they will need to change to their political activism. Some see themselves as future presidents and prime ministers, while others as faithful continuing grass root members, willing to keep coming to meetings without ever trying to 'lead.' Some have come to meet new friends and do not even need their political party any more once their new social networks have been constituted and developed.

Throughout this chapter, we review the findings based upon the answers to our survey question regarding how young party members imagine their political involvement and activism over the next ten years. We also look back at the details of the individual accounts gathered by the in-depth interviews that we conducted. There, young party members tell us about their dreams and imagined futures as 519 young party members across the UK, France, Germany, Spain, Norway, and Hungary opened their hearts to us with regard to the details of their desired futures.

General trends

If the trichotomous model is to be further confirmed, then nowhere will the difference between moral-, social-, and professional-minded young members be more obvious than when they are asked about the future of their political involvement. In many ways, a young party member's stance on his/her political future is possibly the most definitive confirmation of his/her approach to the meaning of party membership. In this respect, hypothesis *H5* suggests that social-minded members will be the least certain about their future, moral-minded members the most likely to intend to complement partisan involvement with non-partisan engagement, and professional-minded members the most likely to intend to run for election or seek positions of responsibility in the future. Table 8.1 illustrates how the three types

Table 8.1 Expected future of membership by type of young party member

Expected form of future involvement	Moral	Social	Professional
Party Member	2.74** (0.55)	2.64* (0.64)	2.66 (0.64)
Elected	1.61 (1.00)	1.47** (0.98)	1.98** (0.94)
Leader	1.68 (0.88)	1.52** (0.85)	1.96** (0.85)
Other	1.66** (1.16)	1.46 (1.15)	1.37** (1.13)

**: ANOVA test sig < 0.01; *: ANOVA sig < 0.05.
$N = 2904$.
Notes: Theoretical range: 0–4. Index score corresponding to each type of respondents' average self perceived likelihood that in ten years, they will (1) still be a party member, (2) will have been elected to a public office or will have run for election, (3) will have taken a position of leadership within the party, and (4) will be a member of another organisation than a political party (pressure group, union, etc).

of young activists see their future. It largely confirms the predictions of hypothesis *H5*. Within the next ten years, professional-minded members are far more likely to expect to run for elections and occupy a position of responsibility. Moral-minded members, by contrast, are far more likely to imagine becoming a member of a non-partisan organisation. As for social-minded members, they are far less convinced that their political engagement will continue altogether. Here again, an ANOVA test confirms that professional-minded members are most significantly different from the rest in all areas of their perceived future involvement, except continuing party membership.

These differences in how the three categories of young party members expect to see their political engagement develop is at the heart of our model. Thus, we proceed to test how powerful young membership types are in explaining a respondent's perceived future involvement in multivariate regression models. The results are reported in Table 8.2. Four separate Ordinary Least Squares (OLS) regressions are run for each aspect of future involvement: party membership, running for election, position of responsibility within the party, and membership of another organisation. In each regression, we include some important control variables such as gender and age, and also length of membership, whether the respondent holds an executive position, and his or her self-assessed levels of activism and efficacy. The results fully uphold hypothesis *H6*. In all four regressions, the type of membership matters in the way that was predicted, with a professional profile making a young party member significantly more likely to think that he will run for election in the next ten years and that he will occupy a position of responsibility within the party. At the same time, moral-minded members are more likely to think that they will join another organisation and also, to a lesser extent, that they will still be a party member by that time. In all four regressions, member type dummies significantly increase the explanatory power of the model, confirming that membership profiles mean and matter more than differences in length of membership, executive positions, activism and efficacy. We are not dealing with types of party members which only matter because they mediate other important membership differences, but rather of a philosophy of membership, which leads to entirely different conceptions in its own right, regardless of the other differences membership practice can make. The three member types mean different frames of mind and expectations. Amongst the significant control variables, activism, and – more marginally – efficacy impact future membership. Younger members are also more likely to think they will join other organisations and men more likely to hope to run for election or seek an executive party position in the future.

Now that we better understand the logic of the way young party members expect their future political involvement to develop, let us take a closer look at the details of the way they project themselves into the future. We will

Table 8.2 Membership type and the future of political involvement

In ten years, how likely is it that you will be…	Regression 1 Party member		Regression 2 Candidate in elections		Regression 3 Position of responsibility in party		Regression 4 Member of other organisation/union	
Professional	-0.03 (0.04)	-0.02	0.39 (0.05)	0.21**	0.35 (0.04)	0.20**	-0.10 (0.07)	0.04
Moral	0.07 (0.03)	0.06*	0.06 (0.05)	0.03	0.10 (0.04)	0.05**	0.21 (0.06)	0.10**
Time Membership	0.01 (0.01)	0.07*	0.02 (0.01)	0.06*	0.01 (0.01)	0.02	0.04 (0.01)	0.12**
Activism	0.08 (0.01)	0.15**	0.20 (0.02)	0.24**	0.18 (0.02)	0.24**	-0.11 (0.03)	-0.11**
Executive Function	0.02 (0.03)	0.02	0.19 (0.05)	0.09**	0.17 (0.05)	0.10**	0.23 (0.07)	0.10**
Efficacy	0.08 (0.01)	0.13**	0.18 (0.02)	0.17**	0.15 (0.02)	0.18**	-0.01 (0.03)	-0.01
Sex	-0.01 (0.03)	-0.00	0.19 (0.04)	0.09**	0.13 (0.04)	0.07**	-0.10 (0.06)	-0.04
Age	0.00 (0.01)	0.00	0.01 (0.01)	0.02	0.00 (0.01)	0.00	-0.04 (0.01)	-0.08**
Constant	2.17 (0.14)		0.15 (0.21)		0.35 (0.19)		2.46 (0.28)	
Adjusted R²	*0.07*		*0.24*		*0.22*		*0.04*	
Change in Adj. R²	*+0.01*		*+0.05*		*+0.04*		*+0.01*	

**: sign < 0.01, *: sig< 0.05.

$N = 2904$.

Note: For each regression, figures in the first column represent the un-standardised regression coefficient with standard error in brackets. The results in the second column represent the standardised regression coefficient. The last row of the table represents the change in the adjusted R^2 when compared to the same regression run without the professional and moral dummy variables.

examine, in turn, five main categories of young party members according to the way they envisage their future. First, there are those who think that they will soon reach the end of the road and stop participating in party politics either to become 'regular' citizens or to refocus on another channel of participation such as a pressure group or trade union instead. Second, there are those who intend to combine partisan activism with one of these alternative modes of participation at the same time. Third, there are those young party members who intend to stick to partisan activism in the foreseeable future but will, as far as they know, remain grass root members without further climbing the ladder of their partisan hierarchy. The fourth type of young activists claim to have originally thought of remaining grass root members but explain that they would now consider 'accepting' positions of leadership as well. The fifth and final group, whose discourse we will analyse, comprises of those who claim that they have, in fact, always wanted to become 'professional' young party members and still intend to do so in the near future.

The end of the road

We have seen in Chapters 6 and 7 that for many young party members, their party, as well as the current state of democracy and the political system are far from perfect and have both come with their string of occasional disillusions and disappointments. From this point of view, it is not really all that surprising to see that a small but not negligible proportion of the young activists that we have interviewed do not expect to remain members of their political party for very long.

First of all, some of them, who, consistently with the results of the survey component of our study, tend to be primarily found amongst the category of social-minded young party members, believe that they have now got what they wanted from their political involvement, and would be better off renouncing intense activism to become regular citizens once again. Those who intend to curtail ties with their parties and direct political involvement altogether give a number of reasons for it. This attitude is even more generalised amongst the members of radical parties – notably on the extreme right – who often believe that their partisan affiliation could cost them a lot professionally almost regardless of their career choices. Some intend to engage in jobs for which, they believe, a partisan affiliation would be an impediment. Others explain that they simply want to retrieve more time for their work and their personal life. Below are a few examples of the discourse of those who believe that the cost of partisan activism is too high – not least professionally – to be sustainable to them in the long term:

> DECO16: In five years, I want to be successful in my job, so my life outside of the party is more important to me.

DEPS37: You need a personal option outside of politics. I want to pursue my career not in politics.

HUPS25: I want to work in the Foreign Office, I like international affairs. I want to get to know the world, I might consider going back into politics later but not now.

FRFN13: I am at a crossroad. I need to choose: Do I want a job or do I want to keep my activism? I can't really stop my activism though, it's in me. If I see a poster and I didn't stick it myself then I almost feel guilty that I didn't. But then I need to eat like everyone else. How do I sort that one out?

FRGR12: I have landed here by taste and by luck and might reroute myself towards law.

NOCO26: I have no political ambitions because I want to work in a completely different arena (business).

UKPS36: I am keener on a 'civilian' career.

UKLB06: I want an academic career not a career in politics.

ESPS43: Since I have to leave the Socialist Youth movement next year, I have been thinking a lot about the future lately. I decided that I will abandon politics completely and that I will concentrate on my personal life and my career instead.

Another number of young party members who believe that they will completely desert the life of political activism explain that they will do so, quite pragmatically, because they have been disappointed by their involvement and the political world and that they do not think of it as a fulfilling and pleasant experience after all. Sometimes, this is said quite simply; other times, it is articulated with a certain bitterness, but either way, the criticism often fails to leave any door open for a change of mind, as illustrated by the following excerpts from our in-depth interviews:

ESCO19: On the whole, my experience disappointed me, so I don't think that I will be in politics at all in the future.

DEPS37: Politics is not all what I thought it would be, so if I were to say it now, I'd say I expect to be less involved in the future.

UKBP21: This was the only party which I thought could bring me something and I ended up quite disappointed. I will leave politics within one or two years.

FRPS18: I have done my time in the MJS and in the PS, now it's time to leave and do something else.

Note that among those who plan to leave because they were disappointed by politics, a number exclude any other form of involvement, but a few wish to try 'something else.' At times, a number of young party members who plan to put an end to their partisan activism have even more specific ideas about how they really intend to try alternative routes to give a new outlet to the political motivation and engagement that, they believe, was not quite matched by what their political party had to offer. Indeed, perhaps a sign of times, in the same way that we have seen a number of young people choose to join a pressure group rather than a political party in the first place, others who have had a taste of party politics now explicitly plan to re-orient their political work towards non-partisan organisations such as pressure groups, trade unions, or direct action groups such as ATTAC. Here are a numbers of testimonies from young party members who intend to follow these routes in the future:

> *ESPS48*: As I'm made to feel that I can't help in the party, maybe I'll become a member of a union.
>
> *ESCO15*: I don't see myself in politics in the future at all. In fact, I am already detaching myself from the party. The only question is whether I stay in politics through another type of group or if I decide that I need the time to do my own things.
>
> *FRGR18*: I have come to the conclusion that party politics is not an efficient way of investing my energy. I plan to focus on joining Greenpeace or ATTAC instead.
>
> *UKPS09*: Having tried to give everything I could to the Labour party, I came to the conclusion that I'd never be able to achieve much here. In one or two years, I plan to move on to union politics instead. I think you can make much more of a difference in people's lives there.
>
> *FRFN32*: I found the party a bit disappointing. Too much talk not much action. I plan to join some groups which are not affiliated with any party but focus on more action and less talk.

Unsurprisingly, the high level of criticism formulated by a large proportion of young party members towards their party or young party organisation leads some to come to the conclusion that it will soon be time to leave. Some plan to give up on active politics, while others will give a chance to unionism, direct action, pressure groups, or other types of unidentified organisations, which are likely to provide 'lighter' structures than political parties and more of a chance to focus on specific causes. In addition, a small proportion of the young activists interviewed about their futures are considering adding such a non-partisan involvement to a continuation of their partisan membership and activism.

The globalisation of political activism

In total, approximately 11 per cent of the young party members whom we interviewed believe that in a few years, they will not be members of their political party any more and that instead, they will either have left politics altogether or that, instead, they will have switched to another category of political organisation. By contrast, the second category of young party members whom we interviewed are planning to let their political involvement grow towards 'global activism', whereby they believe that they will not only remain members of their political party but also intend to join some other organisation, such as pressure groups, trade unions, non-governmental organisations, and direct action groups. This tendency is particularly strong amongst members of left-wing and extreme left-wing parties, especially in France, Germany, Spain, and the UK. By contrast, other groups appear to have less appeal to members of centrist, right-wing and extreme right-wing parties, and young party members from Norway and Hungary.

At times, young activists have clear ideas about which of the two will represent their 'main' affiliation, and which will be secondary; in other cases, they do not start from the assumption that one of the two will be dominant. It is worth noting that amongst those who consider evolving towards this 'global activism', professional-minded young party members are clearly dominant among those who think of joining a trade union on top of their partisan involvement, while, by contrast, moral-minded young activists are significantly more likely to think of joining a pressure group or a direct action group. Let us look at a few examples of young party members who describe their planned evolution towards global activism:

FRCM07: I can't see myself leaving the party but I'll also become active in a worker's union.

ESPS22: I would also like to be in an NGO in the future as well. I'm not sure which one yet.

UKPS32: In years to come, as well as remain active within Labour, I would like to create my own NGO.

HUPS10: I will probably continue in the party and in the workers' union.

FRGR02: I'm considering joining ATTAC in addition to my involvement in the party. I think the two are really complementary because they use combined means to achieve many of the same goals.

FRCM19: As I leave university to become employed, I will also have an interest in taking a prominent position in a union.

Altogether, however, while a small minority of young party members would like to add a second (or more) membership card to their party's, a clear majority continue to despise most non-partisan modes of activism and strictly exclude splitting their allegiance between the party and some other group, regardless of its nature. For many of them, allegiance to the party means a continued membership and maintaining one's status as a grass root member. Indeed, only four per cent of those young party members whom we interviewed believe that they will likely be members of the party and another political organisation at the same time within a few years from now.

Grass root member once, grass root member forever

By contrast, 36 per cent of the young party members whom we interviewed see their partisan future as they know their partisan present. Some of them are in fact quite virulent when presented with the possibility of progressively moving up the organisational ladder of their party to start assuming positions of responsibility and the possibility of a professional political future. Among them, we can distinguish between three categories of objections. First, a certain number of young party members refuse the possibility of an increasing involvement out of ideology and absence of sympathy for those around them who have progressively become professional politicians or permanent local leaders. Second, an equally important part do not wish to dedicate the time and energy that leadership and elected functions would take, not least because they have a clear professional future in sight (or, indeed, already have a job that they like) which they do not wish to sacrifice. Third, a smaller proportion of these faithful grass root members exclude an evolution towards leadership positions and elected functions predominantly because while they openly accept that they would not have minded 'becoming politicians', they simply do not think that this is a realistic prospect for them. Some of them believe that they do not have the background, some that they do not have the networks, some just say that they would never stand the amount of 'kissing up' which they believe is needed to 'get anywhere' in the world of party politics.

There is therefore a mixture of young party members who want to remain grass root members forever because they simply love 'plain membership', and of others who intend to remain base members because, instead, they are clearly not tempted by or do not feel within reach of the possible alternatives. Let us now consider some of the testimonies of those who, precisely plan to remain regular young party members in the future:

ESPS03: If the PSOE really values that I co-operate, then I'll be there for them in good and bad times.

UKLB29: I hope to be a simple member in 5 years from now. I don't want any position of responsibility, I hope I don't have to do this.

ESPS19: I would consider it a success to become councillor but I would prefer to contribute in the shade. I'm not modest, I just don't see myself as a politician. It makes me feel a bit odd.

DECO22: I suppose I will be less active as a party member but I'll definitely still be in the JU.

DEPS05: At a local and regional level results are more visible, so that's something I'll always do.

ESCO23: If you want to get ahead locally, you have to stay put and show stamina.

FRPS11: I see myself as a passive member – I'm realistic.

HUPS09: I don't want to be a politician. There is too much work to do in order to get anywhere.

HUPS24: I don't want to be an MP. I want to be a backstage man. I don't want to be in the front-line but be part of the apparatus.

NOCO19: I will be a member of the party for the rest of my life.

NOCO09: I do not consider myself as a politician i.e public figure. am more of an advisor-type and will seek those kind of challenges from my membership.

HUCO15: I intend to faithfully remain a party member for the rest of my life.

UKLB29: If I climb the ladder, I will feel that I have forgotten the meaning and the purpose of my affiliation.

UKBP29: I'd never become a professional politician.

ESPS11: I like it here and I want to keep militating, but I will try not to assume any responsibility because I need my free time.

ESPS12: As long as I don't get kicked out, I'll be here and in PSOE later.

FRGR08: I am and will always consider myself a base line activist.

ESPS39: I am just helping, like my parents did before me and my grandparents did before them, but I don't see myself as becoming a politician – ever!

DELB28: I really see myself doing exactly what I am doing right now in the party – just helping and being ready for anything the party might ask me to do but while remaining a simple member.

ESCO38: I try to comply with the purpose of my membership. My purpose in being here is to change little things or things that affect people in my district. I think complaining is not enough, and paradoxically, I don't think I could do as much if I took positions of responsibility or ran for elections.

FRCM17: I would not see myself becoming a leader, even locally – you end up spending more time sorting things out, supporting x and y or trying to fight z. You end up acting like a bureaucrat and you don't get a chance to really think about issues.

UKBP19: I don't think I could become a big shot in the party even if I wanted to!

Note the difference between those who glorify grass root activism and those who look at party leaders and professional politicians with extreme suspicion. In the first instance, a few young activists are clear in their discourse about the fact that they simply love being grass root activists and cannot see any reason to change either to do less or to do 'more', since the engagement of a leader is perceived to imply much time spent on internal organisation and administration and less on strict militancy. In many cases, however, other young party members use some rather terse words to describe the political perspective of those who live of politics and strictly exclude being like them in their own partisan life. They believe that they miss the point of partisan engagement and of what some young activists call 'high politics.' They are, to many young party members, the opposite of a role model and thus explicitly represent what they do not want their future to be like.

'Now that you mention it'

For many others, however, in fact 27 per cent of the people we interviewed, the situation is more ambiguous. In relative terms, they constitute the largest group of young party members who do not exclude anything. They are ready to remain grass root members for the rest of their life if need be but do not necessarily say that they do not want to become local leaders or run for elections. In fact, many of them say that they would probably enjoy it quite a bit even though they are not sure that the perspective is realistic. They are the young party members who plan to say 'why not', the ones who do not intend to fight to gain power but will not choose to refuse anything that is proposed to them. They are the young activists who say that they do not seek power but will do anything they are asked to help their party – leadership and elections included, those who always said that they wanted a normal job, but find that normal jobs are underwhelming and consider that more political involvement, if it earned them a living, would simply be more interesting. Or again, they are those who never intended to get involved within the party's hierarchy or through running for elections, but who 'got there' almost naturally, little by little, slowly realising that there is what they perceive to be a natural progression from street militancy all the way to the high spheres of power. All these hesitating, ambiguous young party members present a fascinating picture to us, because even after talking to them for hours through our in-depth interviews, it is not always clear whether they genuinely could not be bothered to run for positions of power – either within their party or through competitive elections – or if, instead, they were always ambitious deep down but end up pretending not to be, either because it 'sounds arrogant', or because they want to avoid aggressive competition, or again because they simply do not want to face the possibility of exposing their ambition openly and then losing the battle to fulfil it.

Indeed, consistently with this uncertainty regarding ambiguously phrased political ambition, these hesitating young party members express a range of different discourses and use a great diversity of tones to explain that they do not know quite yet whether they will remain baseline activists in the future or end up 'jumping in the pool' to face their political destiny as young leaders. A first declination of such a discourse claims that it is simply impossible to know what the future will reserve and that while they are not ambitious or aiming for power as such, they do 'realise' that by the nature of things, soon enough, it will be their turn. This is quite brilliantly summarised by a young party member who explained in the interview that 'it is hard to imagine the future but I am aware that we are the future.' Indeed, this first type of argument rests on the assumption that as ageing elites disappear from the scene, younger generations will soon have to replace them in all corners of partisan activism whether they want it or not. This is illustrated by the following short interview excerpts:

> HUCO13: The older ones will pass on the job to us and I think we have to be prepared for anything.
> FRPS36: It is hard to imagine the future but I am aware that we are the future.
> FRPS10: Maybe they knock on our door and offer to lead the party. You don't know.

Many others, on the other hand, privilege another alternative explanation to justify their ambiguous interpretation of how 'open' they are to the possibilities of an internal evolution within the party. They seem to willingly interpret accession to power in an ultra legitimist way as a process whereby 'the party' or its current leaders ask, invite, or request individual members to step forward and engage in further stages of partisan activism. These references to 'waiting to be invited' were surprisingly frequent in the discourse of the young party members whom we talked to. Here are a few examples provided by our interviewees across countries:

> UKPS33: If they offered me a place on the electoral list, I guess I would take the offer.
> ESPS05: Maybe I will get the offer of running for election.
> DEPS10: I could imagine doing politics professionally, but I would never put myself forward for a post but if asked, I might consider it.
> DEPS05: I think professional politics could be fun, and you earn well. So if I was asked I would be interested but I need to finish my education first.
> NOCO25: If I get an offer to run for elections, I'll say 'yes, why not?'
> ESPS03: If they offer me a place in the lists, I won't say no, but I'm not campaigning for that, and if I never make it, I won't fall into depression.
> FRFN14: I'll be ready for anything they [sic.] ask, but I would prefer to contribute in my own way, as a simple street militant.
> ESCO37: If they propose me a post, I guess that I won't be rejecting the offer, but I would do it more out of party loyalty than out of personal joy.

The connotation varies a little, with some clearly wanting to be asked to engage further, and others suggesting that they would prefer not to be. However, the global perception that is conveyed by young party members in this respect is that many consider that being 'available for anything' is in itself the nature and duty of a grass root member, and is fundamentally different from the attitude of ambitious 'professionalised' politicians who may want to ask for positions rather than be available for them.

A few of the young party members whom we spoke to go further and explain that in a way, the manners in which the party may 'need' its young activists is not only something that they understand and anticipate but something that they have already experienced. Indeed, many young militants insist on the fact that while they never intended to go for positions of responsibility within their political party or run in elections, leadership functions and electoral opportunities have, in fact, come to them. Thus, they see their openness to a more ambitious future as a simple projection of their past experience. The types of comments that young party members make on this occasion imply references to how surprised they have been at how quick their ascension on the party hierarchical ladder has been. They insist on the fact that they 'never' intended to move up within their party and have already done so, and that thus, naturally, they could not exclude similar developments to present themselves either occasionally or repeatedly. The following interview excerpts summarise this particular position:

> UKLB10: I never imagined that within only three years, I would be elected councillor in my home town. I had no interest at all in having responsibilities but I saw myself taking more and more of it.
>
> NOCO02: I have slowly progressed and assumed more responsibility step-by-step. If I get more responsibility I will take it.
>
> ESPS29: I'm mostly a councillor by chance, just because the 4 people higher than me on the list couldn't actually make it!
>
> FRCM10: I joined with the intention to be a simple member, but very rapidly, opportunities to do more proved plentiful and volunteers were lacking. This has shaped the path of my engagement.

In the cases above, young party members explain that they had no real ambition to 'be someone' within their party but that the opportunity presented itself, that they felt compelled to accept it, and, across cases, admitted to enjoy it and now consider doing more. Similarly, another sub-part of the young party members that we interviewed explain that despite them not having started to discover the realm of political leadership within their party and country and not originally intending to discover it, they have progressively become aware of a newly emerging ambition. This is an another important twist that is key to understanding the profile of these 'mildly ambitious' young activists: they are keen on reasserting that they did not join to become politicians but to make a difference in people's lives and in their country policies; however, once they found themselves there, they realised that you can do more if you take more responsibility and their ambition emerged, as exemplified in the following few testimonies, still derived from our in-depth interviews:

FRPS09: My political ambitions were not there initially but they emerged very quickly.
NOCO25: Not something I wanted when I joined but my ambitions emerged a few months ago. The parliament, maybe. But that's not a dream 17 year old should have. You have to start at the bottom.
ESPS29: I wasn't sure before, but my job is boring, so participating in politics means having a more exciting life.

There are many other variations of this discourse on the progressive discovery of one's new ambition over time. The young party members quoted above are characterised by a general tendency to switch from no political ambition to some, but others, similarly, explained that their political ambition got refined, more specific, and that they progressively learnt *how* they would not mind progressing within their political party. Some for instance, would like to specialise in a given policy area, others in a specific level of either political or partisan governance, and yet again, some are of the opinion that they want to advise front-line politicians, or even work for the party rather than seek election themselves. Altogether, we therefore have a significant proportion of young party members who are keen on saying that they do not seek progress in general and for the sake of it, but discovered, through their partisan activism, some specific 'niches' which they would like to explore in the future if given the occasion. The following represent a few examples of this attitude:

FRPS29: I would like to be a local representative, but with the sports portfolio only.
DECO24: I see myself as working for the party but not really as a politician.
ESPS12: I definitely want to become the secretary general of the local youth movement in my area, and then I will see. Maybe I will want to become secretary general at the national level.

Or alternatively, a few other young party members do not specify their ambition in terms of a particular job or function or of a given topic of participation, but, instead, have determined an 'ideal level' of future involvement. They may conceive this ideal involvement in terms of how many hours a week they would like to dedicate to their party, of how much time they want to keep for the rest, or of how many years they want to devote to intense party work before revisiting their life priorities and refocusing on their career, their family, or something else. The following excerpts reflect that sort of thinking on the part of a number of the young party members whom we interviewed:

> FRPS37: I'm really not sure yet. I intend to develop a career as a lawyer. In the future, I would like my life to be half private work and half party work.
> ESCO45: Ideally, I would like to spend eight to ten years in politics and then leave.
> UKBP04: Right now, I tend to dedicate 1–2 hours a week to the party. I'd like to do more, say up to one day a week, but I can't see myself getting more involved than that.

Nevertheless, the clear majority of the young party members who express what we could call 'qualified ambition' is rather different. They do not pre-establish which post they would like to occupy, what amount of time they would like to dedicate, or which policy area they are willing to accept. They do not provide particular dates when their ambition suddenly revealed itself, or describe an event that made them change their perspective on that matter. Instead, they admit to dreaming of experiencing the high spheres of power but without being obsessed by it. They could 'see themselves' as elected members of responsible within the party but they remain shy or uncertain about it. Their core message is: 'I'd quite like it, I'd see the point of it, if I have a chance I'll take it, but of course my first priority in the context of my political involvement was first and foremost ideological, and I have other plans if it all fails!' In short, qualified ambition often comes from the fact that many young party members who would like to gain power and climb the ladder realise that it is not easy, not certain, and not without risks and uncertainty. They are, in fact, entirely unambiguous in their desire to succeed, but more reasoned and moderate in their prediction that they will or not. They want to stress how different they are from highly ambitious young who 'only join for that', but would not mind the said 'that' themselves nonetheless. The way they express their ambition and their reserve is of course extremely diverse, but here are some of the examples we heard when interviewing young party members across the six countries:

> DECO29: I can imagine being elected, I'd like that. Angela Merkel has said, it's good to 'serve Germany' [Deutschland dienen]. It's not a natural progression from party membership to elected office, you can aim for that but it's not guaranteed by any means.

DELB17: I can imagine being a professional politician. My current post in the council could be a step in the direction of a professional post.

FRFN20: I'll have to decide if I want to make the step and become a more 'public' activist later and run for elections. Some people might not understand my membership so I don't know if I want to make my membership known right now.

UKBP14: Climbing the ladder isn't my goal really, even though I accept local responsibilities as well as new exciting national ones.

DECO33: Some people join a party without a particular ambition, just want to support it; others want to join and rise through the ranks very quickly, but they usually fail; I just want to defend my opinions and use the opportunities I get. So yes, I would let myself be elected to a post.

HUPS18: Well, I am open to anything in the future.

ESPS29: I didn't really think of running for Congress, but now that you mention it, why not?!

Altogether, a significant proportion of young party members, more than a quarter of the total, are therefore ambitious but within reason, willing to try more but, at the same time, happy to remain simple grass root activists if their further ambitions are not fulfilled. They are mostly moral-minded young party members and sometimes professional-minded ones, they often are still new within their party or young party organisation, tend to be younger than average, and often never had a chance to experience positions of responsibility as yet, or only relatively minor ones. They represent the fluid, flexible quarter of respondents who could alternatively climb the ladder or remain grass root activists forever. Their discourse and their spirit sounds highly different from that of the last category of young party members that we will look at, those who explain that they have always wanted to become politicians in the future, even though there is nothing to say that their motivation and ambition is in fact much lower than that of those more explicitly driven young party members who only see their future in the world of politics.

'I have always wanted to be a politician...'

The contingent of the most driven, ambitious, and explicitly professional-minded young party members is by no means small. In the context of our in-depth interviews, 22 per cent of the young activists who answered us explicitly admitted that they have more or less always known that they wanted to become politicians in their life. Considering that in Chapter 2, we saw that 29.8 per cent of young party members can be classified as professional-minded, we can very clearly imagine that the great majority of these professional-minded young activists fit within this highly ambitious category, and the rest, mostly among the previous group of young party members who express 'qualified ambition.'

Of course, many types of different discourses are used by those who admit that they want – and have always wanted – to become professional politicians. By and large, a first category of young party members simply explain that they want and have always wanted to become professional politicians or are already half there. By contrast, a second category of ambitious young party members explain that it is the only way to really make a difference and take one's responsibility and is, therefore, a question of coherence. A third category justify their ambition by saying that 'everybody' wants to reach the top of the political hierarchy, and that those who pretend otherwise are either hypocritical or plain liars. A fourth type of discourse comes from those who specifically want to get involved in local or regional politics. They stem from their town, city, or region, it is their place, and they want to make a difference for those who share this local implantation with them. The fifth type of justification for such deeply rooted ambition is provided by those who, on the contrary, want to go 'all the way to the top' at the national level. This shows pure ambition in a way, openly asserted by people who do not blush when admitting that for them the sky is the limit, and the higher the better. Finally, the sixth and last category of ambitious young party members, a variation on the previous kind, openly admit that they like success, like to be liked, do not want power so much for the sake of climbing steps but more because they enjoy being at the centre of things with what psychiatrists would undoubtedly consider a certain hysteric streak.

Wanting to engage in professional politics...

The first type of openly ambitious young party members explain that they have simply always wanted to become professional politicians, that this is the job they want, the work of their life, and that nothing would suit them as much as a professional political function whilst, conversely, they believe that they are more suited for the job than anyone. In a sense, this is the simplest, most technical expression of ambition. Politics is seen as entirely professional, a choice which stems from sheer taste and does not have to be either more or less justified than if these young party members were explaining to us that they really want to become hairdressers, bakers, or actors. Of course, there are a few variations in how these young activists describe and explain their ambition. Some explain that they are already professional or 'semi professional' young party members, others that they believe to be particularly suited for the job, but by and large, the underlying structure of these young militants' discourse is always the same: they like politics and see themselves as professional politicians in the future. The following few examples illustrate their perception:

UKPS28: I like politics, I want to be a politician.

FRPS34: I do see myself as a professional politician in the future.

HUPS26: I am anxious to run for elections; I want to be a professional politician.

DEPS16: My strength is not doing a standard job and routine work. I prefer having new challenges and new responsibilities constantly. I also like meeting people from different walks of life – unemployed people, functionaries. I have always wanted to be a professional politician.

FRPS22: I consider myself a 'semi-professional' politician. I am the national secretary of the MJS.

UKLB17: I know we are the next generation of politicians.

HUCO01: Sooner or later, it will be our turn.

NOCO12: I would like to become a professional politician.

ESPS40: I will definitely become a politician.

ESCO25: My dream is to have more responsibilities in the party, why not, I do see myself as a politician in the future.

NOCO18: I have run numerous times in school and university bodies and in local elections. In fact, everybody knows me since I run for elections all the time here.

Wanting to make a difference

A second variation in the mode of outright ambition consists in the explanation that a young party member's long-held ambition to become a professional politician does not derive from their taste for the job or their impression that it is the one that best fits their career. Instead, it is said to proceed from their embracing the logic of activism as one of trying to make as much of a difference as possible, and that the higher up one is within the political game, the greater the difference he or she can make. Here again, the discourse can vary in terms of its nuances and subtleties. Some explain that trying to go as far up as possible is really the duty and responsibility of a young party member. Others suggest that you need to reach office to change things, or that militants only talk whilst professional politicians – particularly when they hold executive functions – do things. Yet others explain that the logic of their ambition rests in simple coherence as they have done things, like politics and are 'not afraid of power' as one of our interviewees puts it. The gist of the argument, however, is always the same: when you want to make a difference, you need to take your responsibility, and go as high as possible, because the highest jobs provide optimal opportunities to change the life of a nation. This argument, in some of its main variations, is summarised in the interview excerpts provided below:

FRPS01: I sure would like to have more responsibilities.

UKPS26: If you want to change things, you need to be able to reach office.

DECO21: I think it is your duty to do a political job if you're asked to do it. A party is not just any club or association.

NOCO20: You join as a naive 18 year old and think you can change the world. Now I am here to get things to done.

DELB07: I have always wanted to have the power to do things and a voice that can be heard. That way I will do things for ordinary people. I will listen to them and find ways to solve their problems.

ESPS04: Well, I do know that I'll keep participating for my ideals and that I'm not afraid of being closer to power. I don't think power corrupts people; I think it all depends on the kind of person you are. I know that I won't abandon my convictions even if I'm high up on the ladder, so it does make sense to try and be as high up as possible to empower my convictions.

HUPS26: I care about politics so I'll be involved in it in the future. I like it in this party, I don't see myself militating somewhere else, and as I don't want to push my ideals into the background, I'll take my responsibilities.

ESPS07: Well, maybe one can say that I am slightly ambitious, but in any case, I aspire for more positions of responsibility in the future. I'll take the step every time the PSOE will propose me to get more involved, and I will be proposed a good enough position.

ESCO29: Being here is the only way in which you can change things, but it is much better still if you re at the top.

FRGR01: Undoubtedly, if someone asks me to take charge of an issue, I will.

Everybody wants it

The third type of openly ambitious young party members justify their desire to reach the highest possible spheres of politics by saying that, for lack of a better formulation, it is very simply 'natural.' According to them, climbing the ladder is what everybody really wants deep inside. If we remember that the quasi totality of the young activists who claim to have always dreamed of becoming career politicians belong to the category identified in Chapter 2 as professional-minded young party members, this probably makes sense. They joined a political party specifically to become professional politicians for life, and it might make sense that a few of them suspect all the other young members around them to have the same ambition whether they admit it or not. When we consider that the journey to the top is not only long, but also extremely difficult and competitive, there is no doubt that this suspicion is further fuelled by the fear that many fellow young activists who do not admit to their ambition will ultimately compete with the young militant for promotion within the party ranks when they least expect it. Indeed, while some of the people we talked to are mostly keen on justifying their ambition, others cannot help to add that they do not trust those who pretend that they are not ambitious or interested in elective functions and leadership positions. Out of the many testimonies suggesting that ambition is simply natural and the desire to become a professional politician shared by all young party members, we have chosen to highlight the few examples that follow:

> *FRPS27*: It's a natural thing after a while when you are a militant to want to have elected positions.
>
> *NOCO18*: Everybody told me that I would become a politician one day.
>
> *ESPS20*: Yes, of course I'd like to have more responsibilities than now. I'm not afraid of saying this. I think there is a lot to do and I have lots of ideas and of energy to offer.
>
> *HUPS01*: People who say they don't want positions of responsibility are either lying or they don't have anything to offer.
>
> *FRPS22*: I am suspicious of the people who say that they don't want any position at all.
>
> *UKBP17*: I guess it will be natural that I hold a position of representation in the future.

In all the examples above, young party members have provided different types of explanations for the ambition held, for as long as they can remember, to become professional politicians and go high in their party's hierarchy. The three main types of explanations that we have identified so far include (1) the notion that politics is the 'job' that young party members prefer and consider perfect for them, (2) their desire to genuinely change things in their national or local community as effectively as possible, and the belief that the higher up you are, the more you can do for your country, and (3) the certainty that ambition is natural and widely shared by all activists in general and that, in fact, those who claim not to want to become professional politicians are hypocrites or liars. However, the type of political function a militant can hope to achieve over time can significantly vary. In particular, there seem to be significant rhetoric differences in the discourses of those young party members who claim to have always wanted to become politicians at the local level, and those who claim to have always desired to become professional politicians at the national level.

Changing the life of one's community

Across Europe, local and regional politics still represent a certain conception of taking care of one's community in the eyes of many citizens. The reputation of local politics is to be closer to citizens, more hands on, more practical, and less ideological than national politics. In fact, across most European nations, local politics and local politicians benefit from a significantly better image than national politics and political personnel. In terms of territorial attachment, it is also worth noting that in almost all of the European Union member states, levels of attachment to one's town or region tend to be significantly higher than levels of attachment to one's country (Bruter, 2009). In this sense, it is not surprising that a significant minority of those young party members who hope to achieve a career in politics want to do so at the local or regional level rather than at the national one.

Obviously, the status of local and regional politics is not the same across the six countries that constitute the universe of our study. Among territorial communities, local councils are extremely powerful in France, Norway, and Spain, regional or federate units of government in Germany and Spain as well as in Scotland, Wales, and Northern Ireland, and both local and regional institutions are rather weak in Hungary and England. Similarly, local politics in Europe often tends to be far more stable than national party competition. Thus, whilst the members of all major parties may hope that their political formation will possibly end up gaining national power at one point or another in the medium term, the equation is more complex at the local level. A young Conservative would be most unlikely to see his/her party hold a majority in the Scottish Parliament or Welsh Assembly or the Catalan or Basque Cortes in the near future in exactly the same way as a young Socialist would be unlikely to see his/her party manage to conquer the Nice city council or the Land of Bavaria. Majorities tend to be more stable and thus more predictable, and to a certain extent, co-optation can be a relatively sure way of making one's entry into an executive political job if one belongs to the 'right' party in a given region, town or city.

From that point of view, it is undoubtedly unsurprising that a few of the young party members who claim that they have always wanted to become professional politicians in the future have no hesitation about wanting to become local politicians and nothing else. They explain that to them, this is the level of governance where they believe that they will feel at ease, will be able to make a real difference in the life of citizens, and have clear practical ideas about what they want to achieve once in power. The motivation is sometimes social as well, and some young party members have a clear idea about what it will feel like to be a local leader, almost a modern democratic aristocrat. Below are a few examples of these spontaneous self-assured testimonials by those who have never dreamt of becoming anything else than a local mayor, politician, or councillor, liked by his/her fellow citizens, close to them, and dedicated to making their lives happier and their governance better:

> DECO23: I'd like to work in the regional parliament, that's where I see my professional future.
> HUPS04: Everybody has ambitions. I would like to be a local representative.
> ESCO27: I have always wanted to become Mayor of my home town, and I can see it happening after the next elections. I think I am the ideal person for the job.

ESPS36: I would love being an MP in Madrid but I would even prefer being Mayor to be closer to the people and feel or suffer from their problems myself.

Faster, higher, stronger...

In many ways the desired future of those young party members who want to become local or regional high-ranking politicians almost sound like a childhood dream. They know the place, have strong beliefs about what works and does not with it, and have a clear direct perception of how citizens view their Mayor or their councillor, what it means in terms of respect, prestige, and visibility. In many ways, this contrasts with the imagined perceptions held by those who have 'always' – or at the very least long – dreamt of becoming leading national politicians. It would be absurd to claim that the projections of those young activists who want to become local politicians are not highly and obviously fantasmatic, but these fantasies are more likely to be fuelled by direct images than by the even more abstract imagination one may hold of top national politics.

Yet, amongst the many young party members who clearly aim at and hope to become professional politicians, almost three times more hope for top national positions as compared to top local or regional functions. MP, Minister, Prime Minister, or President, such remain the most coveted prizes of political activism in the eyes of the most ambitious of young party members. In fact, many young activists in the interviews did not even speak of specific functions that they would like to achieve, but simply of going as far and as high as possible. What young party members imagine their life as a top level politician to resemble varies quite a lot. Some see themselves as loved by citizens and others as feared, some explain that they will fight other politicians and will be extremely radical, while others expect to sort out disagreements and bring consensus all round. At the same time, some imagine reaching the top levels of their country's political life as a reward, others as a honour, and yet further young activists see it as their 'making history.' Out of such a diversity of equally abstract images and dreams of a glorious future, the following few interview excerpts barely give a sketchy account of a range of perceptions that some young party members were in fact quite willing to talk about for hours:

NOCO36: I want to become leader of UH – go all the way to the top maybe the minister of justice or foreign affairs.
ESPS40: I have always wanted to be in Moncloa [Spanish Prime Minister's residence] in the future.
UKPS39: I do see myself as an MP.
UKLB28: I'd like to contribute with education policies in a future government.

ESPS44: I would love to be an MP for Madrid. I would never stop shouting out my ideas and fighting other Congressmen! I would be very radical, this is what I would like!

ESPS37: I would really like to be a Member of Parliament in the National Cortes. I would prefer to be a member of the opposition though, to fight more!

ESCO07: Since your first ambition cannot be to become Spanish 'President', I hope to be councillor, which is quite probable, and then, when I get the chance, I would also like to be MP, and then, going little by little, Minister, etc.

DECO36: I can imagine being a full-time politician, for example as a Member of Parliament.

NOCO35: I would like to run for election. Not necessarily here in Norway but maybe in the US.

HUPS13: I'd say I am playing politics right now! Being MP would be a great encouragement; I'd see it as the obvious reward, no doubt.

FRFN08: I'll succeed where Jean-Marie Le Pen barely failed!

In fact, when it comes to imagining what it must be like to be 'at the top' of one's country political life, the imagination of the young party members whom we interviewed is almost endless. The level of detail in many of the accounts that we received is almost hard to believe.

In a few cases, however, young party members go even further and instead of simply focusing on the 'level' of their ambition or describing the life which they hope to enjoy once they fulfil their dream, many specifically told us what it is, in power, that excites them so much and grabs their hearts and minds when it comes to projecting themselves into their desired professional political future. Clearly, many imagine and crave the feeling of being centre stage in one of very many forms. For some, thinking of climbing the political ladder to get to the top means imagining victory, and how sweet and wonderful it will be. Many young party members imagine their pride or the pride of their parents, family, and friends. At the same time, a significant number of others recount the dream of their being so loved that people will stop speaking for them, start crying for them, feel their hearts beat for them.

What to make of these testimonials is hard to imagine. Undoubtedly, some readers will find the young party members communicating their hidden dreams touching and moving. Others will consider them somewhere between vain and megalomaniac. Let us bear in mind, however, that the important thing here is not to decide whether young party members' dreams are great or horrid, realistic or not, childish or mature. The most interesting aspect of all, rather, is to understand, very simply, what these dreams are, what drives young party members to be so focused, ambitious, and hopeful for their professional political future. Because these images represent the fragile dreams of as many individuals' hoped futures, it is almost absurd to even try and summarise or synthesise them. To an extent, no two such accounts are exactly alike. However, the following excerpts from the in-depth interviews give at least a very sketchy sense of the range and types of images, hopes, and dreams that haunt our highly ambitious young party members' minds when they imagine their future as a successful top level politician a few years from now:

ESPS38: During elections I handed pamphlets and stuck posters with my picture on them!

DECO23: I think there is a natural progression within the JU, but to get somewhere in the CDU you have to know the right people and do the right deals.

FRFN15: When I attended Jean Marie Le Pen's campaign meeting, I saw hundreds of people crying with emotion. They will cry for me, that's what I want!

ESCO07: Winning elections in university was a huge satisfaction. I want to experience this satisfaction again at other levels.

UKBP12: I know that victory will feel overwhelming. That's what I want to experience.

HUPS01: I used to want to be Primer Minister, but everybody always criticises the Prime Minister and love the President, so now I know I want to become the Hungarian President. I love being loved!

UKPS08: I know how I feel when I win. I just love winning. But I can barely start to imagine how wonderful it will feel to actually win an election! I know I'll love it even more!!

FRPS21: The whole Parliament will be silent and listen to my speech.

HUCO06: I imagine my parents and grand parents being so moved and proud that they will cry on and on. This will be the sweetest feeling ever.

FRGR20: I can see myself leading thousands of people in demonstrations or in rallies, everyone cheering and getting excited as I speak.

FRCM25: I have heard that successful politicians feature in prime position in the fantasies of many girls as the ultimate sex symbols!

This quasi endless list of projective dreams is fascinating to the extent that it gives us a glimpse of what politics, success, and power tend to mean for many professional-minded young party members. By listening to their perceptions of their future, we can understand much better how they view the relationship between leaders and militants, politicians and citizens, winners and losers. The dimension of competitiveness in politics, the concept of political race, take a dimension that very few young party members spontaneously talk about and which, in fact, many claim to dislike, despise, and fail to understand. In this case, these accounts of young militants' dreamed futures give an unprecedented sense of the tension, excitement, and stimulation they receive from political competition and make it extremely difficult to genuinely believe that most young party members genuinely disapprove of their parties' perceived obsession with elections and their leaders apparent lack of restraint when it comes to fighting their political opponents.

Table 8.3 summarises the patterns that we derived from the in-depth interviews whereby young party members developed their dreams about their future. It reinforces the findings based on the quantitative part of the research. Beyond giving us a sense of the relative importance of groups of young party members according to their imagined future, the table gives us further details as to how the three types of young party members that we identified in Chapter 2 see their future. We see that future expectations, even more than present perceptions, radicalise the divergence between social-minded members who are uncertain about their future engagement, moral-minded members who thrive in grass root activism, and professional-minded members who systematically consider or strongly desire a professional political future.

Throughout this chapter, we have approached the fascinating question of how young party members imagine their future. We have seen what their hopes, dreams, and expectations are. We have seen that a relatively small proportion of young party members – about one in ten – expect to leave active partisan politics altogether within a few years, either because the toll

Table 8.3   Summary of young party members' future plans

Expected future plan in ten years from now	%	Likeliness Moral-minded	Likeliness Social-minded	Likeliness Professional-minded
Will leave the party (end of activism or new outlet)	11	−	++	−−
Will remain in the party + join another organisation	4	−/+	+	−
Will remain a grass root member forever	36	++	−	−−
Might become a leader if given a chance	27	+	−−	+
Has always wanted to become a leader	22	−−	−−	++

Note: Percentages and likeliness codes are based on the interviews. Likeliness codes range from −− (least likely) to ++ (most likely).

on their private and professional life is too high, or because they have been disappointed – sometimes gutted – with politics, to the point that they are done with parties. Most of them are either social-minded or moral-minded young activists. An even smaller proportion plan to 'cross the Rubicon' and betray party politics in favour of the other forms of activism – from pressure groups to direct action – that attract so many other young citizens to the despair of many party militants.

The bulk of the young party members whom we surveyed and interviewed, however, think that their political engagement will last forever. A large third of them believe that grass root activism will remain their way to get involved in active politics and will continue to provide them with the life balance, impression of intellectual stimulation and moral fulfilment that they crave through their membership. They mostly tend to be found amongst the category of moral-minded young party members.

Finally, almost half of the young party members we talked to in our interviews – and over half of those who answered our survey – either consider moving on to political leadership or are absolutely certain and positive that they will indeed seek positions of responsibility within their party or seek representative or executive positions through competitive elections. These highly motivated young party members represent the quasi totality of professional-minded young party members and, when it comes to the more ambiguously ambitious of them, an important minority of moral-minded activists. The motivations, stories, and dreams of these young people who want to become professional politicians vary as much as they tend to be rather specific for each individual. First of all, there is a clear distinction between those who can only see themselves as local or regional leaders in the future, and those who, instead can only imagine themselves as national leaders, climbing as high as they will possibly and eventually manage.

The arguments of those who crave a career in politics come in an infinite variety of shades and nuances, from those who think that the ambition to reach the pinnacle of democratic politics is a dream shared by everyone – or at least with all their fellow young party members – to those who already imagine what it will be like to win elections, to see their name known by millions of citizens, and to have parents, friends, and family (or indeed potential boyfriends and girlfriends!) proud and impressed. Finally, some believe that they will change the world, make history, revolutionise things for their fellow citizens and generations to come. Most important of all, however, this insight into the expected and perceived future of young party members gives us an unprecedented sense and a far more refined understanding of what motivates them today, how they hope that they will change the life of others and how they hope that politics will change their life. All in all, these stories of how young activists see their future brings us back to one of the primary original goals of this book: to understand what goes through the hearts and minds of tomorrow's leaders and what awaits our democracies in their future. In the next – and last – chapter, we will turn back and try to understand what we have learnt about the future of our democracies, and how young party members intend to – and indeed are likely to – shape it in years, decades, and conceivably centuries to come.

9
The Future of Our Democracies?

A new model of young party membership

The young party members whom we surveyed and interviewed have taken us on an original and fascinating journey in their hearts and minds: Why and how do they join? What do they do? How does their membership change their life? How do they evaluate their party, and their democracy? And finally, what do they imagine, hope, and dream that their future will be like?

At the heart of the picture that our book has depicted, we have shown that young party members fall into three categories identified by a specific dominant membership drive: moral, social, or professional. Each type of young party member is characterised by different patterns of perceptions, attitudes, activities, and preferences, as well as hopes and expectations about their own future. In particular, the small group of professional-minded members behave like 'mini-leaders' who already consciously prepare what they hope will be their professional political future. The other two types of members also have their own 'story.'

First, a majority of 39.7 per cent of young members join a political party to answer a sense of moral duty. They are the most radical of young activists, the most likely to engage in confrontational forms of participation, and the most likely to consider joining non-partisan organisations. They do not really consider politics a profession and they see their future as 'activists', not 'politicians'. Moral-minded members are motivated and dedicated, potentially 'troublesome' because of their radicalism, but they are not really tempted by serious executive functions or a professional political future.

The second type of young partisans are social minded. They represent 34.2 per cent of our total sample across six countries. They join a party to fulfil their social needs, make new like-minded friends, engage in interesting discussions, and meet stimulating people. They are the least active of all members, the least efficacious, the most critical of the party's organisation, and the least dedicated when it comes to devoting time and energy to its cause. The loyalty of social-minded members is limited and their critical sense towards the party makes them doubt the long-term future of their partisan commitment.

The final type – the least common as it represents only 26 per cent of our total sample– is that of professional-minded young party members. They join political parties with a distinct intention to tie their professional future to politics. Some will fail to gain the confidence of their party or will change their mind later, but some will undoubtedly succeed and progressively become tomorrow's leaders. They want to become politicians, run for election, and quickly access positions of responsibility. They already behave – and, to a certain extent, seem to 'think' – like young leaders in the making. Professional-minded members try to remain close to the median voter, and care about their party's vote-seeking ability and their own office-seeking objectives. They accept to be highly involved in the electoral activities of the party, but shy away from radical modes of participation, they are efficacious and always supportive of the party line, but can be critical of older members with their contrasting perceptions of politics. Professional-minded young party members want to be at the heart of politics. They use a different approach, a different discourse, and abide by the intricate rules and habits of the party and 'political class' they are – and want to be – part of. They believe in professional politics, and their ambition, relationship to the party, and sense of what does not work within it are influenced by their perceptions of what befits a young leader.

The gap between the preferences of each type of young party member and what the literature tells us of their elder counterparts may explain some of the recurrent tensions between a dominant but ageing general party membership, and a small, dynamic segment of young members, which many older members perceive as arrogant and threatening. Young party members tend to primarily engage in intellectual rather than 'physical' partisan activities, and most moral-and social-minded members seem less keen on electoral politics and internal party politics than what we know of the majority of older party members. Next to them, professional-minded members, whilst more dedicated to canvassing duties, make no mystery of wanting to use the party to serve their own professional ambitions and to ultimately want to lead it, thus bypassing grass root members who may have been activists for decades. These professional-minded members are ambitious and demanding, but at the same time necessary to the party. Not only do they represent a dynamic and motivated potential 'main d'oeuvre', but they can improve and rejuvenate the party's image. They could address and potentially convince segments of the population that are least interested in politics, least likely to place their confidence in parties, and hardest to reach. In short, no modern day European party can refuse the luxury of including a few refreshing young faces amongst their most visible politicians, regardless of whether other party members think of them as ambitious, arrogant, and self-serving. These 'leaders of tomorrow', indispensable to major European political parties to change their image as declining, out-of-touch, and 'un-cool' democratic instruments, have very specific ideas about why and how to change politics. They feel different from older members and non-professional young members alike. Ultimately, whilst they already choose to behave like 'young leaders', there is no doubt that they also understand that their future success requires their 'young leadership' style to look and sound different from the conceptions of the politicians they ultimately want to replace.

What have we learnt?

This typology of young party members, developed, explained, and tested in Chapter 2 has allowed us to get a new perspective on our various findings on their background, activism, new life, perceptions of party politics and democracy, and, ultimately on how they see their future and that of our democracies. Let us first remind ourselves of some of the main things that we have learnt about young party members.

After the validation of our trichotomy, the first aspect of our investigation had to do with how some young citizens decide to join a political party to become young militants. In Chapter 3, we looked at the core channels of engagement – with the overwhelming dominance of the family path followed by the influence of friends and a process of organisational contagion whereby some young people arrive into party politics from union or associational organisations. We look at the parallel importance of the imitation of role models and opposition to those anti-heroes whom the future young party members despise. We have also seen that young activists are split between those who have always wanted to join a party and often prove to be professional-minded young party members, and those who, quite often joined following one particular catalytic moment when their political vocation was 'revealed' to them.

In Chapter 4, we looked at the reality of the activism of young party membership. We studied the level of involvement of young activists, which varies quite significantly between social-, moral-, and professional-minded young party members. We also saw that when it comes to the 'nitty gritty' of their activism, young militants differ radically in their commitment. A core of about 10 per cent are hyper active and dedicate time to their party almost every day, and about 25 per cent every week. Next to this large third of very active young party members, 40 per cent remain regular monthly participants, and approximately 25 per cent are barely occasional visitors whom the party cannot really count on. We also looked at the way young party members share their time between electoral, aggressive, pedagogical, and internal activities, and saw how social-, moral-, and professional-minded young militants tend to focus on very different types of duties and modes of action.

In Chapter 5, we moved on to evaluate how partisan activism can durably 'change the lives' of the young party members whom we surveyed and interviewed, and in particular which key events and moments are perceived as directly eye opening by these young militants. We discovered what young party members like and dislike as part of their activism, and how this varies across the three groups of young party members, whether they be moral, social, or professional minded. We also saw that two 'moments' in the life of a young party member can be extremely charged symbolically: their first experience of participating in an electoral campaign on the one hand, and, for those young party members who access leadership positions, this journey to political leadership on the other hand. We also saw that a greater proportion of young party members experience these positions of responsibility than we would expect of regular party members and the consequences that this can have. Finally, we questioned the impact of party membership on young party members' social life, including their networks of friends, and how and why some young activists may feel different, marginalised, or inadequate.

Chapter 6 was dedicated to the question of how young party members perceive their party and its internal structures and internal democracy. We saw that young party members often tend to feel disappointed by their (lack of) ability to change things and be heard within their party, but also that professional-minded young activists tend to be far more efficacious than their social- and moral-minded counterparts. We also asked young party members how they perceive their relationship with older members and saw that many – particularly, this time, amongst professional-minded young activists – tend to feel rather inhibited or at the very least under-evaluated by older members, even though few think of this as a major problem. We looked at the way in which some young party members find a new family in their party and what aspects of it they praise. By contrast, we studied how different young militants tend to be critical of the atmosphere of tension and rivalry within their organisation and young party groups, and of fellow members either because they are seen as unduly ambitious, driven, and self centred, or because they are perceived as incompetent, or because their discussions and debates can last forever and lead to compromises which many partisans see as counter productive.

Chapter 7 saw us move from the realm of partisan introspection to young party members' evaluations of democracy and their respective political systems as a whole. We saw what the policy priorities of young activists are, and how they vary by country and party family. We established that these young militants often wish to primarily devote themselves to restoring a privileged democratic linkage with fellow young citizens. Crucially for our investigation on the future of our democracies, we listened to young party members' ideas, perceptions, and suggestions on the topic of political apathy. We compared the views of those who believe that citizens are really interested in politics but not 'caught' by parties in the present period, and those who believe in political apathy and either attribute it to external factors, proponents of non-partisan participation, the political system, parties, politicians, or citizens themselves. In short, we looked at how young party members read what they often believe to be a current crisis of democracy and representation. We considered the solutions that they hope to put in place, and more generally, how and why they believe that they *do* represent the future of our democracy and will 'change' the way politics are conducted and organised in their country.

Finally, in Chapter 8, we investigated how young party members tend to see their future. We saw that a small proportion of them – approximately 11 per cent – intend to put an end to their partisan involvement, either to drop out of active politics altogether or to 'betray' the partisan channel of political communication in favour of union politics, pressure groups, or some other organised form of direct action. We saw that a very small proportion – approximately 4 per cent of our interviewees, trust that such parallel channels of participation will be combined with continued party activism in their own political future. We then showed that over a third of young party members intend to remain grass root activists for the rest of their life, and why they do not wish to progress in the hierarchy of their own party. By contrast, we found that nearly half of young party members either would consider, or are absolutely keen on entering the world of professional politics, undertaking positions of leadership and responsibility within their party, or elected positions at the local, regional, or national level. We considered the different profiles of the young party members who imagine their future in such different ways, stressing among other things, the unique characteristics of the category constituted by professional-minded young activists.

This cluster of quantitative and qualitative findings provides us with a complex picture of what goes on in the hearts and minds of young activists in 15 different parties from all ideological families in the UK, Germany, France, Spain, Norway, and Hungary. However, these complex results also raise a number essential new questions and paint a series of crucial portraits when it comes to understanding what young party members are really like, where they come from, what they want, what they think, and what role they are likely to play over time. Through these portraits, we can get an unprecedented insight into how young party members intend to shape the future of our democracies, and, to a certain extent, how they will probably do so. Let us now consider the consequences of the many findings that we have derived from these numerous survey answers and interviews, and stress some of the challenges they raise when it comes to understanding, capturing, and modelling the future of our democracies.

Table 9.1 summarises some of our main findings and how our trichotomous model of young party membership proved to structure young activists'
perceptions, preferences, dislikes, and dreams.

The rest of this chapter is therefore dedicated to a short series of spotlights
on particularly paradoxical, puzzling, or enlightening aspects of our findings

Table 9.1 Summary of some key findings on the divergence of moral-, social-, and
professional-minded young party members

Chapter	Moral-minded	Social-minded	Professional-minded
Ch2: Nature & Proportions	Driven by ideology, desire to give meaning to one's life and to be a good citizen.	Driven by desire to meet like-minded people, interesting discussions, people, and fun factor.	Driven by attraction to power and honours, desire to become a professional politician.
	39.7% of total.	34.2% of total.	26% of total.
Ch3: Paths to Membership	Paths: Dominance of family path followed by friends and organisational contagion. Processes: Imitation (dominant) or opposition. Catalyst: Often a catalytic moment, in other cases slow process of engagement. Usually directly to the 'right' party, but occasionally after some hesitation.		
Ch4: Activism & Activities	Intermediary.	Least active.	Most active.
	Strongest on radical modes of activism (demonstrate, fight other parties) and on convincing.	Least involved in almost every mode of participation	Strongest in electoral modes of participation (posters, flyers) and on debates. Least involved in demonstrations.
	Overall frequency: 10% daily party-holics, 25% weekly activists, 40% regular monthly visitors, 25% occasional (less than monthly)		
Ch5: Changing Life	Mostly enjoy debating, ideological stimulation, micro-level democracy, and rebellion.	Mostly enjoy fun factor and feeling of inclusiveness.	Mostly enjoy debates, meeting politicians, internal leadership, sense of power, & networking.
	Impact on social life average. Dominant mode of coping: accommodation.	Impact on social life minimal. Dominant mode of coping: fusion.	High impact on social life. Dominant mode of coping: displacement.

	Most likely to feel marginalised, misunderstood, or depressed	Least likely to feel marginalised.	Most likely to sacrifice a lot of time but unlikely to feel marginalised.
Ch6: Perceptions of Party	Highly policy & vote-seeking.	Policy seeking only.	Most highly office seeking + vote & policy.
	Most likely to feel that leaders are out of tune with members (May law) and to think that membership is interesting, teaches them new things	Least efficacious, least negative towards older members, least convinced they have learnt through membership.	Most efficacious, most likely to think that leaders & members think alike, most negative towards older members. Least likely to find discussions interesting
Ch7: Perceptions of Democracy	Often disapprove of professional politics.	Least clear on professional politics.	Tend to approve of professional politics.
	Often think that citizens are not apathetic or are turned off by politicians. Most likely to want to change institutional structure & feel in touch with citizens.	Tend to think of apathy as somewhat natural. Feel in touch with fellow citizens. Most likely to want to primarily engage with the young.	Often blame citizens' apathy on citizens themselves. Think they criticise & politicians have a rough deal. Most likely to claim that they will change how politics is done.
Ch8: Imagined Future	Most likely to want to remain grass root members or possibly go for low level positions of responsibility if asked to. Most likely to consider other outlets.	Least certain about the future of their engagement. Most likely to consider dropping out of active politics.	Most likely to want a professional political future and/or positions of responsibility. Often claim to have always wanted it.

which, combined, can provide us with some original tools to solve the jigsaw that constitutes the question of how young party members will become, in a few years, the new established leaders of our democracies. We highlight three crucial elements of tension or paradoxes, which have progressively emerged throughout our investigation: a sense of frustration and marginalisation, a belief of representativeness, and an element of pride and righteousness. We will examine how they emerge, how they reinforce the contrast between social-, moral-, and professional-minded young party members, and how they are likely to affect the role young activists want to play in shaping the future of our democracies.

The blues of the young party member

Based on our findings, the first thing, which, we believe, one needs to understand to get a sense of how young activists feel and how they are likely to shape the future of our democratic political systems is what one could call, for lack of a better word, the blues of the young party member.

Throughout the book, we have discovered that despite often being enthusiastic about their engagement itself, young party members are not necessarily very happy about much. Chapter after chapter, we have seen that there is not much young party members approve of in the world they evolve in. Most young party members are very critical of their party – its lack of efficacy, and its occasionally tense relationship between young and older members. Most are unhappy with some of their fellow party members – be it the ambitious ones, the lazy ones, or those who create incessant divisions and rivalries. At the same time, they are not much happier about their political systems. Many are annoyed at other groups – from ATTAC to trade unions through to civic groups – for 'stealing' citizens' attention and capacity for participation. Even more are angry at the media for damaging the image of politics, and nearly as many resent politicians for doing just the same with what they see as their aggressive behaviour, incessant arguments, and incapacity to listen to citizens. At the same time, however, hundreds of the young party members whom we surveyed and interviewed similarly see the same citizens as selfish, lacking social and civic consciousness, and by and large, incapable of focusing on anything else than the hedonistic and materialistic pleasures of their idle lives rather than the greater problems of their fellow citizens and humanity. What is more, their blues and frustration are often related to perceptions that their very interest in the affairs and problems of the polity earns them nothing else than misunderstanding, suspicion, and accusations of being weird, power-driven, dishonest, cut off from reality, in short that they become a target for hatred either within their family and group of friends, or within society as a whole!

In short, young party members cannot imagine doing anything else than what they are doing now, except, perhaps, doing even more of it, but nothing seems to work to their taste either within or outside of their party. In fact, even over and beyond the many problems that we have already reported, young party members report an almost endless series of complaints, disapprovals, and disappointments. Many of them feel grumpy, melancholic, and many of them have the blues. For example, many of them feel discriminated against within their party. Typically, for instance, this can be perceived to be because of their gender, regardless of whether they are men or women:

FRFN08: Being in politics is twice harder for women.

FRPS32: Parity has done a lot of harm to young male militants. Not that I regret it, but old men have been replaced by young women.

UKPS20: In a party that is still vastly dominated by men, you face a lot of unfair hurdles when you are a woman!

UKLB24: To save appearance and give an impression of balance, the party will often choose an ok woman rather than a brighter man.

HUCO25: I sometimes feel that however bright and competent a woman, she will never make it to the top.

HUPS08: I sometimes feel that any woman who opens the door of the party headquarters will be offered to run for some election within two months!

ESPS33: It's sometimes difficult to work the gender issue – many women feel frustrated because they are always in a minority and whenever you are interested in any girl in the party, you run a risk of being accused of harassment.

ESCO23: The relationship between men and women within the party is sometimes tensed. Many men are jealous when they see a woman do well, and I have often heard them inventing rumours on how she must have slept with so and so. Spain is still a very macho country!

Gender is only one typical source of grief and annoyance, which, as illustrated here, has nothing to do with country or party family. More often than not, instead, many young party members' frustration is due to their perception that they are discriminated against not as a member of a group, but, rather, as an individual:

NOCO17: The head of the local party branch hates me. The only way I'll ever get any position on a list is if I go away.

FRCM03: The national level hates our branch because we are seen as 'reformist', this basically means that none of us will ever get a proposition to take an important position.

UKBP09: Tense relationships with your local leader can lead to something being 'found' about you that will ruin your political future.

HUPS14: The head of my section is an ass and he knows I know it.

FRPS12: The people in my section hate me because I am a 'royaliste' [note: not as in a partisan of monarchy but as in a partisan of Socialist high profile politician Segolene Royal!]. In short, even if I say 'I can go and buy a pack of coffee since we've run out', several will look at me with a shameful air and someone will say: 'no, don't worry, I'm passing the shop anyway' as if they feared I would poison them.

DELB03: One person can ruin another's career as I have sadly found out.

FRPS06: Those who pretend to be the greatest democrat in the nation often tend to be the worst dictators for their peers.

ESCO23: He just hates me!

And the angst of the young party member does not stop at the door of the party branch (or, for that matter, of the party's headquarters)! Many have equally if not worse ideas about how society at large hates and misunderstands them. They are seen as selfish and self-centred when they perceive themselves as generous and sociotropic, they are criticised as partisan and rigid when they believe themselves to be intellectually thorough and to simply think and know more about complex issues and about right and wrong, they are despised as power-driven, pretentious, and cynical, when they would swear that they are public-spirited, modest, and idealistic. Throughout the interviews, we could hear a frustration that sometimes transformed into suffering and a great sense of injustice and misunderstanding:

UKLB27: The moment you say that you are in a party, people assume that your dream is really to become a dictator!

FRGR24: One day, when I was handing out flyers on the market, an old lady who I thought looked really nice looked at what the flyer was for and started shouting at me 'you are all fundamentalists!'

HUCO09: One of my parents' friends always teases me when he comes for dinner. He says politicians are rigid and specialise in inventing problems rather than solutions.

FRCM13: I hate it when we campaign and people just say: 'so what about the Soviet Union, heh?' or 'so if you are so clever, why did unemployment grow when you were in power?' They think we're all words and no substance, and I'm fed up with being accused of being a liar.

ESCO44: 'Liars!' is an accusation we hear a lot. People think that because you are into politics you won't take it personally, but in truth, it is insufferable.

UKBP16: People always accuse us of being dictators.

NOCO01: People always tease me saying I'm either power thirsty or money thirsty, this is so unfair.

DEPS08: I start talking to people and I can see they find me nice. Then I say I am in the SPD and they look at me as if I was a hypocrite. People don't really consider you human beings.

FRPS29: The moment you argue, they say: 'you're always the same!!' I'm so fed up, and it is so unfair.

Last but not least, a final aspect of the blues of the young party member is the rather frequent impression that people do not see the truth, that they do not understand why the politics of party x are really very very bad, and that of party y very very good. They similarly complain that people always reproach to them to be confrontational and make a scandal about 'small things' while these 'small things' are really, in their opinion, essential ideas:

ESPS03: It's part of our character – we are unable to tell an opponent 'you are right!'

FRPS33: Politics is a 'rapport de force social.' I am proud to like oppositions, struggles between large groups rather than pretend it is all unanimous and for all.

HUCO24: In politics, confrontation is often crucial.

FRFN11: When you make a point you care about, people accuse you of being extremist.

NOCO15: When I explained that I support a free-er system, a friend of my mother got really angry and said I was trying to destroy what Norway is!

UKLB33: People complain that all parties propose the same thing, and then when you explain that you disagree with a party's policy, they say that you are being ideological and rigid and always look for a fight!

ESCO44: When I say Catholicism has done a lot to our country, people say that I don't realise what Franco has done to our country because I am too young.

HUPS17: Sometimes, when I explain how bad Fidesz policies were, people say that at MSzP, all we do is throwing dirt at the Right and not proposing anything ourselves.

HUPS14: Once I told another student in my school that Orban [Former head of Government from the FIDESz] is a dictator, and she said that without Orban, we would still live under Communism and that's really what I wanted. Of course it was so stupid.

UKPS07: You try to explain, you give arguments, people don't listen. They just don't understand us and they prefer to keep their prejudices against New Labour.

These are not just anecdotal examples of miscommunication between young party members and other citizens. These various elements put together give us an essential insight into how young party members often tend to be dissatisfied and feel misjudged, misunderstood, and discriminated against by society at large. This ingredient is essential in understanding how and why, throughout the book, their relationship to citizens appears so paradoxical and complex, and why so many often seem to always have a need to prove something.

Overall, when we look at the references made in the interviews by young party members, regardless of their object (personal, societal, partisan, etc), in terms of positive and negative connotations, negative references 'win' hands down over positive ones by a margin of 2.2 to 1. The blues of the young party member thus rests at the heart of the way they are likely to shape the future of our democracies. They are deeply dissatisfied, and while this means that they want to 'change' things, it also means that whatever they are most dissatisfied with is likely to partly top their agenda for the future. Listening to young party members' ideas about what should be the future of our democracies, they are therefore clearly in a reactive logic – that is, ideas of what would be an ideal system or an ideal policy, or an ideal organisation of politics weigh nearly nothing in their discourse, as compared to what the worst 'problems' are and how they need to be solved.

Are parties the school of life?

A second crucial point to understand when imagining how they will influence our future and that of our political systems is that a majority of young party members are deeply convinced that party politics is, for lack of a better word, one of the best schools of life. This is another essential ingredient to consider when analysing where young party members will get their inspiration from when they will think on how to reinvent and regenerate our democracies. Moreover, this belief that the party is indeed a fair representation of society tends to be even higher than average amongst professional-minded young party members.

Let us remember what large numbers of young party members told us about their perceptions of the 'vibe' and mood of citizens' desires and problems. In Chapter 7, a number of them claimed to truly understand the real problems of fellow citizens either individually or collectively within their young party organisation. They contrasted their perceptiveness to the disconnection of current politicians and older party members. But importantly, they do not attribute this difference to their infancy in the system but, instead, predominantly, to a fundamental difference in their recruitment, origins, and ethos – in other words, many are of the opinion that they will remain 'naturally' in tune with citizens in the long term as illustrated by the following examples:

FRPS05: We know what people care and worry about. Our concerns are the same as theirs.
ESCO25: In my NNGG group, we are down to earth so I think we will always have a better sense of what people want than they realise!
UKBP26: We are a party of real people.
ESPS46: What I like about the party is that it is very much like a miniature version of society.
UKPS16: We know what the problems are.
HUCO20: The era when party members were not regular citizens is over. We are far more 'normal' than what most people think.

NOCO31: We are just normal young people. We like and do the same things as any other young person. This normality is one of the things that makes UH so special.
DELB03: I don't think I'll ever stop being down to earth.
DEPS13: Jusos is the best school of life!

In other words, young activists do not always see their party as a world which is clearly distinct from society as a whole, but, in a majority of cases as a microcosm of society. Of course, as we have just seen, a large number of citizens do not believe in the least that political parties represent a microcosm of society, or that their members are even vaguely resembling the 'average' citizen. When one thinks of it, the implications of this paradox are potentially huge. Indeed, the belief of many young party members – particularly among professional-minded ones – that their party is a miniature version of society as well as the best 'school of life' is bound to have an impact on where young activists will get their impression. It is not from 'base' citizens but by politically sophisticated fellow young activists that they will get their impressions of what society's worst problems are, of what citizens really want, and of what solutions would work best. In other terms, believing in the a priori representativeness of the party or young party organisation as a group means that young party members can 'save' the effort to go outside of the party to try and find out what citizens want. Much of this was clear from the findings of Chapter 6, but the following interview excerpts reinforce the nature of this paradox:

UKPS27: In our debates, we exchange our experiences about how things work and what makes life hard financially or politically.
FRPS13: I wish politicians would talk with us more often – they would get a better sense of normal Frenchmen's daily reality.
NOCO29: When we debate, all types of people are implicitly represented.
DECO35: I was surprised people were so normal and that they weren't all extremely intelligent. It's not the way you know it from watching TV. The people were very diverse, only about a third study politics and lots of them work.
FRPS37: I don't feel that what I do now is politics really.

In short, the second critical point to bear in mind when thinking about young party members' perception of their potential contribution to the progress of their national politics and democratic systems is that despite not being treated as 'normal' by many others, most of them think that they (at least the young 'they') collectively are 'normal citizens', and that they are already aware of and in touch with people's problems and priorities. Thus, there is a clear differentiation made by many young party members – particularly moral-minded ones – between their own and politicians' perception of society and its problems. There is also sympathy – this time by both moral- and professional-minded young party members equally – for the notion of a priori representativness and awareness of citizens' priorities.

Between pride and happiness

Finally, the third crucial element that transpires from our survey and interviews is a sense of pride and valourisation of young party members. Many of them have the impression to be doing something that is 'right', and that their engagement serves the community. Indeed, many even have the perception and hope that they are participating in – if not altogether making – history.

Throughout the interviews, young party members' historical references were extremely frequent, and often dramatic. History will vindicate them as it has, in the past, vindicated others, and their struggle is the proud continuation of the struggle of some democratic heroes who fought hard battles several years, decades, or sometimes centuries ago. Here again, we can provide some additional examples of this type of relatively frequent discourse:

> *DECO32*: My mother was told that she should not join a party by her mother, who said that joining parties should not be done because of our experience with Hitler. So even though my mother was always interested in politics she never joined.
>
> *ESPS34*: In fact, the ETA are killing less lately. Now, I ask *them* to commit suicide!
>
> *ESPS35*: In 1936, the republicans gave hope to politics. Then after Franco, we had to solve the question of democracy, but after we did, the PP solved the problem of the economy, I must recognise that. Now it is time for the nicest part of all – social progress.
>
> *FRPS31*: I often think that at the MJS, we are the only ones who know of and care about the heritage of the Revolution.
>
> *HUCO11*: My granddad was killed in 1956, and I have no doubt that wherever he is, he is proud of what I am doing now.
>
> *UKPS37*: My family are from Pakistan, so I know all about the duty to fight for democracy.
>
> *FRFN06*: The result on 21 April 2002 [when Le Pen managed to qualify for the second ballot of the French Presidential election] made me feel that I was part of an important moment in history. It was really moving and I thought it would change things.

The pride of being a part of history is key in understanding how young party members view their responsibility to contribute to the democratic politics of their nation. Young party members are not fighting for what they take to be right, they fight for what they take to be the 'sense' of history, and do so with clear pride.

This also means that the desire to 'change things' – a core motor of history – is entrenched in the very conception of their political involvement of many young party members. When it comes to this dimension again, professional-minded young activists are far more likely to talk about this pride and this desire to change things and participate in history than their moral- and social-minded counterparts, as we have seen in Chapters 5 and 8. Once more, they are the most likely to claim a historical significance to their struggle, and to refer to politics as 'high politics' and as some glorious making of democracy that relates to some essential national historical myths and points of reference such as the 1789 Revolution in France, the Civil war and the end of Franquism in Spain, the 1956 events and the fall of Communism in Hungary, or the end of Nazism and democratic reconstruction in Germany.

Reflecting on the co-existence of social-, moral-, and professional-minded young party members

Where does this leave us? We have now seen that three key 'constraints' of the role that can be played by young party members in reinventing the future of our democracies is their general sense of frustration, their perception of being genuinely representative and aware of the real problems of society, and their sense of pride and righteousness, and that their action directly 'fits' in with the course of their nation's history. However, we have also seen that all three elements tend to be particularly critical for professional-minded young party members, more so than for their moral- and social-minded counterparts.

Once again, professional-minded young activists distinguish themselves from the other two types and show that they have different interpretations of the world, of their own involvement, of their goals, and of the meaning of politics and of their political engagement. Social-minded members primarily see their membership as an experience, a chance to meet new people who share some of their interests, but few of them think of its long term consequences. Moral-minded young activists are there because they so deeply believe that a certain ideological fight is right that they want to throw all their weight in the balance to make it win, but their perspective is relatively pragmatic and conceived in the present tense from that point of view, and what they want is to influence policy and elections rather than history. With professional-minded young party members, the perspective is entirely different, whatever they are willing to contribute they will want to contribute with a more complex and difficult-to-read aim than the other two categories. Indeed, they need to think of the symbolic and historical purpose of their

actions at the very same time as they need to deal with its immediate professional and strategic consequences. The following few excerpts from the
discourses of professional-minded young militants are, from that point of
view, symptomatic:

> *ESPS45*: I believe in that old saying that goes: 'if you don't take care of
> politics, politics will take care of you!'
> *ESCO25*: You can dream more in a party, it's absolutely exciting and it is
> beautiful. What is more, you can dream together.
> *UKPS25*: Anyone in the party can do or say something that will ultimately
> change the life of the nation. You need to be careful.
> *HUCO03*: I have lots of goals.
> *FRCM15*: Considering what I want for my future and what I want for the
> future of the country, I often feel that I don't have the right to make any
> mistake.

It would be unfair to only reduce this attitude to vanity or to an excessive
dramatisation on the part of young party members. Rather, it says something
about the calculations that are at the background of professional-minded
young party members when they think about what to do. At the same time,
it so happens that these very professional young activists are the most likely
to represent the future of our political personnel and, in all probability, the
very future of our democracies. We have seen that social-minded young militants are not even sure that they will continue their partisan engagement in
the long term, as for moral-minded members, we have seen that they tend
to remain grass root members in the long run, or to merely occupy low level
local positions of responsibility. Chances are, therefore, that all future leaders – or at the very least an immense majority of them – will be drawn from
the professional-minded category of young party members, who all aim for
an entry into the world of professional politics, and, in most cases, will fight
each other for leading places on party lists and positions of national party
leadership.

What does this all tell us about what they are likely to do in the future?
Professional-minded young party members do not often realise that their
perceptions have little in common with those of most citizens, but at the
same time, many feel largely ostracised and marginalised by them. Their
vision of politics is largely party-centric, and at the same time tainted by a
willingness to protect their party's internal structures. In short, they often
accept the mould of current politics, and, what is more, are rather often
convinced by the righteousness of their priorities and political conceptions.

On the one hand, this may sound bleak and point out a likely repeat of
the same and a lack of true change in what these professional-minded young
activists have to offer to our political systems. Yet, at the same time, they do

want to make history, and from that point of view, the seeds of sometimes radical change are planted in the discourse of these young party members. The fact that they are socialised with highly critical moral- and social-minded young party members should also not be underestimated. Whether they like or despise these fellow young activists, professional-minded young militants will have been exposed, throughout the first few years of their membership to a discourse of great criticism towards current politicians and internal party democracy. Here rests the chance that, despite their willingness to be conformist, these ambitious young men and women who intend to reach the Pantheon of their national politics will find the resources to find ways of reforming internal and external institutional structures to gather the adhesion of their fellow young activists and that of the citizens whose diffidence they suffer from.

The future of our democracies?

What future are young party members in general – and professional-minded young party members in particular – planning for our democracies? It is perhaps by looking at the way professional-minded young activists plan to construct their own future that we can best estimate what their impact might be on the political systems, which, throughout Europe, are currently the target of numerous criticisms, frustrations, and disillusions on the part of citizens. Young party members – and particularly those who are most likely to become our future leaders – say that they are aware that change is needed, that they want to succeed, and that they want to be loved by their fellow citizens. At the same time, however, it is clear that their role models, and their references in terms of institutional practice and decision-making procedures are systematically derived from the past. Like current leaders, they share great levels of suspicion towards grass root activists, who which they perceive as unrealistic and potentially troublesome. Similar to many politicians, they believe that they already have a good sense of what problems their country and compatriots face. In fact, most of the changes that they promise in order to solve what some perceive as a crisis of democracy, involve 'new' solutions to policy problems rather than an improvement of the process of representation. In short, while young party members readily offer their youth, their enthusiasm, and their commitment in order to give voters a new image of politics, it looks like citizens are not invited to return to the heart of the political sphere as the future of our democracies unfolds. In fact, while, over the past 30 years, political parties have sometimes had to learn to live without members, it seems that many of our future leaders expect politics to soon have to learn how to live without citizens.

The Survey

A STUDY OF YOUNG PARTY MEMBERS

We thank you for taking a few minutes to answer the following questions. The study in which you participate is totally anonymous and will only be used for academic purposes. Thanks again for your help!

1 – Are you: A – A woman   B – A man

2 – How old are you? _____ years old

3 – Are you: A – A student   B – Unemployed   C – Self-employed   D – Employed in industry   E – Employed in service sector   F – Employed in Public Services/ administration   G – Other:_____

4 – How long have you been a party member? _____ years

4b – Are you a member of: A – [Name of the party]   B – [Name of the young Party org]   C – both

5 – How active a member would you consider yourself?   A – Very active   B – Quite active   C – Not very active   D – Not active at all   E – Don't know

6 – Do you hold any position of responsibility within the party? If so, which one?

7 – Consider the following possible political priorities. For each of them, could you tell me if you think of them as: essential (write 5), important (4), secondary (3), unimportant (2), undesirable (1)

___ Fight unemployment   ___ Lower taxes and   ___ Protect the environment
                                          charges

___ Further European integration   ___ Fight crime   ___ Reduce inequalities

Any other essential priority:

8 – Among the following possible objectives of your party membership, could you rank them from the most important to the least important (1 being the most important, etc)? Give a 0 to any objective that does not matter to you at all:

___ Help the party I support to win   ___ Help politicians I support to gain
elections   positions of responsibility
___ Obtain positions of responsibility for   ___ Help the ideas I support to triumph
myself

9 – Altogether, do you have the impression that you can influence the choices and decisions made by your party?

___ Yes, a lot   ___ Yes, to some extent   ___ Not really   ___ Not at all
___ Don't know

10 – In ten years time from now, do you think it is very likely (4), quite likely (3) quite unlikely (2) or very unlikely (1) that you will:

___ Still be a party member

___ Will have a position of responsibility in the party

___ Will have been elected/will have run for an election

___ Will belong to other organisations, unions, associations, etc

11 – Consider the following statements. For each of them, could you tell me if you agree strongly (4), agree to some extent (3), disagree to some extent (2), disagree strongly (1), or are unsure or have no opinion (0)?

___ Politics is a profession

___ Party leaders usually listen to the members

___ Being a party member is teaching me things

___ Politicians tend to be more 'centrist' than party members

___ Older party members do not really respect young members

___ Discussions within the party are usually interesting

12 – As a party member, do you often (4), occasionally (3), rarely (2), or never (1) perform the following activities:

___ Putting posters on walls   ___ Handing out flyers   ___ Demonstrating
___ Trying to convince friends and family to your cause   ___ Participating in debates

___ Fight against the activities of other parties

13 – In a broad sense, what do you gain from your party membership? (2: a lot, 1: a little, 0: not at all)

___ Money or material rewards

___ Positions and honours

___ Some friends

___ Some interesting discussions

___ The sense that you help others

___ The satisfaction to influence the politics of your country

___ The privilege of meeting interesting people

___ The opportunity to become a politician later

___ The sense that your life has more meaning

___ The sense that you are a good citizen

Notes

1 Introduction and Background

1. We have updated the IDEA figures with 2004–2008 elections. Turnout declined by 21 points in France in 29 years, 13.4 points in Germany in 33 years, 9.6 points in Italy in 34 years, and 17.6 points in the United Kingdom in 31 years.
2. The ratio (party members/electorate) declined from 5.05 to 1.57 in France, 4.52 to 2.93 in Germany, 9.66 to 4.05 in Italy, 10.66 to 6.38 in Switzerland, and 4.12 to 1.92 in the United Kingdom between 1978 and 1998. Country-specific accounts of the crisis of membership include Pedersen et al. (2004), Gallagher and Marsh (2004), and Heidar and Saglie (2003).
3. 2005 general elections in the United Kingdom according to the British Election Study, Italy, the Netherlands, Switzerland, and so on.
4. The same discrepancy exists in most other countries: 58 per cent vs 33 per cent in Germany, 47 per cent vs 25 per cent in Finland, 31 per cent vs 15 per cent in Luxembourg, 40 per cent vs 23 per cent in the Czech Republic, and so on.

2 Model and Methods

1. No reliable data on the characteristics of the young party members population exists, so one would have to rely on parties' volunteered information to construct a random sample of members and test their representativeness. This would be most problematic. Instead, we constructed samples based on the aggregate characteristics of party branches – city size, the known characteristics of party members at large, the party's strength in different areas of the country, and internal party politics, we came up with a representative sample of branches, and asked for the questionnaire to be circulated to all members aged 18–25 within these branches. Of course, we cannot, strictly speaking, derive from the characteristics of the branches some inferences about the characteristics of members. However, the large number of branches targeted for each party and comparison of the characteristics of the members surveyed suggests that the samples for each party do not differ from the extent of our knowledge of the target population. We also tested for a number of possible sources of bias by comparing branch-based results, but not difference was statistically significant.
2. The survey was conducted throughout 2006–2007.
3. Four parties refused to take part in the study: British Conservatives, French UMP and UDF, and German Greens. Two of these parties are relatively minor, but this means not all parties are included for each system. We must consider all comparative tables with caution. Results might have changed if these parties had been included. However, the study already includes a much larger and more varied set of parties than most existing studies of party members, and the core of our analysis is centred on the differences between the three main types of young party members, with differences confirmed across countries and party families. The parties are weighted in the comparative tables.
4. See endnote 6.

5. Response rates by party varied from 54 percent to 83 percent with the bulk of the parties between 65 and 75 percent. There is no significant difference in means between the various countries or the various party families included in the study.
6. Note that unlike the case of the survey, which had rather homogeneous samples for each of the parties included, the numbers interviewed varied by party. They stand as follows: Spain: PP: 49, PSOE: 48; France: PS: 37, PCF: 27, Les Verts: 26, FN: 32; UK: Labour: 39, Liberal Democrats: 35, BNP: 32; Germany: SPD: 38, CDU: 36, FDP: 31; Hungary: MSzP: 26, Fidesz: 27; Norway: Høyre: 36. Total: 519.
7. All correlations are significant at 0.00 level.

3 Becoming a Young Party Member: Inheritance, Paths to Membership, and Political Socialisation

1. We exclude from the count membership to compulsory, quasi-compulsory, or 'social' organisations such as the Communist youths or pioneers in Hungary.
2. We have removed the name of the small village for purposes of anonymity.

Bibliography

Alesina, A. and Rosenthal, H. (1995) *Partisan Politics, Divided Government, and the Economy* (Cambridge University Press, Cambridge).

Almond, G. and Verba, S. (1963) *The Civic Culture: Political Attitudes and Democracy in Five Nations* (Princeton University Press, Princeton, New Jersey).

Bax, E. (1990) *Modernization and Cleavage in Dutch Society: A Study of Long Term Economic and Social Change* (Avebury, Aldershot).

Bhavnani, K. (1994) *Talking Politics: A Psychological Framing of Views from Youth in Britain* (Cambridge University Press, Cambridge).

Blais, A. (2000) *To Vote or Not to Vote? The Merits and Limits of Rational Choice Theory* (University of Pittsburgh Press, Pittsburgh).

Blais, A. (2004) 'Where does turnout decline come from?' *European Journal of Political Research*, vol. 43, no. 2, pp. 221–236.

Bilstein, H., Hohlbein, H., and Klose, H. U. (1971) *Jung Sozialisten, Junge Union, Jungdemokraten* (Opladen, Leske Verlage).

Braungart, M. and Braungart, R. (1990) 'The life-course development of left- and right-wing youth activist leaders from the 1960s', *Political Psychology*, vol. 11, no. 2, p. 243.

Bruter, M. (2009) 'Time bomb? The dynamic effect of news and symbols on the political identity of European citizens,' *Comparative Political Studies*, vol. 42, no. 12 (December).

Buckingham, D. (2000) *The Making of Citizens: Young People, News and Politics* (Routledge, London).

Butler, D. and Ranney, A. (1992) *Electioneering: A Comparative Study of Continuity and Change* (Oxford University Press, USA).

Butler, D. and Stokes, D. (1974) *Political Change in Britain*, 2nd ed. (Macmillan, London).

Bynner, J. and Ashford, S. (1994) 'Politics and participation: Some antecedents of young people's attitudes to the political system and political activity', *European Journal of Social Psychology*, vol. 24, no. 2, pp. 223–226.

Cannon, D. (1995) *Generation X and the New Work Ethics*. Working paper (Demos, London).

Clark, P. and Wilson, J. (1961) 'Incentive systems: A theory of organizations', *Administrative Science Quarterly*, vol. 6, no. 2, pp. 129–166.

Clarke, H., Kornberg, A., Ellis, F. and Rapkin, J. (2000) 'Not for fame or fortune: A note on membership and activity in the Canadian Reform Party', *Party Politics*, vol. 6, no. 1, pp. 75–93.

Cross, W. and Young, L. (2008) 'Factors influencing the decision of the young politically engaged to join a political party: An investigation of the Canadian case', *Party Politics*, vol. 14, pp. 345–369.

Dalton, R. (2001) *Citizen Politics*. Third edition (Chatham House Publishers, New York).

Dalton, R. and Wattenberg, M. (2000) *Parties Without Partisans* (Oxford University Press, Oxford).

Dalton, R. J. and Weldon, S. (2005) 'Public images of political parties', *West European Politics*, vol. 28, pp. 931–951.

Deschouwer, K. and De Winter, L. (1998), 'La corruption politique et le clientélisme: le spectre italien?', in M. Swyngedouw and Martiniello (eds), *Où va la Belgique? Les soubresauts d'une petite démocratie européenne* (L'Harmattan, Paris), 139–152.

Detterbeck, K. (2002) *Der Wandel politischer Parteien in Westeuropa* (Opladen, Leske & Budrich).

Detterbeck, K. (2005) 'Cartel parties in Western Europe?' *Party Politics*, vol. 11, no. 2, pp. 173–191.

Diani, M. and McAdam, D. (eds) (2003) *Social Movements and Networks Relational Approaches to Collective Action* (Oxford University Press, Oxford).

Downs, A. (1957) *An Economic Theory of Democracy* (Harper and Rowe, New York).

Duverger, M. (1954) *Political Parties: Their Organization and Activity in the Modern State* (Wiley, Methuen).

Electoral Commission (2001) *Election 2001: The Official Results* (Politicos, London).

Ellis, C. (2005) 'No hammock for the idle: The Conservative party, "youth" and the Welfare State in the 1960s', *Twentieth Century British History*, vol. 16, no. 4, pp. 441–470.

Eulau, H. and Karps, P. (1978) 'The puzzle of representation: Specifying components of responsiveness', in H. Eulau and J. Wahlke (ed.), *The Politics of Representation* (Sage, Beverly Hills), 55–69.

Fendrich, J. M. and Turner, R. W. (1989) 'The transition from student to adult politics', *Social Forces*, vol. 67, pp. 1049–1057.

Franklin, M. (1996) 'Electoral Participation', in L. LeDuc, R. Niemi and P. Norris (eds), *Comparing Democracies: Elections and Voting in Global Perspective* (Sage, Thousand Oaks).

Franklin, M. (2001) 'The dynamics of electoral participation', in L. LeDuc, R. Niemi and P. Norris (eds), *Comparing Democracies 2* (Sage, Thousand Oaks).

Franklin, M., Mackie, T., and Valen, H. (1992) *Electoral Change: Responses to Evolving Social and Attitudinal Structures in Western Countries* (Cambridge University Press, Cambridge).

Gallagher, M., and Marsh, M. (2004) 'Party membership in Ireland: The members of Fine Gael', *Party Politics*, vol. 10, pp. 407–425.

Galston, W. (2001) 'Political knowledge, political engagement, and civic education', *Annual Review of Political Science*, vol. 4, pp. 217–234.

Gauthier, M. and Pacom, D. (2001) *Spotlight on Canadian Youth Research* (Les Presses de L'Université, Laval).

Gidengil, E. et al. (2001) 'The correlates and consequences of anti-partyism in the 1997 Canadian Election', *Party Politics*, vol. 7, no. 4, pp. 491–513.

Gokalp, C. (1981) *Quand Vient l'Age des Choix* (PUF-INED, Paris).

The Guardian Newspaper (2005) 'New labour in Britain' (http://politics.guardian.co.uk/labour/story/0,9061,1274855,00.html) accessed 1 February 2007.

Heath, A. and Taylor, B. (1999) 'New sources of abstention?' in G. Evans and P. Norris (eds), *Critical Elections: British Parties and Voters in Long-Term Perspective* (Sage, London), 164–180.

Heidar, K. and Saglie, J. (2003) 'A decline of linkage? Intra-party participation in Norway, 1991–2000', *European Journal of Political Research*, vol. 42, pp. 761–786.

Hirczy de Miño, W. (1995) 'Explaining near-universal turnout: The case of Malta', *European Journal of Political Research*, vol. 27, pp. 255–272.

Hooghe, M. and Stolle, D. (2003) 'Age matters. Life cycle and cohort differences in the socialisation effect of voluntary participation', *European Political Science*, vol. 3, no. 2, pp. 49–56.

Hooghe, M., Stolle, D. and Stouthuysen, P. (2004) 'Head start in politics the recruitment function of youth organizations of political parties in Belgium (Flanders)', *Party Politics*, vol. 10, no. 2, pp. 193–212.

Hopkin, J. (2001) 'Bringing the members back in? Democratising candidate selection in Britain and Spain', *Party Politics*, vol. 7, no. 3, pp. 343–361.

Inglehart, R. (1971) *The Silent Revolution: Changing Values and Political Styles amongst Western Publics* (Princeton University Press, Princeton, New Jersey).

Inglehart, R. (1990) *Culture Shift in Advanced Industrial Societies* (Princeton University Press, Princeton).

IDEA (2004) 'Voter turnout in Western Europe' http://www.idea.int/europe_cis/vtwe04.cfm posted 15/4/2004, accessed on 17 May 2009.

Jennings, M. K. (1987) 'Residues of a movement: The aging of the American protest generation', *American Political Science Review*, vol. 81 (June), pp. 367–382.

Jennings, M. K. and Stoker, L. (2002) 'Generational Change, Life Cycle Processes, and Social Capital'. Presented at Citizenship on Trial: Interdisciplinary Perspectives on the Political Socialization of Adolescents. McGill University, Montreal, Canada.

Katz, R. and Mair, P. (1994) 'How parties organise: Change and adaptation in party organisations in Western Democracies', *Comparative Politics*, vol. 11, p. 384.

Katz, R. et al. (1992) 'The membership of political parties in European Democracies, 1960–1990', *European Journal of Political Research*, vol. 22, pp. 329–345.

Kitschelt, H. (1989) 'The internal politics of parties: The law of curvilinear disparity revisited', *Political Studies*, vol. 38, pp. 400–421.

Lijphart, A. (1968) *The Politics of Accommodation: Pluralism and Democracy in the Netherlands* (Berkeley University Press, Berkeley).

Lijphart, A. (1994) *Electoral Systems and Party Systems: A Study of 27 Democracies, 1945–1990* (Oxford University Press, Oxford).

Lipset, S. M. and Rokkan, S. (eds) (1967) 'Cleavage structures, party systems, and voter alignments', *Party Systems and Voter Alignments: Cross-National Perspectives* (Macmillan, London).

Mair, P. (1997) *Party System Change* (Oxford: Clarendon Press).

Mair, P. and van Biezen, I. (2001) 'Party membership in twenty European Democracies, 1980–2000', *Party Politics*, vol. 7, no. 1, pp. 5–21.

Margolis, H. (1982) *Selfishness, Altruism and Rationality* (University of Chicago Press, Chicago).

Marsh, D., O'Toole, T., and Jones, S. (2007) *Young People and Politics in the UK: Apathy or Alienation?* (Palgrave, New York).

Martin, A. and Cowley P. (1999) 'Ambassadors in the community? Labour party members in society', *Politics*, vol. 19, no. 2, pp. 89–96.

May, J. D (1973) 'Opinion structure of political parties: The special law of curvilinear disparity', *Political Studies*, vol. 21, pp. 135–151.

McCarthy, S. (ed.) (2000) *Youth Cultures, Lifestyles, and Citizenship* (Council of Europe, Strasbourg).

Meisel, J. (1991) 'Decline of party in Canada', in H. Thorburn (ed.), *Party Politics in Canada*, 6th ed. (Prentice-Hall, Scarborough).

Merkl, P. (1977) 'Trends in German political science', *American Political Science Review*, vol. 71, no. 3, pp. 1097–1108.

Milbrath, L. W. and Goel, M. L. (1977) *Political Participation: How and Why Do People Get Involved in Politics?* 2nd ed. (Rand McNally, Chicago).

Miller, W. E. and Stokes, D. E. (1963) 'Constituency influence in Congress', *American Political Science Review*, vol. 57, no. 1, pp. 45–56.

Mueller, D. C. (1989) *Public Choice II* (Cambridge University Press, Cambridge).

Narud, H. M. and Skare, A. (1999) 'Are party activists the party extremists? The structure of opinion in political parties', *Scandinavian Political Studies*, vol. 22, pp. 45–65.

Nevitte, N. (1996) *The Decline of Deference. Canadian Value Change in Cross-National Perspective* (Peterborough, Broadview Press).

Nie, N. et al. (1996) *Education and Democratic Citizenship in America* (University of Chicago Press, Chicago).

Offe and Fuchs (2002) *A Decline of Social Capital? The German Case* (Oxford University Press).

Olson, M. (1965) *The Logic of Collective Action* (Schocken Books, New York).

O'Neill, B. (2001) 'Generational patterns in the political opinions and behavior of Canadians', *Policy Matters*, vol. 2, no. 5, pp. 1–48.

Panebianco, A. (1988) *Political Parties: Organisation and Power* (Cambridge University Press, Cambridge).

Park, A. (1999) 'Young people and political apathy,' in Jowell, R., Curtice, J., Park, A., Thomson, K., and Jarvis, L. (eds.), *British Social Attitudes: The 15th Report*, Vol. 16 (Ashgate: Aldershot).

Pattie, C. J. et al. (2004) *Citizenship in Britain: Values, Participation and Democracy* (Cambridge University Press, Cambridge).

Pedersen, K. et al. (2004) 'Sleeping or active partners? Danish party members at the turn of the millenium', *Party Politics*, vol. 10, pp. 367–383.

Putnam, R. (1993) *Making Democracy Work: Civic Traditions in Modern Italy* (Princeton University Press, Princeton, New Jersey).

Putnam, R. (2000) *Bowling Alone: The Collapse and Revival of American Community* (Simon and Schuster, New York).

Putnam, R. (ed.) (2002) *Democracies in Flux: The Evolution of Social Capital in Contemporary Society* (Oxford University Press, Oxford).

Rahn, W. M. and Transue, J. E. (1998) 'Social trust and value change: The decline of social capital in American youth, 1976–1995', *Political Psychology*, vol. 19, no. 3, pp. 545–565.

Riker, W. and Ordeshook, P. (1968) 'A theory of the calculus of voting', *American Political Science Review*, vol. 62, pp. 25–42.

Rothstein, B. and Stolle, D. (2002) 'How political institutions create and destroy social trust'. Paper prepared for the 98th Meeting of the American Political Science Association in Boston, MA. 29 August–2 September 2002 accessible online at https://www.apsanet.org/~ep/papers/2003winner.pdf.

Salzinger, S., Antrobus, J. and Hammer, M. (1988) *Social Networks of Children, Adolescents and College Students* (Hove, Lawrence Erlbaum, Hillsdale).

Samms, C. (1995) *Global Generation X: Their Values and Attitudes in Different Countries* (Demos, London).

Scarrow, S. (1996) *Parties and Their Members* (Oxford University Press, Oxford).

Scarrow, S. (2000) 'Parties without members? Party organization in a changing electoral environment', in Russell Dalton and Martin Wattenberg (eds), *Parties without Partisans* (Oxford University Press, Oxford), 79–101.

Scarrow, S. and Gezgor, B. (2006) 'Trends in party membership and membership participation', Paper presented at the annual meeting of the Midwest Political Science Association, Chicago.

Schaffer, H. (1971) *The Growth of Sociability* (Penguin, Baltimore).

Schlozman, K. et al. (1994) 'Gender and the pathways to participation: The role of resources', *Journal of Politics*, vol. 56, pp. 963–990.

Seyd, P. and Whiteley, P. (1992) *Labour's Grass Roots* (Clarendon Press, Oxford).

Seyd, P. and Whiteley, P. (2004) 'British party members: An overview', *Party Politics*, vol. 10, pp. 355–366.

Sigel, R. (ed.) (1989) 'Introduction: Persistence and change', *Political Learning in Adulthood* (University of Chicago Press, Chicago).

Skocpol, T. (2002) 'United States: From membership to advocacy', in R. Putnam (ed.), *Democracies in Flux* (Oxford University Press, Oxford).

Squire, P. (1997) 'Another look at legislative professionalisation and divided government in the states', *Legislative Studies Quarterly*, vol. 22, pp. 417–432.

Stouthuysen, P. (1991) 'The Belgian peace movement', in Bert Klandermans (ed.), *Peace Movements in Western Europe and the United States* (JAI Press, Greenwich), 175–199.

Strøm, K. (1990) 'A behavioral theory of competitive political parties', *American Journal of Political Science*, vol. 34, no. 2, pp. 565–598.

Tullock, G. (1971) 'The paradox of revolution', *Public Choice*, vol. 11, pp. 89–99.

Verba, S., Nie, N. and Kim, J. (1978) *Participation and Political Equality* (Cambridge University Press, Cambridge).

Verba, S. et al. (1995) *Voice and Equality* (Harvard University Press, Cambridge, MA).

Verkade, W. (1965) *Democratic Parties in the Low Countries and Germany: Origins and Historical Development* (Leiden Presses Universaires, Leiden).

Webb, P. et al. (2002) *Political Parties in Advanced Industrial Democracies* (Oxford University Press, Oxford).

Whitaker, R. (2001) 'Virtual political parties and the decline of democracy', *Policy Options* (June), pp. 1–22.

Whiteley, P. (2007) 'Are groups replacing parties? A multi-level analysis of party and group membership in the European democracies', Paper presented at the ECPR Joint Sessions, Helsinki.

Whiteley, P., Seyd, P., Richardson, J. and Bissell, P. (1994) 'Explaining party activism: The case of the British conservative party', *British Journal of Political Science*, vol. 24, pp. 79–94.

Wring, D., Henn, M. and Weinstein, M. (1999) 'Young people and contemporary politics: Committed scepticism or engaged cynicism?' *British Elections and Parties Review*, vol. 9, pp. 200–216.

Young, L. and Cross, W. (2002) 'Incentives to membership in Canadian political parties', *Political Research Quarterly*, vol. 55, no. 3, pp. 547–569.

Young, L. and Everitt, J. (2004) *Advocacy Groups* (University of British Columbia Press, Vancouver).

Youniss, J. and Yates, M. (1997) *Community Service and Social Responsibility in Youth* (University of Chicago Press, Chicago, IL).

Index